Family and Farm

SUNY SERIES ON EUROPEAN SOCIAL HISTORY

Leo A Loubère, Editor

Family and Farm

Agrarian Change and Household
Organization in the Loire Valley
1500-1900

JOHN W. SHAFFER
Department of History
University of California at Chico

State University of New York Press

ALBANY

To Susan, whose love and support made this book possible

Published by
State University of New York Press, Albany

© 1982 State University of New York

For information, address State University of New York
Press, State University Plaza, Albany, N.Y., 12246

Library of Congress Cataloging in Publication Data

Shaffer, John W.
    Family and farm.

    (SUNY series on European social history)
    Bibliography: p. 238
    Includes index.
    1. Sociology, Rural—France—Loire Valley. 2. Loire Valley (France)—Rural
conditions. 3. Community life. 4. Family farms—France—Loire Valley—History. I.
Title. II. Series.
HN438.L54S48   306.8′5   81-9335
ISBN 0-87395-562-5   AACR2
ISBN 0-87395-563-3 (pbk.)

Contents

Tables

Figures

Maps

Illustrations

Preface

No intellectual endeavor is ever the product of a single individual. This book would not be complete without acknowledging those persons whose assistance and ideas contributed to it. Lutz K. Berkner first nurtured my interest in family history and the study of peasant societies. This thesis is, in a very real sense, a humble effort at repaying an enormous intellectual debt that I owe him. Temma Kaplan provided invaluable criticism and generous encouragement when I needed it most. Robert Brenner forced me to take a more careful look at the questions of tenure and class relations. Much of the thesis is a product of a dialogue carried out over the past five years with Nancy Fitch, whose work so closely paralleled my own.

A Fullbright-Hays Grant and a Shell Oil Foundation Fellowship provided funding for my research in France. Madame Chabrolin, directress of the Archives départementales de la Nièvre graciously assisted my research. Messieurs Vachez, Roy and Noizet, and Mesdames Guyot, Bouquinet and Vincent made my research both worthwhile and pleasant. Susan Shaffer spent many hours coding data at the departmental archives in Nevers. Dee and Claude Gramond opened their hearts and their home to my wife and me during our stay in France. Nancy Riley and Soledad Wright heroically proofread and typed what was too often a confused and jumbled manuscript; Virginia Waring assisted in the design of drafting of the charts, tables and maps. My mother and father gave me unwavering support throughout. To all these people, I am grateful.

CHAPTER ONE

Modernization Theory and Changes in Family Patterns

Selon l'ancien établissement du ménage des champs, en ce pays de Nivernois . . . plusieurs personnes doivent être assemblées en une famille pur demener ce ménage, qui est fort labourieux et consiste en plusieurs fonctions en ce pays, qui de soi est de culture malaissée: les uns servans pour labourer et pour toucher les boeufs . . . les autres pour mener les brebis et moutons, les autres pour conduire les parcs. Ces familles ainsi composées de plusieurs personnes . . . sont régles par un seul qui s'appelle *Maître* de communauté, élu a cette charge par les autres, lequel commande à tous les autres, va aux affaires qui se presentent es villes ou es foires, et ailleurs; a pouvoir d'obliger ses parsonniers en choses mobilieres qui concerrent le fait de la communauté, et lui seul et nommé es ròles des tailles et subsides. Par ces arguments se peut connoitre que ces communautés sont vraies familles et collèges qui, par consideration de l'intellect, sont comme un corps composé de plusieurs membres, combien que les membres soient séparés l'un de l'autre; mais par fraternité, amitié et liaison économique font un seul sorps.

Guy Coquille, *Questions et responses sur la Coutumes de France* (1612)

Je savais que . . . dans une commune appelée Saint-Benin-des-Bois, existait enore, malgré nos cinquente années de révolution dans les moeurs et dans les los, une des ces *anciennes communautés* si usitées en Nivernois parmi les familles de laboureurs . . . L'éxistence de cette communauté date d'un temps immemorial . . . Dans l'origine, le maître naturel de la communauté fut le père de famille; ensuite son fils; et cette héredité naturelle se continua aussi longtemps que se maintint la ligne directe, et que l'on put distinguer un ainé doué de la capacité convenable . . . la principale

1

charge du maître est de faire les affaires du dehors, d'acheter et vendre le
bétail; de faire les acquisitions au nom de la communauté . . . Le fonds de la
communauté se compose 1) des biens anciens, 2) des acquisitions faites
pour le campte commun, 3) des bestiaux de toute nature, 4) de caisse
commune . . . Le nombre des membres n'est que 36, grands et petits . . .
Tous les communs vivent suivant la loi de leur association, *au meme pain,
pot, et sel . . .*

Letter from . Dupin to M. Etienne (1840)

Anyone reading these passages cannot help but be struck by the
complexity of family life that existed in this region of central France.
Neither description was an idealized portrayal of some mythical form of
household organization of the past, but were based on direct, first-hand
observations by men who had lived in the Nivernais for most of their
lives. Guy Coquille was a renowned jurist and legal commentator of the
late sixteenth and early seventeenth centuries; Dupin, a prominent
lawyer and influential politician of the nineteenth. Separated as they are
by three and a half centuries, the passages underscore a remarkable
continuity in household organization in the Nivernais, a continuity that
spanned the collapse of the Old Regime and the birth of modern France.

Widespread in China, India, and eastern Europe, such joint households existed in western Europe only in northern Italy and central and
southwestern France. *Communauté*, a term borrowed from Old Regime
legal terminology, denoted joint ownership of property by two or more
persons. It eventually came to be identified in France with large peasant
households in which several kin-based families resided together, held
property in common and divided work tasks among themselves. They
lived *au même feu et au même pot*, shared the same hearth and ate from
the same pot. By no means even loosely democratic, the *communauté*
was administered by the *maître de communauté*, usually the father or
eldest sibling—only rarely, it appears, simply by the most capable. All
members were expected to submit to his authority and defer to his
judgment.

The *communauté* described by Dupin gives some idea of the size and
complexity of these households. The Jaults were a landowning *communauté* residing in the commune of Saint-Benin-des-Bois. At the time of
the 1831 census, the *communauté* was composed of seven families:
Claude Lejault, the *maître*, his younger brother Claude, their four
married sons, and their widowed sister-in-law. In all, there were
thirty-one members, not counting household servants. The association
owned only 27 hectares of arable land plus a vineyard. Its main source of

wealth came from raising cattle, which were grazed on 204 hectares of communal land to which they held use rights. Communal rights on an additional 153 hectares of woodland provided the household with fuel and timber. Dupin estimated the total value of the land, cattle, and buildings at about two hundred thousand francs.[1]

In fact, the Jaults were an exception, both because of their wealth and long history (the elder Claude could trace the *communauté's* origins to the fifteenth century). This distinctiveness, which was one of degree rather than of kind, had earned them a wide reputation that extended beyond the Nivernais itself. Indeed, Dupin's purpose in visiting the family had been to announce to them that Princess Adelaide, the sister of Louis Phillippe, was to present them with a medal in recognition of "her esteem and encouragement to preserve a mode of life based on concord and the spirit of association and of the family."[2] There were other reasons for such attention. The Jaults were considered to be one of the few remaining *communautés* in a province where such associations had until only recently been both widespread and common. In the decades after 1840, however, the *communauté* as an institution virtually disappeared from the province. Indeed, the presentation of the medal to the Jaults came just in time, for less than four years later, they dissolved their association and divided their property among its members.

While the Jaults were certainly not the last *communauté* in the province—indeed, Dupin himself pointed out that many others existed throughout the Nivernais—their breakup came to symbolize the decline of the institution. "Soon," lamented Dupin, "it will pass into legend." For him the demise of the *communauté* by no means represented the passing away of yet another quaint agrarian tradition. He saw the *communauté* as the very embodiment of benevolent paternalism, filial piety, and family solidarity. Dupin's views were shared by many of his contemporaries, so much so that the *communauté* in the Nivernais attracted the attention of politicians, legal historians, and social scientists from throughout France. The attention focused on the institution at precisely that point in time when it began to disappear is indeed fortunate, for much of what we know today about the *communauté* is derived from the observations and studies carried out by individuals vitally concerned with its passing.

Dupin and his contemporaries were in fact witnessing a phenomenon that has been confirmed by recent anthropological and sociological research on the family in all parts of the world. In societies as disparate as those of Europe, Asia, and Africa, industrialization, urbanization and the commercialization of agriculture are transforming and shaping family patterns on a scale hitherto unprecedented in world history. Whatever the nature of the family and society subjected to these developments, there is now a growing emphasis on the conjugal family, a family with fewer ties to distant relatives and one composed solely of parents and their unmarried children.

The history of the *communauté* in the Nivernais is best understood within the context of the impact of modern social relations on family and household organization. Why, after an existence that can be traced as far back as records allow, did the *communauté* in the Nivernais begin suddenly to disappear during the middle decades of the nineteenth century? The question itself poses the problem of how to account for its existence in the first place. For it is futile to attempt to determine why certain family types give way to others without fully understanding how the earlier mode of household organization came into existence and the ways in which it served the needs of its members. What must be understood are the reasons why families in this region of France adopted the specific residential patterns and property arrangements that characterized the *communauté*. In short, how do we account for the existence of the *communauté* in the Nivernais?

Theoretical Models of the Extended Family

Family structure and household organization have been investigated intensively during the past decade. These studies have stressed that extended family structure is predominantly a phenomenon occurring among the landed peasantry and in societies where landholdings are passed more or less intact to succeeding generations. The heir, or heirs, remains with the parents after marriage, eventually assuming control of the farm. Those excluded from succession to real estate and who receive only movable property have the alternative of marrying into another household, establishing their own independent household, or remaining celibate. The key question here is not necessarily direct ownership of the land. Among tenants, extended families can be organized around the succession to the leasehold if it is a long-term, secure contract. Families working short-term insecure leases do not usually follow this pattern, since the expectation of eventual succession to the holding cannot be assured.[3]

Demographic conditions also play an important role in structuring extended family forms in any society, particularly in preindustrial societies characterized by high mortality. Some couples will have no children survive to adulthood, while in other families the parents will die

4

before the heir marries. Marion Levy has argued that even in societies where extended family formation is the norm, never more than half the households will have three generations coresiding at any one time.[4] Recently, Levy's theory has been shown to be statiscally correct.[5] Nevertheless, the crucial factor appears to be whether land is transmitted intact.

Until quite recently, the study of the extended family in western Europe remained almost synonymous with that of the stem family, that is, a household composed of parents and one married child. Because of the importance surrounding the disposition of land, it has been argued that, among peasant proprietors, impartible inheritance practices will lead to a greater frequency of extended families while partible inheritance will lead to nuclear families. In fact, nearly all peasant societies are characterized by partible inheritance customs of some sort. In the case of impartible inheritance, the land itself is not divided, since the integrity of the holding can be maintained simply by dividing only movable property or paying off other heirs with cash. The practice of impartibility itself may be a result of manorial restrictions, statute or customary laws, or economic necessity. Where none of these operate and the land is divided among several heirs, the necessity of residing with the parents to succeed to the holding is eliminated and the likelihood of such a society producing a large proportion of extended families is thereby reduced. While such practices of partible inheritance have been associated with regions where new economic opportunities, such as the development of rural industry, allow subsistence to be maintained on smaller holdings,[6] Lutz Berkner has demonstrated that partibility can operate independently of such influences.[7] Moreover, it has been argued that the development of rural industry can be limited in regions of strict impartibility since there will be fewer opportunities to establish new households necessary for economic expansion.[8] Thus, the framework of inheritance practices has come to be seen as a critical factor in determining family structure.

With the advent of studies dealing with joint households in past European societies, the theoretical problems have become more complex. Anthropologists, of course, have been studying the joint family for decades. While there is some disagreement as to the precise definition of what constitutes a joint family, most scholars in the field distinguish the joint family from other forms of extended households by both its compositional structure and the nature of property relations among its members.[9] According to the most widely accepted view, the joint family is one in which parents and two or more married children, or two or more married siblings, reside together while at the same time holding property in common. Thus, coparcenary property rights constitute an important defining characteristic of the joint family. As T. N. Madan explained:

> Two criteria seem to be in the minds of most writers when they write on the joint family. These are: first, the existence of a familial group larger than the nuclear family and second, the existence of some property relations, if not joint, coparcenary rights, between all the members, or at least some of them . . . A great deal of confusion and uncertainty can be avoided if the terms joint family and extended family are not used synonymously. The joint family should be used with the ownership of joint property rights (and obligations) as the sole referent. Any particular type of composition of a familial group should not be regarded as an essential criterion for it to be called the joint family.[10]

This distinction can be shown to be empirically correct. In studies of family structure among European peasants, property rights differ sharply between members of stem and joint families. In regions where stem families predominate, the son or daughter who marries and remains with the parents is given outright ownership of the family's property. The parents are provided with a specified pension or may for a time retain use rights until they formally retire.[11] Thus, while sharing residence, ownership of the family patrimony is transferred to the new couple rather than shared. Among joint families, on the other hand, rather than transferring property between generations, new members are incorporated into an association in which property rights are shared equally by all members, in most cases for as long as the members reside together.[12]

In terms of actual family structure, this distinction is never so clear-cut. The structural composition of a household will not always enable the researcher to distinguish between "joint" and "stem" families. As has been repeatedly stressed by scholars, family structure constantly changes as children mature, marry, have children of their own, and the parents die. Because of this developmental cycle, the overall structural evolution of a family may be missed when its composition is viewed at a single point in time.[13] The household that at one point is a joint family may, at another, appear structurally like a stem family simply because only one child has married. In terms of the property relations among members, however, the joint family will always differ from the stem, even when they appear structurally alike.

Clearly, the formation of such family associations entails practices of partible inheritance. In fact, as the recent survey of some forty-six peasant societies by Walter Goldschmidt and Evalyn Kunkle has shown, joint families are found only where partible inheritance practices are carried out.[14] In this respect, the strategy leading to the formation of joint families resembles that which leads to nuclear families. In both cases, succession devolves more or less equally on several heirs. The two strategies differ fundamentally, however, on the actual practices regarding the disposition of the landholding following the settlement. Where land is divided outright, nuclear families are more likely to be formed than extended families. Where the integrity of the holding is preserved, the sharing of property rights tends to keep the coparceners together and joint families are likely to result. It is in this latter sense that stem and joint families resemble one another, since in both cases extended family formation hinges on the indivision of the landholding. Stem families are a consequence of a strategy by which the holding is passed onto a single heir in order to maintain this indivision. The joint family, on the other hand, is fostered by a strategy of equal partition of property rights among several heirs, but which is at the same time centered on the indivision of the land.

It is this combination of centrifugal and centripedal forces within the joint family that makes it both unique and fascinating. Both these characteristics are underlined in studies of the joint family undertaken by anthropologists and historians. The similarities between the developmental cycles of the joint family in such diverse societies as those of eastern Europe, China, and India are striking. As the children marry, first one, then another, are incorporated into the family association. Eventually, the cohesiveness of the family is broken as quarrels break out between the members. The tensions are heightened as grandchildren begin to reach maturity and the pressure on limited family resources is greatest. The authority of the father acts for a time to suppress such tensions, but after his death the quarrels develop to a point where continued coresidence becomes impossible. At this point the family breaks up.[15] The dissolution of the joint family is therefore as integral a part of its cycle as its initial formation. The strategy of succession leading to stem families produces tensions, especially when the transfer of control of the farm is delayed longer than the heir feels is appropriate. But the dissolution of the stem family occurs naturally with the death of the parents. The joint family is its own gravedigger. The basis for the tensions that inevitably lead to its breakup is created precisely at the moment that a second heir is incorporated into the association. The intriguing problem, therefore, is to explain this initial formation of joint family relations.

In discussing the dissensions generated by joint family ties, Eric Wolf remarked, "Taking these tensions into account we may expect that a society containing such family units will have to provide strong reinforcements to keep the units from flying apart."[16] In attempting to identify such reinforcements, anthropologists and historians have considered a number of factors and conditions which could account for the existence of the joint family within a society. These may be classified into two categories: those which are based on economic foundations or rooted on tenurial restrictions, and those based on cultural predispositions of a society.

Among those who have argued that the crucial factors fostering joint family ties are found within the economic and social structures of a society, the conditions most often cited are those of the ratio between land and labor and the specific tenurial relations under which peasants hold the land they farm. E. A. Hammel has argued that the availability of land enabled Balkan peasant families to increase their economic base and thereby avoid the dissolution of the joint household, or *zadruga*.[17] The severe population declines of the late Middle Ages created similar conditions in Lanquedoc, the Bordelaise, and Tuscany. In order to ensure a sufficient work force for their now enlarged holdings, peasants formed joint families and relied primarily on the labor of adult kin.[18] In their survey of peasant societies, Goldschmidt and Kunkel noted that joint families existed only in regimes characterized either by an abundance of land or by recent availability of land.[19]

While high land–labor ratios may explain the initial development of joint families in a society, they obviously cannot explain their persistence in societies where increasing population exerts pressure on land resources. Yet, as Andrejs Plakans has demonstrated, these were precisely the conditions under which the joint family flourished in Kurland during the eighteenth century. Unlike Lanquedoc, where the joint family subsequently disappeared under the impact of population pressure and the continued division of landholdings, large, complex families were maintained by the Kurland peasantry.[20] The key to their survival lay in the tenurial relations existing in the region during that period. As serfs subject to the dictates of a vigorous manorial regime, peasant families in the Kurland were forbidden to divide their fairly substantial farms in order that these would be able to support the considerable *corvée* demands imposed by the lords. Without control over the disposition of land, the underlying conditions of labor demands necessary to work both the farms and the lord's *domaine* persisted throughout succeeding cycles of family expansion and fission. In this case, the restrictions imposed by the manorial regime acted to ensure the survival of joint family relations under demographic conditions which might otherwise have spelled their doom. In central France and in Italy during the eighteenth and nineteenth centuries, sharecropping acted in precisely the same way, by removing from peasant families any control whatsoever over land, thereby assuring the persistence of joint family ties.[21] It is significant that where such restrictions were absent, population increase has resulted in a decline in joint family formation. This occurred not only in sixteenth-century Lanquedoc, but in the Balkans during the nineteenth century. There, in one of the classic regions of the joint family, population pressure acted to transform the *zadruga* from joint to stem family structures.[22]

For many cultural anthropologists, however, neither land availability or restrictions imposed on the disposition of land are sufficient by themselves to account for variations in family structures among societies. Underlying the economic and social structures of any society rests the more important realm of cultural values and traditions. Culture, as defined by this school, is an organized system of knowledge and beliefs whereby a people structure their lives, experiences, and perceptions. A society's cultural values provide the standards by which alternative actions are formulated and chosen, and influence not only patterns of behavior but social organization as well. As one leading American anthropologist explained:

> On the [cultural] level there is the framework of beliefs, expressive symbols, and values in terms of which individuals define their world, express their feelings, and make their judgements; on the [social] level there is the ongoing process of interactive behavior, whose persistent form we call social structure. Culture is the fabric of meaning in terms of which human beings interpret their experience and guide their actions; social structure is the form that action takes, the actually existing network of social relations.[23]

In terms of the joint family, so the argument goes, cultural values and beliefs provide the rewards and sanctions that cement the bonds among kin. These may be found, as Wolf suggests, in the ceremonial sphere where rewards and punishments are provided for what is considered proper or improper behavior. Or, these can be found in the realm of socialization, which may render the individual dependent upon the domestic group and reinforce the tendency to continually seek support from within the family unit.[24] This latter argument has been adopted by Peter Laslett as the basis for defining the point at which a particular form of family structure can be said to be the predominant form for a society.

9

A form of the coresident domestic group can be said to be *the* familial institution of a society in permanency over time if a sufficient number of persons being born into that society are being continuously socialized within domestic groups of the structure nominated. Only this will ensure that such a familial form is a fact of their experience in the particular sense which is necessary if that familial form is to be present as an established norm of behavior. Under these circumstances alone will the whole society be dominated by individuals who, when they have to make decisions as to where they will live after marriage, or whether to permit or encourage their own relatives to reside with them, or their children to join their spouses to the familial group, will tend to make those decisions in such a way as to reproduce the familial form in question. [25]

A similar argument has been invoked by Robert Wheaton to explain the cultural basis of the joint family. After examining several economic and social variables which may have given rise to joint families, Wheaton concludes that none were in themselves sufficiently strong to support such ties without the reinforcement of a system of kinship already predisposed toward strong patrilineal ties favoring solidarity between fathers and sons and especially between brothers. "Where a society opts for the joint household system over any period of time, the system must be supported by elements in kinship structure which reinforce and support certain roles and relationships. As these elements become institutionalized in law and embodied in custom, they build into the culture a bias in favor of that household system". [26]

Neither Wheaton nor those who argue along similar lines deny the importance of the effects of economic factors on family structure. In virtually every study of the joint family or of extended family structure where wealth or class has been employed as a variable, the extended family has been shown to be a class-specific phenomenon occurring mainly among the wealthier peasantry and rarely among those without land or without direct access to it. The response to this evidence has been that class differentiation in family structure is due more to the economic limitations imposed by poverty than by differences imposed by labor needs, property relations, or even preferences. According to this view, family formation is seen as a factor of cultural emulation in which the poor strive to imitate the norms of social behavior established by the wealthy, usually with little success. [27]

One of the weaknesses of the emphasis on family structure apart from tenure or property is that such arguments fail to show causality or explain change over time. Wheaton, for example, notes (erroneously) that the joint family in western Europe disappeared after the sixteenth century, yet offers no explanation for such a fundamental change. If, as he argues, the crucial factor underlying their existence was the solidarity between related males, especially brothers, then logically the decline of such families could only have been a consequence of a declining value placed on such bonds. Where such cultural changes have not taken place, for whatever reasons, the extended family will continue to flourish.

This is precisely the question around which the debate over the joint family in India raged a decade ago. Because the weakening of ties beyond the conjugal group was considered by many to be a critical factor behind economic development (historians will recognize this as the growth of individualism), the question was whether, or to what extend, the persistence of the extended family in the subcontinent might pose a hindrance to Indian economic development. The most influential statement of the view that the cultural predispositions underlying the extended family can have a detrimental effect on economic development was William Goode's *World Revolution and Family Patterns*. Goode posed the problem in these terms:

> We can . . . assert that Western family systems have had an effect on industrialization. To make an extreme comparison, Western industrialization would have developed more slowly if those family systems had perhaps been patriarchal and polygymous, with a full development of arranged child marriages and a harem system . . . . It seems plausible, then, that by the early period in the industrializing Western World some changes in family patterns had already occurred which, to some extent, prepared the lower strata of workers for industrialization.[28]

The origin of such a change, for Goode, was the rise of individualism resulting from the Protestant Reformation. Goode then attributed responsibility for retarded economic development in the Third World to the extended family and its culturally determined ties of kinship.

> It must be conceded that in modern work enterprises in underdeveloped countries there is no general shortage of labor . . . but instances abound of workers returning to their villages and families when they are needed at the factory, or earning enough for a family obligation and then quitting, or exhibiting a low commitment to the factory job because their primary responsibility lay with their extended kin and its obligations.[29]

This is, of course, an extreme view and results in part from a complete misreading of both family structure and kinship in European history. Yet precisely the same accusation has been recently made by Alain Corbin in his study of economic development in the Limousin during the nineteenth century. According to Corbin, innovations such as new crop rotations and more rational farm methods failed to gain rapid acceptance in the region in large part because of the extended family's emphasis on paternal authority and family cohesiveness rather than on individual self-motivation.[30] Retarded economic growth was, for Corbin, a consequence of the "traditionalism" of the joint family.

Thus, most social scientists have argued that the transformation of family systems is largely a function of ideological and cultural changes associated with the impact of modern social relations. Economic development presupposes greater economic efficiency. Traditional value systems emphasizing the importance of kinship ties and respect for parental authority, so it is argued, have no place in a society where behavior is geared towards maximizing economic returns to the individual or his immediate family. The weakening of kinship ties beyond the nuclear family therefore presumes a transformation of cultural values. Underlying the theory of modernization is an assumption that economic development is contingent on a transformation of mentalities, that greater economic efficiency can be achieved only when people consciously renounce or are forced to renounce cultural values not aimed at the rational maximization of monetary income and profit. So-called traditional societies are viewed as being characterized by values diametrically opposed to such aims. Social status, obligations to kin, attitudes toward other members of the community are governed by measures and sanctions that often have little to do with mere pecuniary gain. As the process of modernization takes hold, such traditional value systems give way to modern ones, obligation towards distant kin give way to individual self-interest, and the large, extended household gives way to the nuclear family.

Even when a decline in traditional cultural values is linked to broader economic transformations—the rise of markets is the usual villain—the changes are seen as the result of an intrusion of new ideas into "traditional" societies. The conflict between the two value systems is often described as protracted, with "traditionalism" fiercely resisting the onslaught of "modernization." While traditional culture may survive in various forms and practices, the outcome is never in doubt. Modernization always emerges as triumphant.

The Nivernais as a Case Study in Family Change

The Nivernais offers an excellent opportunity to test these theories. Extending east from the Loire River, the Nivernais is a region of gently rolling hills separated by broad valleys. The province of the Nivernais was largely created by the counts of Nevers, later elevated to the rank of dukes in the sixteenth century. During the Middle Ages, the various ruling houses of Nevers pursued a policy of territorial expansion, acquiring new lands through marriage alliances or outright conquest. By the twelfth century the political boundaries of the Nivernais were definitively established. The province included, in addition to the county of Nevers, the barony of Donzy, the county of Château-Chinon and several smaller *châtellenies* and *seigneuries* to the north and across the Loire to the west. The present-day boundaries of the *département* of the Nièvre roughly parallel those of the former province.

Because the medieval expansion of the Nivernais was governed by political opportunities rather than economic necessity, the province retained little in the way of geographic unity or economic integration. In fact, the Nivernais straddles the geographic division between the broad plains of northern France and the uplands of the Massif Central. The northern third of the Nivernais, characterized by open-field farming and nucleated villages, had for centuries possessed close economic ties to the Paris Basin. The Nivernais has long been one of the most heavily forested regions of France, yet it was only the north, where the river system flows into that of northern France, that was able to capitalize on the province's woodlands. Since the early sixteenth century trees were felled and floated down the Yonne River to the city of Clamecy. There the logs were formed into rafts and steered to Paris, providing the capital with fuel and lumber.

The southwest Nivernais, however, was linked economically to the Berry, the Bourbonnais, and other regions of central and western France. Its exports consisted primarily of cattle, sheep, and pigs. Here forests were employed chiefly in fueling small, primitive iron foundries manufacturing farm implements and other products for the local market. The eastern third of the Nivernais, known as the Morvan, is often referred to by writers as the Scotland of France, and with good reason. With its sheep, rugged mountains and dense forests, this area had for centuries remained isolated from the rest of France. Well into the nineteenth century its people spoke a patois that could be understood only with great difficulty by outsiders. Whatever economic ties it did possess with the outside world were largely with Burgundy to the east.

Indeed, the Morvan had at one time been ruled by the dukes of Burgundy until the region was absorbed by the counts of Nevers.

Apart from the small metal industries scattered throughout the forests of the southern Nivernais, the economy of the province was entirely agarian and essentially geared for local markets. Up to the 1830s the only

Map 1. The Nivernais

————— Département of the Nièvre

— — — Duchy of the Nivernais

means of communication and transport were provided by the Loire River, unnavigable during the summer months, and a single royal road skirting the river on its eastern bank. Aside from the export of cattle and lumber, the only markets for agriculture were a dozen or so towns of two to three thousand inhabitants and the city of Nevers, with a population of some thirteen thousand.

Economic isolation seems to have brought with it a kind of indifference to national politics. In 1814 the prefect for the Nièvre noted that "the *département* will never have a public spirit which it can call its own since it is impossible for it to have the least influence on events which decide the fate of France. It follows movements, never leads them."[31] The one notable exception to this political apathy was the rebellion by the raftsman of Clamecy against the coup d'etat of Louis Napoleon in 1852. Each year these men guided rafts of lumber and fuel to Paris, where frequent contact with working men's associations generated a political awareness that distinguished them from the passive peasant farmers. The uprising of 1852 was one of the bloodiest in France that year.[32]

If the political significance of the Nivernais was rather limited, the region possessed at least one institution which has aroused the interest of social scientists and legal historians. This was, of course, the *communauté*. As early as the sixteenth century, jurists such as Coquille commented on the uniqueness of such a form of household organization. Yet sustained interest in the *communauté* developed only in the nineteenth century, when the institution became a focal point of French conservative ideology. Whatever one's overall assessment of nineteenth century conservatism, it must be acknowledged that social scientists in general and students of the family in particular owe a great deal to the social theories developed by French conservatives of that era. These individuals, of whom Frederic LePlay was the foremost and best known, initiated the first anthropological field studies in history and developed a theoretical framework that continues to influence social science to this day.

Reacting against the social dislocations that accompanied economic development, conservatives in France formulated a fairly coherent ideology to account for the political and social instability of their country. This instability, in their view, resulted from the breakdown of time-honored institutions, customs and traditions that had, at one time, fostered social harmony by integrating each individual into a large community. The patriarchal family, the church, the village community, the benevolence of a paternalistic landlord or employer, and above all, the force of custom, had together served as powerful social controls over a human nature that was seen as essentially corrupt and evil. Urbanization, industrialization, and the rise of the modern bureaucratic state, by promoting individualism and self-interest, had uprooted the individual from the community, weakened the restraining force of custom and led to social conflict, class antagonism and moral degeneration.

Of all the institutions promoting social harmony, conservatives had the greatest respect for the family. By this, they meant the large, partriarchal extended family presided over by the eldest male, and within which the role of each person, kin and servant alike, was clearly defined. And it was precisely this institution that, in their view, was being destroyed most rapidly by the impact of modern, individualistic society. LePlay spent much of his life attempting to define precisely the characteristics of the patriarchal family. Indeed it was LePlay who first formulated the distinctions between extended, stem, and nuclear families. It was his aim to show how, when the family was reduced to the conjugal unit of parents and children, the moral function of the family was seriously jeopardized. For LePlay, the crass individualism that was undermining the mutual respect of employer and employee had its origins in the disintegration of family solidarity, paternal authority and filial devotion.

LePlay consistently argued that the root cause of these problems lay with the laws regulating succession adopted by the National Convention and incorporated into the Napoleonic Code. By instituting forced equality between heirs, the new laws struck at the basis of family stability: the integrity of the patrimony. At the same time, the abolition of parental rights to pass on the family estate to the most capable heir or heirs was contributing to moral decline. "Young people, secure in their birthright, pretend to enjoy from their very birth the wealth created by their elders. They feel not in the least inclined to show themselves worthy by virtue of work. Rebelling against the authority of their parents, they abandon themselves to sensual appetites and passing fancies."[33] Throughout his life, LePlay sought to cure the social ills of his time by reinstituting parental testamentary rights. Once restored to its former stability by such actions, the family would serve as a model for all social relations, creating a natural harmony among all classes.

Such views gained a considerable influence and LePlay attracted numerous followers and supporters, the most ardent of whom grouped themselves around the journal *La Réforme sociale,* founded the year of LePlay's death. The journal achieved immediate success and continues to be published even today. Throughout the 1870s and 1880s, clubs and associations were established to promote reform along the lines advocated by LePlay. Some of the most influential notables from the *département* of the Nièvre were drawn into the movement. Indeed, it was within the sociological framework established by LePlay that most of the early studies of the *communauté* in the Nivernais were written,

The theories advanced today that changes in family patterns are largely the result of a transformation of values, customs, and traditions thus had its origins in the interpretation of social change advanced by LePlay; only the value judgments have been eliminated. However, the closer attention one pays to the actual function of kinship ties, family structure, and household organization in any society, the more the distinction between "traditional" and "modern," between gemeinschaft and gesellschaft, begin to disappear. So-called traditional family patterns emerge as adaptations to the political, legal, and economic environments in which families live, adaptions which have essentially one goal, the continued survival of the family and the individuals who comprise it. When the legal or economic environment is altered, as with industrialization, families will, of necessity, readapt to meet the new demands posed by social change, and establish new strategies and practices to fit the new environment.

In this book I will concentrate on one aspect of the way in which families in peasant society have adapted themselves to meet the demands posed by the physical, social, and economic environment in which they live, that of the household organization. The term is here used to mean not simply household structure per se—that is, how many and which relatives coreside in a given household—but rather the entire network of property rights accorded family members, the division and allocation of family labor, and the uses to which family income is employed. The peasant family must be considered as a single unit of production aiming to provide subsistence for its members. Peasant families may employ any number of a variety of strategies regarding the organization of property rights, labor, and income, but all have a common aim in securing their own livelihood.

The title *Family and Farm* is intended to reflect the principal argument of the book: that peasant household organization is intrinsically linked to the farm that provides subsistence for the family. A thorough understanding of peasant household organization cannot be achieved without careful analysis of the peasant farm. It is the farm, after all, that maintains the family and it is the property rights of family members to the farm, the way in which family labor is allocated, and the uses to

17

which farm income are employed that determine household organization. The peasant farm, however, cannot be examined simply in terms of its mere physical nature, the size or the character of the land. A farm is much more than its fields, meadows, and buildings; it is the way in which these are utilized. A farm worked by oxen-drawn plow, hoe and spade is obviously something different from one worked by tractor and combine. Household organization is effected not only by the size of the farm but by the level of agricultural technology as well. Farm methods requiring considerable inputs of labor mean that families must, in some way, provide the labor, whether by relying on hired hands or on kin. In either case, income and property rights must be employed in such a way to satisfy these needs. By the same token, technical changes will necessitate a change in household organization.

Yet, the characteristics of the peasant farm encompass much more than its physical nature and the level of agricultural technology. Peasant societies, by their very definition, exist within a political, social, and economic framework extending well beyond the individual peasant community. Anthropologists usually distinguish peasant societies from food cultivators in general by their integration into a larger society comprising a dominant aristocracy, a large centralized state, urban centers, or all of these combined. Such was the intended meaning of Alfred Kroeber when he referred to peasantries as "part societies" and of Robert Redfield's distinction between the "Great Tradition" (the laws, customs, and ideologies of the large society) and the "Little Tradition" of the individual peasant community.[34]

The peasantry, as such, is subject to the demands and sanctions of a social stratum existing outside the peasant class itself, sanctions maintained either by force, economic necessity, or both. Whatever the means by which peasants are incorporated into a larger society, these ultimately center on the status accorded the land. The demands of the state for taxes, of a landlord class for rents, dues, or services, or of urban centers for disposal surpluses subsume the peasantry in a network of rights and obligations that specify and define control over land. Tenural relationships are the most obvious and evident form this control may take. Yet the charges levied by political states over so-called free peasants with direct and outright ownership of the land must be included in this system of control. Indeed, it is often just such demands that integrate peasantries into national economies where surpluses can be exchanged for cash needed to pay taxes.

All these elements—the physical nature of the farm, the way the land is worked, and the legal obligation under which the land subsumed—

constitute the peasant farm as such. And it is within this framework that the peasant family must organize itself. The history of the joint family in the Nivernais is largely the story of how individual families organized themselves in order to cope with the problems of wresting a living from their farms, and how changes affecting the nature of their farms forced them to continually readapt the organization of their household. Different forms of household organization were adopted, not because of the dictates of culture or tradition, but because these enabled individual families to meet the demands imposed by the social, economic, and physical environment in which they lived.

CHAPTER TWO

The *Communauté,* Customary Law, and Feudal Tenure

Any investigation of household complexity in the Nivernais must begin with an examination of the term *communauté.* Virtually the entire body of source materials, and most French historians as well, employ this term to describe complex households rather than the more precise terms of "stem family" or "joint family." It must be understood that the terms joint household and *communauté* are by no means synonymous. The word *communauté* itself is a legal term describing any group sharing property; it does not describe any particular kind of household structure. In fact, it need not even describe the property relations of related persons, since it could be employed by nonrelated businessmen to describe their commercial ventures. Pooling their capital into a common fund, such persons would establish a *communauté* for a given period of time, after which profits—or debts—would be divided by the members.[1]

Among related persons, the term *communauté* was employed to describe the sharing of property rights between husband and wife, between parents and children, or between more distantly related kin. To have incorporated a specific set of kinship relations into the legal definition of *communauté* would have restricted its usefulness with respect to families. Household composition is far from static. It continually changes as parents age, children are born and mature, marry and have children of their own. The legal term denoting the co-ownership of property by kinsmen had to be loose enough to allow for such an evolution, since membership in the *communauté* would change as new members were incorporated from within by birth and from without by marriage. As Dupin put it, "When *[a communauté]* lasts for a considerable time, and especially if it does so for several centuries, what is each person's share? What belongs to whom? Everyone is related, but to what degree? All this would be impossible to define and unravel. The only thing one knows is that one is *en communauté*."[2] The mere existence of a *communauté*, therefore, does not describe any particular form of household structure. It merely denotes certain aspects of property relations among members, relations which can link a wide range of persons.

Up to the sixteenth century, customary law in much of France assumed that anyone living together for a year and a day, and who had shared property and income during that time, had in effect formed a *communauté* by tacit agreement. Since there was no written contract involved, it was called a *communauté tacite* or *taisible*. During the fifteenth century such *communautés taisibles* came to be viewed with increased disfavor by jurists since common residence after the pre-scribed period could be used by persons to claim rights in a relative's property even if this had not been their original intention.[3] One attempt to prevent frauds of this kind was the Ordinance de Moulins, issued in 1566. It did not seek to destroy the *communauté taisible,* as was sometimes claimed, but sought to put an end to conflicts and injustices that could be provoked within them by ordering that any agreement involving property valued at one hundred *livres* or more would require a written contract.[4]

More forceful attacks on the *communauté taisible* were carried out when the various customs of France were codified during the sixteenth century. Many prohibited the *communauté taisible* outright while others severely restricted it to specific sets of kin. In some cases, the final codifications of customary law imposed restrictions on the *communauté* which had not existed in earlier versions. The first edition of the customs of Nantes in 1506, for example, had allowed the *communauté taisible* between the parents and affines; all that was required was common residence and the mixing of *meubles,* or personal property. The version finally drawn up in 1560, however, stated that no *communauté* could exist without a written contract, regardless of who had lived together or for how long.[5] In the Nivernais the *communauté taisible* was also restricted, but much less so than in most other provinces. A *communauté taisible* could be formed by four categories of people: married persons, widowed persons and their children, adult brothers, and between parents and their sons- or daughters-in-law.[6] Coquille in fact was not at all happy with these restrictions. He argued that a contract existed, even if unwritten, between any persons who had lived together and had shared property and income for several years. "A convention can be expressed or tacit, because intention and consent are also reported and proven by deeds and by words.'' How far Coquille's interpretation was accepted by other jurists is open to question. It may well have existed in the popular mentality, for there is considerable evidence that people felt threatened by the mere fact of coresidence, even when they lived with persons whose relationship to them specifically precluded the existence of a *communauté taisible*. Notary acts exist in which persons living with fairly distant kin, even servants, filed a *contradiction de communauté* to insure that no claim could be leveled against their property.[8]

Whatever the precise legal distinctions between a *communauté* established by written contract and a *communauté* established by tacit agreement, it must be stressed that the word itself denotes nothing at all about kinship or family structure as such. It was simply the legal term for a group sharing property and income. Nevertheless, in the Old Regime it was usually associated with a family or a group of kinsmen living together. Its importance, in terms of family organization, lies in the degree to which property rights were extended to members of the kin group. In northern France, the *communauté* usually comprised only parents and children; in the Pyrenees, Lanquedoc, and Provence, *communautés* were formed as stem families, uniting parents and one married child; in much of central France, including the Nivernais, they were often the basis for the joint family.

It would be erroneous, however, to view the varying provisions of *communauté* as *the* factor determining household structure. The *communauté* was only a part of the overall system of legal provisions regulating family property and must be interpreted within a context that also includes the settlement of inheritance. The relationship between inheritance practices and family structure has been noted by both anthropologists and historians. The important factor is whether land itself is divided, with impartible inheritance usually linked to stem families and partible to either nuclear or joint families.[9] Nivernais customary law governing inheritance gave parents a great deal of leeway in determining the disposition of the family patrimony by allowing them to favor one child at the expense of their others. Parents were free to pass on the vast bulk of their estate to a single heir by donation or testament if they so chose, the only restriction being that those excluded had claim to their *legitime,* defined as one-third to one-half of the share they would have received had the estate been divided equally.[10] Inheritance customs in the Nivernais, therefore, would not *necessarily* give rise to joint households. While a father could incorporate two or more of his children into the *communauté,* he could just as easily exclude all but one from the inheritance settlement, a practice which would lead to stem families. Even beyond the problem of inheritance practices is the more crucial question of whether property, once the settlement had taken place, would be held jointly. The determining factor appears to have rested on the tenurial status of the family's property.

The Evolution of Feudal Tenure in the Nivernais

At the time of the codification of customary law in the sixteenth century, the most common form of tenure in the Nivernais was known as *bordelage,* a mitigated form of serfdom.[11] The leaseholder, or *bordelier,* paid an entrance fee *(entrage)* plus a fixed annual rent in money and in kind. In return, he held the property in perpetuity for himself and his heirs. While *bordelage* property could in no way be damaged or rendered less productive by the leaseholder, he could make any improvements he desired without fear of an increase in dues. This apparent security of tenure, however, was subject to certain restrictions. Failure to pay dues for three consecutive years could result in the reversion of the property to the *seigneur.* The property, when returned in this way, was free and clear of all debts and obligations that the *bordelier* may have incurred on the property. The *bordelier,* however, continued to be held responsible for all arrears and could be pursued in court to force payment. Probably the most significant restrictions posed by *bordelage* were the provisions governing succession to the leasehold. First, succession to *bordelage* property required that the heir be living in a *communauté* with the leaseholder at the time of his death. Second, it was forbidden to permanently divide property held under *bordelage.* Failure to adhere to these provisions meant that the property reverted to the *seigneur,* again, free and clear of all obligations levied against it, including any rights of dower claimed by the widow. "In short," wrote Coquille, "*bordelage* amasses all the harshest conditions to which other tenures are subject."[12]

Bordelage has been cited almost universally by historians as the most crucial factor that fostered the large complex households of the Nivernais. "Their origin," stated Victor de Cheverry, one of Frederic LePlay's associates, "is to be found in *Bordelage.*"[13] Half a century later, the same conclusion was reached by Dr. Turpin in an excellent monograph on *communauté* in the Nivernais: "The aim of the *communauté* was to make possible the contracting of *bordelage;* by the same token, *bordelage* was the basis of the *communauté.*"[14] These findings were arrived at not without some justification. The link between the *communauté* and *bordelage* seems obvious. The overriding concern governing succession to the leasehold was the existence of a *communauté* between the leaseholder and his heirs. Legally, the existence of a *communauté* held more weight in this question than degree of kinship tie. The closest relative of a *bordelier,* if not his coparcener, would see the property pass to a more distant relative if this latter were a member of the deceased's *communauté.*[15] Hereditary rights to land held under *bordelage,* therefore, were directly dependent on having coresident heirs. At the same time, the constraints against partition of *bordelage* property made it entirely consistent with a system of succession based on exclusion. For while succession to *bordelage* depended on the existence of a *communauté,* a *bordelage* leasehold had to pass onto successive generations intact. Even the largest holding had an upper limit on the number of people it could support, so that some children would have to be settled with nonlanded property. Thus both the inheritance preferences given to coresident heirs and the exclusion of other children were well suited to the restrictions imposed by *bordelage.*

It is certain, however, that the *communauté* existed long before *bordelage* itself became widespread in the Nivernais. Up to the fifteenth century the most common form of tenure in the province was *mainmorte personnelle,* or personal serfdom. The importance of *mainmorte* is indicated by the care given by jurists who drew up the first written body of customary law for the Nivernais in 1490. These customs contained more articles governing serfdom than any other form of tenure. Further evidence of the predominance of *mainmorte* over *bordelage* comes from a *terrier* compiled in 1288 for the Bishopric of Nevers.[16] At that time, only thirty-one *bordelage* tenures existed on the five manors of the bishop compared to 1,449 servile tenures. In fact *mainmorte* acted in such a way as to continually expand the serf population of the province. Unlike provinces such as Champagne where a child was considered free so long as one parent was free, personal serfdom in the Nivernais was governed by the rule "le pire y emporte le bon." That is, a child was considered a serf if only one of his parents was a serf.

Until the fifteenth century serfs were considered "taillable et explectable à volonté." That is, the levies and charges imposed by their lords were not subject to any formal restriction whatsoever. Furthermore, virtually all the restrictions on peasant control over property that *bordelage* attached to the land were, with *mainmorte,* attached to the person of the serf. Succession by serfs to their parents' holding was subject to greater restrictions than that of *bordelage* because of the precarious nature of the servile *communauté*. Like *bordelage*, failure to have an heir residing in common with the parent at the time of their deaths meant that the entire holding reverted to the lord. *Mainmorte* differed from *bordelage*, however, in that its restrictions on the various members of the *communauté* were far more strict. Governed by the rule "un party tout party," a servile *communauté* was deemed dissolved by the absence of any member for more than a year and a day and could be reconstituted only with *seigneurial* permission. The severity of this rule was tempered by a statute issued in 1235 by Mahaut de Courtenay, countess of Nevers, stating that the marriage of children out of their parents' *communauté* would in no way threaten the integrity of the association.[17] Thus the rule "un party tout party" was applied only in cases where formal division of the *communauté* took place.

Because of the nature of these restrictions on the servile *communauté*, the ability of *seigneurs* to exact fines of this kind tended to increase with the structural complexity of the peasant household. If a serf holding passed intact to a single heir no fines could be levied by the *seigneur*. However, when two or more heirs were incorporated into the *communauté*, the natural tendency towards dissolution characterizing all joint families created opportunities for *seigneurial* exactions. Brothers who at one time had been incorporated into their parents' *communauté* would eventually have to dissolve the association as their own children began to grow into adulthood and the pressure on family resources increased. When this occurred the lord had the right to levy a fine. Examples of such transactions exist in numerous documents surviving from the late Middle Ages. When the *communauté* of Estienne Folot and his two brothers, serfs of the manor of Beldeduit, was divided in 1443, their lord granted Estienne the right to form another *communauté* in exchange for six salus of gold. He further stipulated that the members of the newly reconstituted *communauté* were "communs san partaiges à faire de temps advenir et demourent heritiers et successeurs les uns et les autres."[18] That is, the lord made sure that in any future divisions, he would be able to collect similar fines.

Lord-serf relations in the Nivernais were abruptly transformed by the general crisis of the late Middle Ages. With the Black Death and repeated outbreaks of plague and epidemics throughout the fourteenth and fifteenth centuries, population in the Nivernais declined dramatically. In some villages population may have dropped by as much as sixty to seventy percent.[19] Compounding the effects of plague and disease were the disruptions caused by the Hundred Years' War. The Nivernais, which had passed to the dukes of Burgundy in 1384, figured as a major battlefield during this period and suffered further in the struggles between the crown and the Burgundian dukes. The disruptions caused by troop movements, pillaging, and sieges left the province devastated. Farms were abandoned and whole villages deserted by population loss and peasant flight. Numerous documents from the period attest to the severity of conditions brought on by war and pestilence. In 1474 the inhabitants of Château-Chinon declared the countryside surrounding their town to be utterly desolate.

> Because of the recent wars and divisions, the inhabitants have had to sustain several great losses and inestimable damages because the town of Château-Chinon is situated on the frontier of France. During these wars and divisions, the French have continually raided and pillaged the countryside, so much so that the inhabitants were totally ruined, their goods and chatel lost, their homes and buildings burned, their houses demolished. Most have been led away as prisoners, for which they have had to pay large sums. . . . Because of these wars they had been forced to flee their villages and towns and go to live elsewhere in great poverty and misery.[20]

The survivors who remained were faced with increasing financial burdens as their lords sought compensation for declining revenues brought about by population decline and peasant flight.[21] The dukes of Burgundy spearheaded the movement by imposing extraordinary levies on the province in order to finance their war effort. Local lords followed suit, both by increasing tallages at will and through a bold-faced attempt to nullify the statute of 1235. Throughout the Nivernais, lords claimed the right to impose fines whenever children of serfs married outside their parents' *communauté*. Thus the priors of Saint-Révérien and the lords of Corbigny and Lormes declared that serf *communautés* were deemed dissolved with the marriage of children outside the association. The duke of Burgundy also tried to override the 1235 statute by attempting to exact a twelfth of a bride's dowry if she left her parents' *communauté*.[22]

In the face of growing levies, tallages, and threats to the integrity of their *communauté*, peasant discontent erupted into open rebellion. In the words of Andre Bossuaf, "Peasants did not discuss the conditions of serfdom; they simply rejected it outright."[23] The people of the county of Château-Chinon not only refused to pay the new charges demanded by the duke of Burgundy, but declared themselves to be free persons and therefore not subject to arbitrary tallages or servile restrictions.[24] The duke's officers were able to carry out their leader's *arrêt* only by physically commandeering the movable property of the inhabitants.

Fighting repeatedly broke out until, in 1447, peasants won the right to a fixed *taille* as well as the right to determine its distribution. At Saint-Révérien, Corbigny, and Lormes the same demands were voiced by peasants whose *seigneurs* claimed the right to tax their subjects twice a year, "une fois plus et l'autre moins comme bon leur semble." A protracted struggle between the prior of Saint-Révérien and his peasants began in 1410 and lasted for forty years. The intervention of the Paris Parlement to restore order resulted in a decree granting peasants the right to have their daughters marry without fines on their *communautés* but upheld the right of the prior to impose arbitrary taxes. However, continued peasant resistance appears to have prevented the last part of the decision from being enforced. At Crux disturbances over the same issues resulted in yet another intervention by the royal courts. In 1459 the Parlement declared further tallages would be levied only once a year and with the consultation of representatives of the local inhabitants.[25]

In countless similar struggles servile charges were progressively attenuated as peasant resistance, flight, and the intervention of royal courts to maintain order forced lords to accede to peasant demands. The *seigneur* of Apremont freed his subjects in 1426 because he was unable to prevent their flight: "Due to the conditions of *mainmorte*," he declared in their charter, "many men flee and continue to flee each day to reside in the nearby Bourbonnais. . . . The land, which ought to be of great value, diminishes every day."[26] A *terrier* for the fiefs of Concley, Luzy, and Lanty in the Morvan drawn up in 1488 initially stated that the tenants there were "taillable, corveable et exploictable"; a year later these words were replaced with "à volonté raissonable."[27] A *dénombrement* for the *seigneurie* of Marcy dated 1409 declared that the peasants of the manor were "mainmortable et taillable à volonté." Beginning in 1459, however, individual serfs were freed in growing numbers. By 1542 when another *terrier* was compiled for the manor the tenants were stated to be *censitaires*.[28]

In addition to franchises granted to entire communities, there is evidence of countless individual families negotiating directly with their lords in order to obtain their freedom, to fix permanently their dues, and to transform their holdings into *censives* or *bordelages*. In 1457, for example, Jean Millin and his family, serfs of the priory of Saint-Pierre-de-Decize, were able to secure the right to marry children freely and to fix tallage exactions by ceding to their lord a hectare of land and meadow. Other families simply denied outright their servile status, took their cases to court and were able to win their freedom. At Decize, Huguenin, Philibert, and Andre Courrault, "cousins et communs parconniers," denied the claims of their lord, Jean du Pre, that they were "his men and of servile condition . . . *mainmortables* and subject to *corvées* and *tallages* at the rate of thirty *sols tournois,* or another sum greater or less, such as it pleases their lord." The Courraults had refused to pay their dues for several years and in the meantime had brought suit against du Pre after he had seized part of their holdings. Du Pre, apparently unable to show written proof of his claims, agreed to free the Courraults in exchange for half a hectare of meadowland and further transformed their lands into *bordelage* leaseholds.[29]

In some cases the confusion brought about by peasant flight and the leasing of abandoned tenacies to new immigrants resulted in conflicting claims over the status of individual families. Thomas Dodin and his *communs personniers* had immigrated from Burgundy in the late fifteenth century and established themselves at Maulois in the southeast Nivernais on "heritages vagues, non tenus ne occupes par aucunes persones." After several years their new *seigneur,* Jean de Saint-Amour, claimed that the Dodins were his serfs and had been for "so long that there was no memory of the contrary." The Dodins countered by claiming that they had occupied their holding according to the custom of Burgundy, "by which it is said that tenancies are servile and not the person." They agreed to pay all dues arising from the land but denied that their persons were subject to the restrictions imposed by Nivernais law. When the case was taken finally to Parlement, the claims of the Dodins were vindicated and their lands declared to be *bordelage* leaseholds.[30] In all these cases the transfer of tenant holdings to *bordelages* achieved the principal demands voiced by peasants. It eliminated the threat posed to their *communautés* by the rule "un party tout party" and fixed their dues once and for all. In the end, the attempt to revise marriage restrictions on the servile *communauté* also failed. When customary laws were codified in 1534 the right of serfs to freely allow their children to marry out of their *communautés* was confirmed.[31]

With the cessation of hostilities in the Nivernais after the defeat of Burgundian forces in 1475 and the death of Charles the Bold two years later, *seigneurs* embarked on a vigorous campaign to reconstitute deserted holdings. However, new tenancies were now leased out under *bordelage* contracts rather than under *mainmorte*. This reconquest of deserted farmland can be documented from surviving manorial records. All the new tenures granted after 1439 at the manors of Prye and Azy, just east of Nevers, were *bordelage* leases, usually on lands described as "terre en desert" or "terre en friche."[32] At the barony of Vitry in the southeast Nivernais near Burgundy a similar pattern occurred. A *terrier* dated 1438 listed only forty-seven tenants while another compiled between 1526 and 1533 listed on hundred and fifty-one tenants. Several villages and hamlets appearing in the later document had not been listed in the earlier survey, indicating either the reoccupation of deserted villages or the opening up of new lands.[33] By the early sixteenth century *bordelage* appears to have been widespread throughout most of the Nivernais. One writer at that time asserted that three-fourths of the territory surrounding Nevers was held under *bordelage*.[34] The claim has support from manorial records of the eighteenth century. A *terrier* drawn up in 1780 for the manor of Saint-Baudiere, just west of Nevers, shows thirty-eight of fifty-six articles subject to *bordelage*.[35]

By the eighteenth century, when manorial documents become not only more numerous but more detailed, *bordelage* is shown to have been extensive in most of the Nivernais. I have examined the *terriers* and *dénombrements* of several manors and fiefs measuring the amount of land held by each tenant. All date from the years 1771 to 1779.[36] The largest is a *terrier* for the *châtellenie* of Decize written in 1775. The document delineates the holdings of one hundred and twenty-four tenants whose *seigneur* was the duke of Nevers. In all some two thousand hectares were subject to the *châtellenie*, divided into eight manors lying along the Loire between the town of Decize and the barony of Vitry to the southeast. The next is a *dénombrement* for the fief of La Forêt located in a region known as the Bazois, a lowland area just north of Decize and bordering on the Morvan to the east. The remaining records are *dénombrements* for three fiefs situated in the Morvan near the neighboring villages of Chiddes and Larochemillay, all held by the marquis Bruneau de Vitry.

The proportion of land held under each form of tenure for these manors is shown in table 1. The figures reveal considerable variation in the extent of *bordelage,* ranging from less than ten percent of the land at Decize, Champvert, and Devay to the entire territory of the fiefs of La Villette and Champrobert. At Charrin half the area was subsumed under *bordelage* and at Saint-Hilaire three-fourths. Clearly, there existed a great deal of regional variation in the extent of *bordelage*. It is probably safe to estimate the total surface area covered by *bordelage* in the province at somewhere between one-third and one-half.

Bordelage and the Communauté

The arguments linking *bordelage* and the *communauté* rest on a vast body of literature and documents. Marriage contracts, *terriers,* leases,

Table 1. Distribution of land tenure in the eighteenth century

| | Percentage of territory under: | | | |
Manor or Fief:	bordelage	cens	rente or direct	total hectars
Châtellenie de Decize (1775):				
Decize	6.9%	93.1%	–	101
Tannay	–	100.0	–	108
Champvert	2.8	62.7	34.4%	272
Devay	8.5	90.4	1.1	365
Gannay	21.5	75.7	2.8	312
Saint-Hilaire	49.7	22.0	28.3	167
Charrin	25.5	58.3	16.2	600
Cossaye	76.3	23.7	–	67
Fief de La Forêt (1775)	37.8	58.7	3.5	135
Fief de La Verechêre (1771)	66.5	–	33.5	112
Fief de Champrobert (1779)	100.0	–	–	70
Fief de La Villette (1779)	100.0	–	–	50

acts of association, and innumerable other sources testify to the existence of large households organized into *communautés* and farming lands held under *bordelage*. Turpin's study of the Petiots, a wealthy *communauté* living in the village of Magny, traced its origin to the fifteenth century when they began taking up *bordelage* leaseholds. In a marriage contract from the seventeenth century the *communauté* was listed as numbering sixteen married couples, two widowers, one widow, as well as the betrothed who were to enter into the association after their marriage![37] In another study, Réné de Lespinasse described the Braudeauls, a *communauté* residing in the Morvan during the fifteenth century: "There were some twenty families, grandparents, children and nephews, 'posterité et lingée,' all directed by one elder and one younger member who held the confidence of all. This association constituted a veritable force, dependents of several lords [and which held their lands] 'à titre et nature de bourdelaige'."[38]

By their size, such households were undoubtably exceptional, yet there can be no doubt that complex households were widespread during the fifteenth and sixteenth centuries. Manorial records from this period give some idea of their extent. Tables 2 and 3 show the distribution of family types as indicated in leases taken up at the manors of Prye and Azy between 1439 and 1793, and by those listed in two *terriers* drawn up for the barony of Vitry in 1533 and 1607.[39] At Prye and Azy, two-thirds of the one hundred and fourteen leases contracted between 1439 and 1500 were either to *communautés*, coresident brothers, or multifamily households. In the villages comprising the barony of Vitry over half the tenants in each *terrier* were listed as so-and-so "et ses communs," "et ses commons personniers," or "et les siens."

Table 2. Bordelage leases established at Pyre and Azy

Leaseholders:	1439–1499	1500–1549	1550–1599	1600–1649	1650–1699	1700–1749	1750–1793
Single individuals	22	9	5	2	10	7	2
Communautés	7	14	2	1	3	2	–
Brothers	12	7	2	–	–	2	–
Multiple families	18	8	6	–	2	2	–
Nobles and bourgeois	–	1	1	1	4	2	1
	59	39	16	4	19	15	3

Table 3. Tenants at Baronnie de Vitry

Tenants:	1533	1626
Single individuals	36.4%	49.0%
Communautés	27.8	42.3
Brothers	2.6	1.9
Multiple families	33.1	6.7
Total tenants	151	104

Given such evidence it would appear that the restrictions imposed by *bordelage* against the division of holdings, together with the requirement for heirs to reside in common to assure succession to the leasehold, were crucial in fostering large complex households in the Nivernais. However, it must be remembered that *bordelage* became widespread largely as a result of peasant actions aimed at loosening restrictions on their control of property. Indeed, the severity of *bordelage* itself seems to have been weakened precisely during that period when it was expanding through the province. Evidence of this comes from a comparison of the various editions of customary law drawn up for the province. In the earliest version, compiled in 1490, no heir, regardless of his or her relationship to the *bordelier,* could succeed to the leasehold without the existence of a *communauté* between the two. In the final codification, completed in 1534, this was mitigated by excluding the *borderlier's* immediate offspring from this prohibition.[40] Thus, children who were not coresident with their parents could inherit *bordelage* property without fear of reversion.

Nor was this the only difference between the two versions of customary law. An even more significant change appearing in the final body of law concerned the restrictions prohibiting division of *bordelage* holdings. To fully understand this change, it must be pointed out that not all families necessarily held land from a single manor or even by a single contract. Indeed, a family could take up any number of *bordelage* leases even from the same person, with each separate contract covering a different piece of property. In fact, it appears that most *bordelage* leases were for distinct fields or meadows rather than for a single tenement composed of scattered plots.[41] The jurists who set out to compile customary law in the fifteenth century clearly recognized this and sought to prevent the division of such holdings as much as possible. The 1490 version of the customs stated, "If *bordeliers* hold several *bordelages* from one or several *seigneurs*, they can divide them in such a way that each can have one or several *bordelages*, but they cannot separate them without the consent of the *seigneur* or *seigneurs*."[42] The *seigneur* therefore retained a clear interest in the property as a whole and could levy fines or prevent its partition outright. However, in the final version issued forty-four years later, the clause providing the *seigneur* with this right was deleted, thereby restricting his power of prohibiting division solely to the specific property covered in the individual contract.[43] The ability of families to divide holdings composed of several distinct *bordelage* leaseholds was underlined by Coquille; "In this case," he wrote, "the *seigneur* has no interest, because each tenement must be considered as separate and distinct."[44] The prohibitions against division of property so often ascribed to *bordelage* could not, in fact, prevent a family from dividing their patrimony by simply parceling out among several heirs the various fields comprising it, if each was held by a separate lease.

These far-reaching relaxations in the severity of *bordelage* were followed by further important modifications in its application. During the seventeenth century, jurisprudence in the province interpreted customary law in such a way as to allow persons to pass on *bordelage* property by donation or testament to individuals not living in common with them. An *arrêt* of 1690 stated unequivocally that reversion could take place only when the *bordelier* died *ab intestat* and without an heir in common.[45] The legal basis for this ruling was a rather broad interpretation of that section of customary law dealing with testaments. Article One of Chapter Thirty-three permitted disposal by testament of all "biens meubles et conquêts, et de la cinquième partie de son héritage." Since it did not specifically exempt *bordelage* property, testamentary rights were thus defined as extending over all property, regardless of its status. Whether this was the intention of the jurists who originally drew up the customs is doubtful. They were, after all, quite specific about the conditions required for succession to *bordelage,* the crux of which was the existence of a *communauté*. In fact, the decision continued to be challenged well into the eighteenth century by *seigneurs,* indicating that the ruling was never entirely accepted. These challenges nevertheless met with consistent failure as the courts continued to uphold *bordeliers'* rights to dispose of their property in this manner.[46]

The cumulative effect of these developments meant that, by the eighteenth century, the various restrictions on the disposition of land at one time imposed by *bordelage* had been weakened to such a degree that any legal buttress fostering the joint family in the Nivernais had all but disappeared. Not only was the existence of a *communauté* unnecessary for a *bordelier*'s immediate offspring, but it was no longer even required of any heir so long as property was passed on by testament or by donation. Furthermore, the family patrimony, when made up of properties leased out by several *borderlage* contracts, could be divided and redivided virtually at will. Yet the prohibition against division of property held by a single lease continued to remain in effect and was never challenged. Was this prohibition sufficient to preserve the extended family?

Co-ownership of real estate by siblings would certainly be a necessary consequence of partible inheritance practices if the land with which the settlement was made was a single *bordelage* leasehold. In fact, a conscious desire on the part of parents to split a settlement between their children was not even necessary for such a scenario to occur. Under customary law, *ab intestat* successions resulted in the division of the family patrimony by equal shares among all children, male and female. The division among several heirs of a single *bordelage* leasehold could thus be brought about by the unforeseen death of the parents. But did the necessity of co-ownership resulting from such a situation entail coresidence as well? There is considerable evidence that it did not. A *reconnaissance de bordelage* taken at Limanton in 1782 shows that while a piece of property itself may not have been divided, the *rights* to it were. For one *charetier* of meadow (approximately a fifth of an acre) the rights were distributed as follows:

> Jean Thomas, carpenter at Chaumont, an Jeanne Thomas his sister; both for one-fourth of the total.
> Claude Baudequin, carpenter at Montembert and Charles Thomas, day-laborer and proprietor at Champardolle, together for one-fourth and one-tenth of one-half.
> Edmee Gagnard, widow of Toussaint Thomas, at Chaumont, for two-fifths in one-half.
> Pierre Michot, weaver at Chaumont, acting for Jean Michot, for two-fifths in one-half.
> Guillaumin Boulin, plowman at Vauvelles, acting for Charles Michot, his brother-in-law, for one-fourth in one-fifth in one-half.

33

Pierre Gateau, tailor at Nantilly, acting for Charles Michot and Louis Martin, each for one-fourth in said tenth.

Francois Menant, day-laborer at Chaumont, for himself and for Toussaint Lavault, day-laborer at Chaumont, for one-fourth in the total.

These individuals did not share residence although they did hold property in common. The rights to this particular plot, already quite complex, would certainly become even more intricate with succeeding generations. Little imagination is needed to envision how such a division of rights could complicate the landholding pattern of an entire village. Just how entangled the network of property rights could become under *bordelage* is revealed by the *dénombrement* for La Verechère in the Morvan.[48] Some one hundred and sixty-five parcels of land are enumerated in the survey, one hundred and twenty-four of which were listed as being held individually by one of the eighteen heads of household residing on the manor. However, the remaining forty-one parcels, covering over half the territory of the fief, were held jointly by some combination of the residents. While one field might be held by Denis Dubras and Lazre Bonnot, another was held by the same Lazre Bonnot and Jean Durand; another by Lazare Marechal, Jean Laudet and Denis Dubras, while yet another by Lazare Bonnot, Lazare Marechal, Denis Dubras, Pierrette Bonnot and the widow of Pierre Bonnot. In one extreme case, a single field less than one-tenth of an acre in size was held jointly by seven different families!

In some cases common surnames among families owning land jointly indicate that common ownership and kinship were in some way linked to one another. The eight Godard households not only stand out as the largest landowners in the village, but were linked together by the greatest number of ties based on co-ownership of land. Other groups of families, however, such as the Marechals, the Laudets, and the Dubras, do not appear to have been directly related. That is to say, they did not share the same surname. Since wives were not listed in the survey, it is entirely possible that these families were linked by female ties.

Similar patterns of land ownership are revealed in numerous other documents dating from the eighteenth century. In some instances, it appears that *seigneurs,* rather than attempt to sort out such complicated mazes of property rights, were content simply to specify the dues owed by the manor or fief as a whole, leaving the leaseholders themselves to determine who owed how much for what land. According to the 1779 *dénombrement* for Champrobert, a few miles from La Verechere, some seventy hectares were held under *bordelage* by thirteen families.

Although each plot was carefully delineated, the tenants were simply listed as "les habitants de Champrobert conjointement et indivisement"[49] Exactly how such networks of co-ownership were translated into the actual practice of farming is in itself an intriguing question. Were fields worked alternately by each family, or did one family compensate other co-owners with annual payments? However these problems were resolved, the essential fact is that while individual *bordelage* holdings were not themselves physically divided, the rights to them were. By the eighteenth century, *bordelage* tenure no longer made succession or even co-ownership synonymous with coresidence.

This is not to say that *bordelage* restrictions had become a dead letter altogether. Under certain circumstances, *bordelage* could continue to pose a significant threat to a leaseholder's property. The one area where *bordelage* restrictions continued to operate in full force was that of collateral succession. According to customary law governing succession, in the event that a person died without either ascendant or descendant heirs, his nearest male collaterals or their descendants succeeded to the inheritance (females were excluded from collateral succession).[50] It was in such situations that *bordelage* could threaten a family's patrimony. An individual who shared a *bordelage* leasehold with his brother who died without lineal heirs would very likely see their leasehold revert to the *seigneur* if the two had not established a *communauté*. Complaints against such a threat literally reverberate through the *cahiers de doleance* compiled in 1789. "This odious measure," cried the inhabitants of Neuffontaines, "has no other end, in the case of the death of the proprietor, than to despoil the legitimate heirs of the heritages and property belonging to them by the rights of blood-ties. . . . Families are often reduced to a life of begging because of it!"[51] Even noble status could not serve as protection against such a disaster. When Jean-Marie Sallonier, *seigneur* de Montagne, died in 1781 without heirs in the direct line, his properties at Couloise reverted to the Baron de Vitry.[52]

The threat of reversion in cases of collateral succession was therefore quite real. On the other hand, for reversion to occur for lack of heirs living in common required the conjuncture of a fairly unique set of circumstances, and depended not only on both the specific tenurial conditions of the property in question and the arrangements regarding the disposition of that property already carried out by the family, but on the vagaries of demography as well. That reversion did occur is clear from both manorial records and other sources. Yet these same sources testify to its sporadic nature. During the last two decades of the Old

Regime, the *Contrôle des actes notaires* for the Bureau of Larochemillay registered fewer than ten reversions, most of which were for nonpayment of dues.[53] The infrequency of its occurrence, of course, may have made it all the more onerous. Nonetheless, it would be fair to conclude that, by the last century of the Old Regime, the threat of reversion posed by *bordelage* had been reduced to fairly narrow limits.

The natural tendency of joint households is toward ultimate dissolution. Only the existence of a tenurial regime maintaining the impartibility of peasant holdings will ensure their continued formation. *Bordelage* was not the tenurial foundation of joint households as so many historians have claimed. Its provisions placed only minor restrictions on peasant disposition of land, sanctioned the division of peasant holdings, and did not require coresidence of family members to assure succession except in a few limited circumstances.

Nevertheless, the joint family in the Nivernais continued to flourish, even into the nineteenth century after both *bordelage* and customary laws favoring joint ownership of property had been abolished. Such households survived because a fundamentally new element was introduced into the social relations surrounding land. This new tenure was *métayage,* or sharecropping. While *métayage* certainly existed even before the earliest codification of customary law in the fifteenth century, it was not until the seventeenth century that it came to be practiced on a large scale in the Nivernais. Under *métayage* peasant control over land was entirely eliminated, thereby ensuring that holdings would not be subject to division with each inheritance settlement. *Métayage* had a decisive impact on family relations in the Nivernais. Without its appearance it is conceivable that the large complex households of the region would have completely disappeared by the sixteenth century. The development of sharecropping in the seventeenth century is therefore of fundamental importance for a clear understanding of household organization in the Nivernais.

CHAPTER THREE

State Taxation and Primitive Accumulation in the Seventeenth Century

For Karl Marx, the decisive stage in the development of capitalism occurred in England during the sixteenth century. Huge tracts of land formerly controlled by peasants were absorbed by the nobility and landed gentry, thereby eliminating petty modes of production and establishing the agricultural basis for capitalist economic development.[1] This creation of ever-larger units of production, which Marx called primitive accumulation, also took place in the Nivernais during the seventeenth century and on a scale every bit as momentous as in England. However, the conditions under which agrarian change occurred in the two areas differed sharply.

In England the successful accumulation of capital developed in response to market forces. The sixteenth century price rise created incentives not only for farm engrossing but for the implementation of productivity increases as well. The seventeenth century was for the Nivernais, as for all of France, a period of economic stagnation. Peasant expropriation and the reorganization of agrarian social relations were not induced by the market but resulted instead from growing peasant indebtedness stemming from a massive increase in state taxation. The state, not the market, was the driving force of agrarian change in the Nivernais. In the absence of a vigorous demand for agricultural products, farm production in the Nivernais stagnated, geared largely for local markets. At the end of the century, the *intendent,* or royal governor, was able to name only ten grain merchants at Nevers with commercial connections to the Paris region.[2] Indeed, the most destructive harvest crises in the Nivernais occurred in the 1690s and early eighteenth century, well after property relations had been restructured.

The conditions under which primitive accumulation occurred in the Nivernais had profound consequences on peasant household organization. Peasant control over land was entirely eliminated as their holdings passed into the hands of the nobility and the bourgeoisie, who consolidated them into large farms operated under sharecropping arrangements. The tendency towards division of holdings at each peasant succession was thereby forestalled. However, in the absence of any market incentives for the introduction of more efficient labor-saving methods of farming, agriculture continued to rely on techniques requiring considerable inputs of labor. On the newly created large farms, this labor was secured by tenant reliance on the adult members of their families, and as the size of farms increased, so too did the size of the families. The *communauté* evolved under conditions in which primitive accumulation not only failed to eradicate reliance on primitive farm methods, but actually expanded the scale on which they were employed.

The Crisis of the Seventeenth Century

The impoverishment of rural society in the Nivernais was the direct result of a crushing burden of taxation imposed in order to finance the wars of the seventeenth century. While the entire century was characterized by heavy increases in the *taille* and other direct taxes, two periods stand out on which the intensity of the state's demand was at its greatest. The first and most severe coincided with France's entry into the Thirty Years' War and dates roughly from 1631 to 1650. In the Generality of Moulins, which compromised the Nivernais and the province of Bourbonnais, directly to the south, the *taille* alone increased by sixty percent between 1607 and 1621 and between 1635 and 1647 by 133 percent![3] The period of peace following the Fronde, coupled with the reform of finances undertaken by Colbert in the 1660s, alleviated somewhat the tax burden in the province. This "relaxation" in the level of state taxation in fact meant that no major increase in direct taxes was demanded. Yet at no time during this period did the amount of the *taille* levied on the inhabitants of the Nivernais drop below the level demanded prior to the commencement of hostilities in 1631. And the respite was only temporary. With the outbreak of the War of the League of Augsburg in 1688, the demands of the state were renewed. By 1698 the combined direct taxes of the *taille, capitation,* and *utencile** had risen to a level almost as great as in 1647 when the amount of direct taxes had reached its greatest height during the century.

Compounding these difficulties were the problems created by the inequities in the distribution of the tax burden itself. The deficiencies of the French tax system under the Old Regime are all too familiar to historians. Cities and towns were invariably assessed at rates inferior to those of rural areas. Nobles and much of the bourgeoisie were all but exempt from direct taxation despite repeated efforts by the crown to eliminate tax privileges.[4] Thus, the burden of the state's demand fell almost entirely on the shoulders of the peasant.

Problems of this kind were common to peasants throughout the century. For the peasants of the Nivernais, however, it was far more acute because the province was subjected to a greater tax burden than the rest of France. This can be shown by comparing the level of taxation per household and per capita for the various provinces of France during the seventeenth century. The Table 4 has been constructed by using available population figures for the various generalities of France for the year 1625, 1664, and 1696 and dividing these into the amount of the *taille* and other direct taxes levied against the generality for the same years.[5] The available sources sometimes failed to give the number of households or persons for a particular province, so there are a number of gaps in the table. Nonetheless, the inequities and distribution of state taxes at the provincial level are clear. Not only were the central regions of France assessed at higher rates than those of the north and east, but the generality of Moulins was consistently subjected to the highest rates in the country.

It is unclear whether these inequities were due simply to a bureaucratic inability to determine more uniform tax rates or were the result of a deliberate policy on the part of the state. The question is only indirectly related to our subject. Nonetheless, it is conceivable that in an attempt to avoid social unrest and tax rebellions at the periphery of the country where the king's armies were most actively engaged, the crown placed as much of the tax burden as possible on the central regions. As Boris Porshnev has shown, the almost endemic tax revolts of the seventeenth century were indeed largely confined to these areas.[6]

Compounding the problem of crushing taxes was the steady contrac-

*The *capitation* and *utencile* were extraordinary taxes levied in the latter seventeen century on inhabitants of those provinces in which royal troops were stationed.

Table 4. Direct taxation in the généralité de Moulins

Year	Taille	Rate of Increase
1607	601,460 *livres*	100
1621	949,400 *livres*	158
1636	1,009,445 *livres*	168
1639	1,369,324 *livres*	228
1647	2,352,914 *livres*	291
1665	1,248,500 *livres*	207
1688	1,244,693 *livres*	207
1690	1,333,406 *livres*	222
1694	1,330,189 *livres*	221
1696	2,340,619* *livres*	289

*Includes *utencile* and *capitation*, later introduced in 1695

tion of the tax base itself. The population of the Nivernais declined dramatically as successive waves of plague struck the province in 1601, 1606, 1628, and again in 1667. Just how serious the demographic crisis was is difficult to determine precisely. No figures on population for the Nivernais exist prior to 1664. At that time, an inquiry ordered by Colbert and apparently based on *gabelle* lists reported a population of 73,649 persons living in 14,608 households for the seven *greniers à sel* of the Nivernais.[7] A later enumeration in 1686, based this time on *taille* lists, showed a total of 16,200 households for the *élections* of Nevers and Château-Chinon, which encompassed the same jurisdiction as the *greniers*.[8] Ten years later another inquiry, also based on *taille* lists, reported a population of 72,986 persons and a total of 17,971 households.[9]

The pattern of development revealed by these figures is somewhat confusing; a steady increase in the number of households at the same time that the population stagnated or perhaps even declined. However, the *intendant* for Moulins in 1696 claimed that serious omissions in the enumeration had occurred and that as much of a sixth of the population had not been counted. If this were so, then the actual population at that time would be over 85,000. While the accuracy of such figures is certainly questionable, the direction of their movement seems clear. Population between the 1660s and 1690s may have increased but at an extremely modest rate.

The same cannot be said for the first half of the century. Unfortunately, for the earlier period, we lack even the questionable evidence of *taille* or *gabelle* lists. The only available information on population that exists is indirect evidence derived from *gabelle* sales around 1625. In 1628 Lazare Ducrot, a lawyer attached to the king's private counsel, published the number of *muids* (about 1,800 liters) of salt sold in the twelve generalities of France subject to the *gabelle*.[10] Emmanuel Le Roy Ladurie and Jeannine Recurat have demonstrated how such sales, while not the equivalent of population enumerations, can serve as rough approximations of population levels.[11] The official per capita ration of salt in the seventeenth century was figured at $1/14$ *minot* per year. At 48 *minots* to the *muid,* this would mean 672 "official rations" for each *muid* sold. Le Roy Ladurie and Recurat suggest that because of animal consumption and the use of salt in manufacturing, this should be reduced to 623 rations. Ducrot reported a total of 152 muids of salt sold in a seven *greniers* of the Nivernais, which would give a figure of 95,696 official rations.

This figure, when compared to the 73,649 persons listed in 1664, indicates a severe decline in the province's population during the second quarter of the century, a decline of perhaps as much as one-fourth. Again, however, it must be emphasized that the figures cannot be taken as anything but the most crude approximations. But how approximate? The 1696 inquiry reported a total of 219 *muids* of salt sold in those *élections* of the generality of Moulins where the *gabelle* were voluntary rather than fixed.[12] Based on Le Roy Ladurie's calculations, this would come out to 136,437 official rations. At the same time, the intendant reported the population of those *élections* at 139,273, suggesting that estimations based on *gabelle* sales undervalued the population by only two percent.

As already noted, the *intendant* himself tended to doubt the accuracy of returns that year. If he was correct in his argument that as much of the sixth of the population had not been counted, then the level of inaccuracy of estimations based on *gabelle* sales increases. In fact, this is to be expected. The *gabelle* was a tax, perhaps the most hated in all of France. Smuggling and even underconsumption of salt were the most common means of avoiding the tax and there is no question that local officials in the generality considered both to be problems.[13] Yet, if smuggling was widespread, it would mean that the estimation of populations derived from the *gabelle* sales actually under estimate the population by a greater margin, which in turn makes the demographic crisis of the second quarter of the century only that much more severe.

While the amount of smuggling could have increased over the course of the century, it is unlikely that increases in contraband salts could have accounted for the kinds of declines in *gabelle* sales registered in the Nivernais between 1625 and 1696. According to the figures listed by Ducrot, some 313 *muids* of salt were sold in the entire generality in the late 1620s. By the end of the century, the amount of salt sold by the state had fallen to 234 *muids*. In the *élection* of Vezeley alone, some 60 *muids* of salt had been sold in 1625, compared to only 30 in 1696.[14]

Taken together, the evidence points to a severe population decline during the second quarter of the century, perhaps as much as twenty-five percent. Population growth after 1660 only partially compensated for the losses sustained during the early and middle decades of the century. Thus, the survivors of plague and pestilence faced not only successive increases in taxes by the crown, but an even greater increase in the actual rate of taxation. The combined affects of taxation and population decline not only ravaged the population, but virtually eliminated peasant ownership of land in the province.

The Erosion of Peasant Proprietorship

Debt is a perennial problem in peasant societies. The death of livestock or a poor harvest may force a family to borrow in order to obtain seed for the next season. Indeed, harvest failures were frequent during the seventeenth century, with severe crop failures striking the Nivernais in 1635, 1661, and 1694. To such unforeseen calamities were added the strains on family fortunes that occurred even under normal circumstances. When children reached marriage age, daughters had to be provided with dowries and the claims of other heirs met. In the seventeenth century however, peasant indebtedness in the Nivernais became so severe that the financial stability and economic position of peasant families at all levels of rural society were undermined. For as the demands of the state steadily increased, peasant families were forced to alienate an ever greater share of their landholdings in order to meet their obligations.

Growing peasant indebtedness and the accumulation of peasant lands by noble and bourgeois purchasers have been well documented for much of France during this time.[15] However, the process appears to have occurred on a greater scale in the Nivernais and Bourbonnais than in any other region of the country. This was the result of several factors, the most important being the greater share of the tax burden levied on the region. In addition to this, the particular terms of *bordelage* (which closely resembled *taille reèlle* in the Bourbonnais) provided unusually fertile means for expropriation. *Bordelage* was a prescriptive tenure, which meant that its terms were determined as much by actual practice as by the contract itself. If a reduced rent had been accepted by the lord for a space of thirty years, the new level of rent was considered legally binding on both parties. A clever lord could therefore lull his tenant into complacency by accepting reduced payments for several years, even for two generations, and then call in arrears and thus force the *bordelier* to sell out. Jean Baptist de Las, the lord of Prye and Azy, waited twenty-nine years before calling in all back payments due by one of his tenants in 1646. Unable to meet this demand, the tenant was forced to alienate his property to the lord.[16]

Such practices were rare, however. Generally, appropriation of peasant holdings occurred through the forced sale of land by peasant families unable to meet the demands of the state, their creditors, or their manorial dues. In each instance, the terms of *bordelage* restricted the ability of peasants to raise cash to meet their obligations. At a time when the state was demanding an ever growing portion of peasant income, failure to pay *bordelage* dues for three consecutive years meant immediate expropriation. The only course open to families outside of outright abandonment of the holdings was to borrow. But as families sank ever deeper into debt, the only means by which they could free themselves from these obligations was by alienating their property. Here, too, *bordelage* proved an obstacle. The transfer fee, or *tiers denier,* levied at every sale or exchange of the leasehold, was fixed by customary law at one-half the value of the property.[17] The aim of this clause, which even Coquille found to be repugnant, was to prevent the alienation of land by the original *bordelier* and his family by making it difficult to sell. It certainly achieved this purpose. Even at the end of the eighteenth century, the *tier denier* was denounced because of the restrictions it opposed on the marketability of land.[18] Creditors, on the other hand, would find little difficulty in accepting *bordelage* property against unpaid obligations since the value of land in such cases would not be determined by its true market value, but by the amount of the debt. If the land was seized for nonpayment of debt, the clever creditor could receive the property for half its value by simply paying the *tier denier.*

Manorial records from this period are littered with references to peasants contracting debts and being forced to alienate property to meet the demands of creditors. In one case, the *communauté* of Jean Michot, *bordeliers* at Brinay, was forced to repeatedly borrow money for seed and livestock during the early decades of the century. Unable to meet these obligations when they fell due, Michot's widow contracted further debts with the local lord in order to avoid the seizure of her property by creditors. Further borrowing occurred until Michot's son and son-in-law were forced in 1634 to alienate their land in order to acquit themselves of their debt.[19] In another case, the Rousseaus, a *communauté* at Saint-Jean-aux-Amognes, saw its harvest seized on four separate occasions between 1647 and 1655 for failing to pay off debts the *communauté* had incurred. Finally, in 1660, the property of the *communauté* was seized at the request of creditors.[20] A similar fate struck the Poideloups, a landowning *communauté* in the parish of Alluy. Between 1643 and 1659 the *Maître de communauté,* Jean Poideloup, contracted several debts with the local lord. On one occasion he even had to borrow money from the parish priest in order to pay his tax assessment. In the meantime the family had repeatedly been forced to sell off parcels of land. By 1660, a year before his death, Poideloup and his family had sunk so low into poverty that the tax assessors of his district accorded him an exemption from taxes.[21] The level of debt which families such as these contracted is sometimes astounding. In less than two years one *communauté* at Saint-Jean-Aux-Amognes borrowed over 2,000 livres from a merchant.[22] In another case, Jean Guyonnin and his *commons personniers* were hauled before the royal court at Saint-Pierre-Le-Moutier in 1661 for failure to pay back debts they had incurred. Their lands were seized and distributed to five different noble families that had lent them money.[23]

The extent to which bourgeois and noble moneylenders benefited from financial problems of peasant families may be measured from the accounts left by one family, that of Jean Despres, *Commissaire de la Marechausseire* de Château-Chinon, and his wife, Madelaine Delaporte.[24] Despres' family already owned a considerable amount of land, most of which had been purchased piece by piece in the sixteenth century. The debt crisis of the peasantry in the next century afforded them with a far cheaper means of property accumulation. In some cases, Despres acquired lands from peasants who alienated their properties in exchange for an annuity, or *rent constituees.* More often, they acted as moneylenders to peasants in several localities throughout the province. On numerous occasions, they had to go to court to force these debtors to pay up, and in at least twenty-one different instances the court ordered the debtor's property to be seized for nonpayment. For Despres, loaning money to peasants was virtually a form of land investment. Yet there were times when peasant debt could become a problem even to creditors such as Despres. In 1658 Madelaine's second husband, Pierre de Noury, had to go to court to try to *prevent* the creditors of one of his own tenants from seizing the peasant's harvest and personal property. His tenant, Jean Pouliet, had been unable to pay off debts to both de Noury and his other creditors and Noury feared that if Pouliet's property were seized, he would never be able to fully recoup his own loans.

Land records for the manors of Prye and Azy provide a unique account of the alienation of holdings by peasant families and their accumulation by noble and bourgeois investors. In the sixteenth century, most *bordelage* tenures were held by peasants, a fact which Coquille emphasized when he remarked that most of the representatives from the Third Estate who gathered to compile the customs in 1534 had not come from the *mene people* who held *bordelages*.[25] Coquille's remark is supported by the class distribution of *bordeliers* at Prye and Azy, where virtually all those who contracted leases before the seventeenth century were listed as *manouvriers, laboureurs,* or local parishioners. During the next century, although few new leases were contracted, a growing proportion of these were taken up by nobles or bourgeois.

Records pertaining to the transfer of lease holdings, as opposed to the establishment of new tenures, reveals to an even greater extent the process of primitive accumulation. *Bordelage, as a feudal tenure,* carried with it both direct and use rights, the former held by the *seigneur* and the latter by the *bordelier.* When the use rights were sold or exchanged by the *bordelier,* the *seigneur* could lay claim to the transfer fees. These have survived for the manors of Prye and Azy and vividly chronicle the accumulation of land by the bourgeoisie and nobility.[26] Land transfers have been broken down by sellers and purchases for each fifty year period after 1550 and the results are displayed in Table 5. Between 1550 and 1559, nearly half the acquisitions made through land *1599?* transfers within the manors were by peasants, all of whom were listed as *chefs de communauté* or *laboureurs.* During the next fifty years, not only did the number of transfers almost double, but virtually all the purchasers were merchants, lawyers, or nobles. Thirty-four of the sellers were peasants and while only five *communautés* had sold property in the previous period, fifteen *chefs de communauté* were listed as sellers during this time. In both succeeding fifty-year periods, the number of land transfers fell back to below thirty. Yet nearly all involved cases of peasants selling land to nobles or bourgeois.

Table 5. Land transfers at Azy and Prye

Years:	Sellers			Purchasers			
	Manouvriers, widows	Communautes, laboureurs	Nobles and bourgeois	Manouvriers, widows	Communautes, laboureurs	Nobles and bourgeois	Total transfers
1550–1559	20	5	2	–	12	15	27
1600–1649	25	15	6	5	1	40	46
1650–1699	18	3	6	5	–	22	27
1700–1749	12	2	9	2	–	21	23
1750–1793	4	–	4	–	–	8	8

The developments at Prye and Azy were by no means isolated. At the Barony of Vitry in the southeastern Nivernais, nobles, bourgeois, and royal officers comprised only six percent of the tenants listed in the *terrier* of 1553. When the next *terrier* was compiled in 1626, the overall number of tenants had declined by a third while the proportion of nonpeasant tenants had increased to thirty percent. Although no later *terriers* exist for the barony, manorial records show that the process continued throughout the rest of the century. Numerous documents record changes in the possession of tenancies after 1626 and these have been traced for each landholding up to 1669.[27] Only seventeen of these were granted in favor of peasants, while twenty-five were in favor of either merchants or lawyers, six were to royal officials and nine to nobles. The same pattern of active acquisition of peasant land in the seventeenth century has been documented for the neighboring province of the Bourbonnies directly bordering the Nivernais to the south. Before the seventeenth century, there is little evidence of direct possession of land by the bourgeoisie. It is estimated that by 1660 perhaps three-fourths of the area was owned by this class.[28]

The forced liquidation of peasant property had its political consequences as well. The inhabitants of the Nivernais repeatedly rose up against the growing fiscal demands of the state. Large-scale rebellions in the province broke out in 1629, 1636-37, and 1640.[29] The uprising of 1636-37 was only part of a widespread series of antitax revolts involving virtually all central and southwestern France. According to Porshnev, it was "the most important peasant uprising in the history of France."[30] In each instance, the authority of the state was reestablished and with it the ability to impose more taxes.

Yet reaction to the state's demands for revenues cannot be measured by large-scale rebellion alone. When not in open revolt, rural unrest posed a continuous threat to the state's ability to administer the province. Local officials repeatedly warned that the hardships created by increasing taxes could not be borne by the inhabitants indefinitely. As one officer pleaded to Chancellor Seguier in 1647:

> The cruelties and inhumanities committed by the soldiers employed in collecting the *taille* in the generality of Moulins has forced me to write these lines. I ask you only to favor these poor people, who suffer from the cruelties of such people, by informing His Majesty of their miseries which they hope will soon be alleviated because they cannot believe His Majesty would abandon them to persons who could not be worse than the enemy himself, were he in France.[31]

Such pleas went unheeded. During 1648 and 1649, rural unrest in the Nivernais was a constant fact of life, as royal officials, tax collectors, and peace officers were faced with unrelenting acts of violence and small uprisings. Hardly a week went by in 1649 without some malefactor being brought to trial before the royal court at Saint-Pierre-Le-Moutier.[32] On February 11 Gilbert Lebreton, a tailor, was tried for attacking a salt-tax official. Three days later, Francois Gody, a farmer, was tried for assaulting a royal notary and a clerk at the *grenier à sel.* The next day four peasants were hauled before the court and tried with "rebellions and assaults." On February 27 Jean Guipier was tried for assaulting a tax official in Château-Chinon. The next day another peasant was convicted of assaulting a royal notary charged with seizing his property. Two weeks later a peasant was brought before the tribunal, also for attacking a tax collector attempting to seize his land. The list goes on and on.

Violence of this sort declined after mid-century, although sporadic and isolated instances continued to plague officials. The resumption of hostilities in the last decade of the century brought about renewed outbreaks of violence. The *intendant*'s reports to the crown repeatedly refer to problems occasioned by the imposition of new taxes or the drawing up of tax rolls. In 1687 the *intendant* had to meet personally with the inhabitants of several "mutinous parishes" in order to pacify their agitation over taxes. The next year brought renewed disorders. The *intendant* was further dismayed to find himself personally named in a lawsuit brought by the inhabitants of several parishes angered over the inequities in the tax distribution. "The insolence of these people," he fumed to the controller-general. "I trust you will support me and make an example of these mutineers."[33]

Relief came only with the cessation of hostilities. At the end of the century, when the tax burden began to subside at last, the *intendant* breathed a notable sigh of relief. In his report on state finances for the generality during the century, he "recalled with sorrow the taxes which have caused so much misery for those who have been obliged to pay them. Many have been forced to live on the barest of necessities. Others have lost all their property, and with it the hopes of their families. The greatest number even lost their daily bread and were reduced to begging."[34]

The extent to which former peasant holdings had been absorbed by the nobility and bourgeois is evident from the testimony of travelers who later visited the province. Indeed, the Nivernais acquired a certain notoriety because of the extent to which property was concentrated into larger holdings. In 1769 one traveler wrote that most people in the Nivernais were employed as lumberjacks, charcoal-burners or day-laborers rather than farmers. "Not that the land is poor, but because the properties are so little divided. In most cases, three or four lords own the territory of an entire village so that there are very few proprietors."[35] The large, compact farms of the Nivernais attracted the attention of the agronomist Francois Quesnay. When he became wealthy enough to acquire land for himself, he bought several farms in the village of Saint-Parize-Le-Chatel.[36] Even Arthur Young was tempted when offered the opportunity to purchase a *domaine* in the province. Only old age and the outbreak of the Revolution changed his mind.[37]

This concentration of property is evident in the *terriers* of Decize, La Foret, La Verechère, Champrobert, and La Villette. In Table 6, the amount of land held by peasants, bourgeois, and nobles has been calculated for each manor with the Morvan fiefs of La Verechère, Champrobert, and La Villette grouped together. At La Foret and Decize, both in the rich lowlands of the Nivernais, only a minimal amount of land was under peasant ownership. Moreover, as shown on Table 7, the overwhelming majority of peasant holdings at Decize were only a few hectares in size. The exception to this pattern in property distribution were the manors located in the Morvan. There the bulk of land was controlled by peasants. Exactly why the Morvan failed to develop along lines similar to those of the rest of the Nivernais is

Table 6. Property distribution by class

Terriers:	Percentage of Territory Held by			
	Nobles	Bourgeois	Peasants	Total Hectares
Decize (1774)	23.0%	63.5%	13.5%	1,959
La Forêt (1775)	81.8	17.0	1.2	134
Morvan Fiefs (1771–1779)	22.4	–	77.6	267
N of Tenants	26	48	126	2,358 Hectares

Table 7. Distribution of size of holdings Châtellenie de Decize

Class of Tenants:	Hectares								
	− 1	1–5	5–10	10–20	20–30	30–40	40–50	50 +	Total
Nobles	2	3	2	3	–	1	2	4	17
Bourgeois	5	8	3	6	5	7	3	7	44
Peasants	21	25	9	6	2	–	–	–	63
	28	36	14	15	7	8	5	11	124

unclear. The explanation may very well lie in the nature of the region itself. The Morvan is one of those classic backwaters of France, heavily forested with near-sterile soils and steep, hilly terrain. Probably the very poverty and isolation of the region made the acquisition of land by nobles and bourgeois undesirable. Whatever the cause, the distinction between the Morvan, with small, family-owned farms and the large, noble and bourgeois-owned properties of the *plat pays* of the Nivernais continues even today.

Métayage and the Communauté

The erosion of peasant proprietorship in the rest of the Nivernais had profound effects on tenure relationships in the province. Former peasant holdings were consolidated into large, compact farms, or *domaines*, of between fifty and seventy-five hectares, with some of one hundred hectares or more. Bourgeois and noble purchasers who were not the direct *seigneurs* of acquired *bordelage* holdings would often negotiate with the *seigneur* to free the property of its servile status by commuting it to the equivalent of a *cens*. At Vitry fifty-five *affranchissements* were made during the seventeenth century, most taking place between 1633 and 1653.[37] Thirty-nine of these were in favor of noble or bourgeois purchasers of servile holdings formerly in the possession of *communautés* or other peasant families. For example, in 1649 the property of the Marechaux, a *communauté* residing at Montigny, was seized by court order and sold to Valentine Challemoux, sieur de Brouillot. Challemoux immediately obtained the commutation of his newly acquired lands from Henri de Saulx-Tavannes, baron of Vitry and lord of Montigny. During the next three years Challemoux made several more purchases at Montigny from various *communautés*, obtaining the commutation of these lands as well. Similar transactions appear to have occurred at the Châtellenie of Decize. Some forty percent of the area under *bordelage* there was listed as *cens-bordelage*, virtually all of it held by nobles or bourgeois.

Whether commuted or not, the newly consolidated *domaines* were leased out under *métayage* contracts to peasants. In part, the adoption of *métayage* resulted from legal prohibitions against subleasing property subject to *seigneurial* rights under forms of tenure, such as *bordelage*, which would have imposed an additional layer of *seigneurial* rights on the same property. To do so would have compromised the rights held by the original *seigneur*.[38] But beyond these considerations was the fact that by the seventeenth century, *métayage* had become far more profitable than the fixed terms of *bordelage* or even *fermage*. Even *seigneurs* who had acquired the holdings of their own tenants switched to *métayage* rather than relet them out under *bordelage*.

At Varzy, a town in the northern Nivernais, bourgeois families significantly increased their investments in land during the seventeenth century.[39] Occasionally these lands would be let out for a fixed price, but this was the exception. Most were leased "à moitié emblure et deblure," with the owner and the *métayer* sharing costs and harvests equally. These contracts show clearly the advantages offered by *métayage*. Most often paid in kind, *fermage* usually averaged about two *boisseaux* of grain (about twenty-four liters) for each *journal* of land rented. With yields of around four for one in a normal year, a *journal* would produce something like two and one-half hectoliters of rye or oats. Subtracting rent (a quarter-hectoliter) and seed (just over half a hectoliter), the *fermier* would be left with about one and three-fourths hectoliters of grain for each *journal* rented. However, under the three-field system employed in the area, at least a third of the arable land would be under fallow, reducing the *fermier*'s profit by at least as much. Even so, his share would be twice that of the owner. The landlord clearly had much more to gain by leasing his property under *métayage*.

The process described here is perhaps best illustrated by a single example.[40] In 1573 Pierre Bernard, a meat merchant from Nevers, made seveal purchases of peasant land in the hamlet of Rancy, near the town of Saint-Benin-d'Azy. The price paid for these properties was one hundred and thirteen *livres*. In 1621 his son Pierre l'aîné made further purchases for fifty *livres*. Between 1629 and 1633 several more acquisitions were made at Rancy, this time by Bernard's son-in-law, François de la Collancelle, a master apothecary at Nevers. François' son-in-law, also a master apothecary, continued the family tradition at Rancy by making purchases totaling two hundred and twenty-six *livres* between 1644 and 1664. In all, these acquisitions involved properties held under *bordelage* by ten different families at Rancy, including three *communautés*. Many of these lands were alienated in order to cancel debts to the buyers. Pierre Loquerau, for example, a *laboureur,* was forced in 1646 to sell all the land he possessed at Rancy in order to meet the obligations he had contracted with De la Collancelle.

As early as 1622 the family began leasing their holdings at Rancy to tenants as a single, consolidated farm. The contracts were always sharecropping agreements and were often taken up by the very families who had been forced to sell their lands. Neither De la Collancelle nor his widow were comfortable holding land under *bordelage* and in three separate agreements with the *seigneur* in 1631, 1640, and 1645, they were able to have their properties commuted to *cens* in exchange for 1,700 *livres*. Although no further purchases are recorded after 1664, the descendants of the family continued to lease out their *domaine* at Rancy until 1731, when it was sold for 10,000 *livres*.

The creation of the *domaine de Rancy* was anything but a haphazard affair. The investments and transactions carried out over three generations reveal a single-minded effort at farm engrossing. But as determined as these efforts were, they could never have been accomplished without the growth of peasant debt. Primitive accumulation was achieved only because the level of state taxation grew to a point at which the peasantry was simply overwhelmed and forced to alienate the very foundation of its livelihood.

By the end of the century the transition to *métayage* appears to have been all but complete. In 1696 Marechal Vauban, Louis XIV's minister of fortification, carried out a survey of the population and economy of the *élection* of Vézelay in the northeastern Nivernais.[41] One of the reasons for the region's poverty, he reported, was the widespread use of *métayage,* which kept the peasant in constant debt to his landlord and prevented any sort of improvements from taking place. Vauban should have known, for he was himself a local *seigneur.* This transformation of land tenure in the Nivernais during the seventeenth century is of fundamental importance for our subject. The weakening of *bordelage* meant that the legal basis for forming *communautés* had all but disappeared. But the size of the *domaines* created in the seventeenth century meant that *métayers* would need a considerable labor force for their operation. This work force was created by the association of parents, their adult children and their spouses into a *communauté.* Thus, while the joint family had been linked at one time to the conditions of servile tenure, it was well suited for sharecropping the large farms and so continued to thrive.

Sharecroppers, of course, could have relied on hired labor, and to some extent did. But the cost of labor fell entirely on the sharecropper. Yields were low and the *métayer* not only paid half the crop to the lessor, but a rent for farm buildings, interest on the value of livestock, farm equipment and tools, and a proportion of all courtyard products. In addition, he was held to perform a stipulated number of *corvées* for the lessor as well as any number of cartings demanded. What was left after all these deductions often barely exceeded subsistence, so the cost of paying for day laborers or farm servants could very well mean the difference between a small profit and a loss. Sharecroppers therefore depended on the labor of their own families. Such associations were no longer corporate groups concerned about land inheritance, but were labor-sharing groups held together by commercial agreements or unwritten understandings.

At Rancy it is possible to see this transition in the basis of the *communauté*. As noted above, the *domaine* there was created in part from the properties alienated by landholding *communautés* in the hamlet. Once constituted, the *domaine* was leased out under *baux à metairie* to families who also organized themselves into *communautés*, as the following list of *métayers* at Rancy indicates:

1622 Etienne Gamard and his children and *commons personniers,* Pierre and Andre Gamard.
1627 Jean Loquereau and his son Pierre.
1631 Jacques and Martin Barillow, brothers and *commons personniers.*
1663 Jean Barillot and Philibert Moreau, his son-in-law and *common personnier.*

Tenurial change did not spell the doom of the joint household. With the labor demands of the *domaines* a new, purely economic factor fostering their formation had arisen in place of *bordelage*. It can be argued that tenurial change strengthened the continued existence of the joint family in the Nivernais by entirely eliminating any control by peasant families over the disposition of the land they farmed, and thereby any potential tendency towards fragmentation of holdings. Household organization came to be determined solely by the size of the *domaine* and its attendant labor requirements.

What we should like to know is the extent to which the specific economic conditions of labor demand had supplanted customary law as the basis for the joint household in the Nivernais by the eighteenth century. To what extent did the weakening of *bordelage* restrictions affect peasant family structure? Did the strategies of household formation differ between *bordeliers* and *métayers,* and if so, to what degree? What was the role of kinship ties within the household? To answer these questions, we must move from the study of legal systems and tenure developed thus far and descend to the local level, to examine individual families within the context of the social, economic, and physical environment of the village in which they lived.

CHAPTER FOUR

The Dynamics of Peasant Household Organization

The commune of Larochemillay lies in the southern reaches of the forest-covered uplands known as the Morvan, and the way of life of its inhabitants typifies that led by people throughout the region. Dominated by stands of oak, beech, and pine, it is the forests of the Morvan which give the country its incontestable beauty, and its people the only source of livelihood outside of agriculture. As early as the sixteenth century, the trees of the Morvan were felled and then floated down the Yonne River to Clamecy, formed into rafts and steered to Paris, providing the capital with lumber and fuel. Seasonal work as a lumberjack was a vital supplement to the meager living that the inhabitants wrested from the infertile lands of the Morvan. The thin, siliceous soils of the country are almost devoid of lime and only stubbornly yield crops of the poorest grains—rye, millet and buckwheat. Only at the base of narrow valleys cut from the hills by streams and creeks have fairly fertile soils been deposited. This geography dictated the adoption of an infield-outfield system of cultivation in which precious bottomland fields were planted continuously, while hillside plots were cropped for two or three consecutive seasons. Once exhausted, these were then left fallow for five or six years, after which time the brush and undergrowth would be cut and burned, and the cycle repeated.

In terms of both geography and property distribution, the Morvan may be divided into two distinct regions. In the Upper Morvan, beginning at an altitude of about four hundred meters, the terrain is at its most rugged. Woodland is extensive, covering as much as half the territories of some communes, with farmland restricted to narrow valleys lying between steep, wooded hillsides. In the Lower Morvan, the terrain is less severe. Valleys are generally more broad, thereby enabling a greater expanse of farmland. Overall, landownership throughout the Morvan is fairly widespread. "There is hardly any Morvandiaux who is absolutely without property," remarked Dupin in 1853. However, proprietorship was far more extensive in the Upper Morvan than in its lower reaches. Census returns for 1820 reveal a close relationship between geography and property distribution.[1] In the communes of the Upper Morvan, over forty percent of all household heads were listed as *proprietaire*. In the commune of Arleuf, at 550 meters above sea level the highest commune in the *département,* eighty-one percent were listed as proprietors. In communes lying below four hundred meters, landownership was less widespread, ranging from a quarter to a third of all families. Below three hundred meters, proprietors rarely constituted more than twenty percent of all household heads.

Property size showed a similar pattern. Table 8 shows the distribution of property for communes lying below the three-hundred meter level,

Table 8. Geography and property size in the Morvan in 1835

Altitude of communes (in meters)	Percentage of Côtes paying				
	− 10f	10–50f	50–300f	+ 300f	total côtes
above 400 m	60.6%	31.4%	6.6%	1.4%	2,038
300 to 400 m	63.1	27.3	7.2	2.4	2,222
under 300 m	62.2	27.0	8.2	2.6	2,161

between three and four hundred meters, and above four hundred meters. The figures are based on the amount of taxes paid for individual pieces of property, or *côtes,* in 1835.[2] A *côte* is not the equivalent of an individual proprietor. It signifies a single piece of property, and as a proprietor could hold several different properties, there are often more *côtes* for a given commune than adults. Very small properties paying less than ten francs in taxes were numerous in all regions of the Morvan. Both medium and large properties—those paying three hundred francs or more in taxes—were more widespread in the lower, less rugged terrain of the country, the regions Dupin called "The Good Morvan." These differences in property distribution undoubtedly had their origins in the transformation of rural society in the seventeenth century. Both the isolation and rugged terrain of the Upper Morvan make its farmland the least valued in all the province. Peasants who managed to retain possession of their holdings probably did so only because their lands

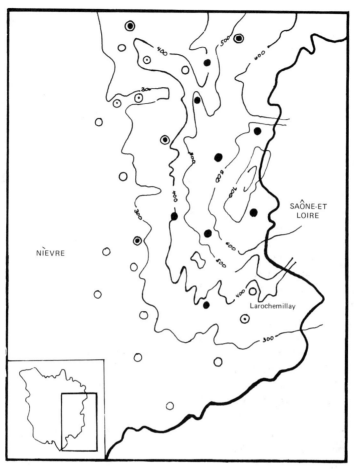

Map 2. The Morvan

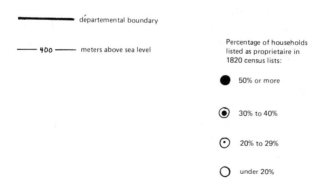

———————— départemental boundary

——— **400** ——— meters above sea level

Percentage of households
listed as propriétaire in
1820 census lists:

● 50% or more

◉ 30% to 40%

⊙ 20% to 29%

○ under 20%

were of so little value that their purchase was not worthwhile. In a cruel irony, their very poverty protected them from expropriation.

Indeed the poverty of the Morvan and its inhabitants was so profound as to be proverbial: "Il ne vient du Morvand, ni bonnes gens ni bon vent." In 1829 Jean Baudiot wrote, "The inhabitants of the Morvan are as miserable as their country is sterile . . . they carry the very soil they cultivate on their countenances, revealing their sadness and suffering."[3] Over a century and a half earlier Vauban had described the Morvan as "poorly cultivated, the people so faint-hearted and lazy that they do not even try to rid their fields of stones, which are left to brambles and worthless shrubs. They are without industry, arts or manufactures of any kind which could fill the void in their lives."[4]

Like much of the Nivernais the Morvan is a region of scattered farmsteads and small hamlets. In all, less than a third of the population lives in the chief bourgs of their commune.[5] In fact, the bourgs of most communes include only the church, the school, a few houses and perhaps an inn, and in terms of size are indistinguishable from surrounding hamlets. The bourg of Larochemillay itself is actually a small hamlet. Its inhabitants rarely comprised more than fifteen percent of the commune's total population of fifteen hundred.[6] It was not for its size that the hamlet of Larochemillay came to be the *chef-lieu de la commune*. Rather, it was because it lies immediately beneath the Château de la Roche Millay, residence of the marquis Laferte-Meun, one of the largest landowners in the area. As the former manorial center for the surrounding farms and hamlets, Larochemillay developed into the only settlement in the vicinity resembling a town. Here resided all those who could lay claim to the title of bourgeois: two *notaires,* an innkeeper and a few *rentiers* and well-to-do *proprietaires.* After the Revolution the list was expanded to include the *maire,* throughout the entire century one of the wealthier landowners of the commune and, after 1870, the *instituteur* and his family.

The earliest extant list for Larochemillay is that of 1820. It gives a total population of 841 persons living in 115 households. The overwhelming importance of agriculture in the local economy is reflected in the occupational distribution of the inhabitants. Seventy-one percent of the households were headed by persons directly engaged in agriculture. Eighteen were listed as *proprietaires* (excluding the local nobility, who were not listed at all); thirty-six were listed as *laboureurs,* all certainly sharecroppers, and twenty-seven as day-laborers. Twenty-one percent of the households were listed as artisans. Other than a few weavers, two smiths, and a tailor, most of these were *sabotiers,* an occupation which was widespread throughout the Morvan up until the turn of the century. Seven families were listed as indigent, most of whom were widows living alone or with their children.

When the cadastral survey was completed in 1845,[7] fully thirty percent of the commune was forest. Just over half was arable and twelve percent meadow and pasture, with the remainder consisting of waste, gardens, orchards, buildings, and roads. The terrain is fairly rugged, made up of steep forest-covered hills between which lies the commune's farmland. Ownership of this land was divided among two hundred and eighty individuals. Two hundred and eight owned less than five hectares, twenty-two between five and ten hectares, twenty-three between ten and twenty hectares, eight with holdings between twenty and fifty hectares, and nineteen persons with over fifty hectares. Together, these last nineteen proprietors owned sixty-two percent of all the land in the commune. Two families, the Laferte-Meuns and the Bertrand de Rivières, held over 1,500 hectares, about a third of the commune.

Lands held by large proprietors were organized into compact *domaines* of fairly uniform size, usually between sixty and seventy-five hectares. Each was made up of about three-fourths arable land, one-fourth meadow and pasture, and included farmhouses, barns, stables, and other buildings. These were leased out by verbal or written sharecropping agreements, generally for six-year periods. The owner would furnish the first year's seed, farm stock, and equipment, in return for which the *métayer* would turn over half the crop as well as a portion of all courtyard products and interest on the stock and equipment. An important aspect of *métayage* for both parties was the terms regarding the *domaine*'s livestock. Usually governed by the clause *à moitie croit profit et perte,* the *métayer* was legally free to buy and sell animals. In fact, such transactions were usually carried out directly by the owner or his agent. *note*

Cattle sales were a crucial source of revenue for the *métayer* because in addition to half the crop he paid a rent, or *bellemain,* for the use of farm buildings. On a typical *domaine,* the *bellemain* could be as much as two hundred francs per year, a heavy charge for the *métayer.* To the *bellemain* would be added the state's direct taxes. It was through sales of cattle that the *métayer* derived the cash to meet these demands. All costs of operating the farm were the *métayer's* responsibility. At the end of the period covered by the contract, the terms would either be renewed for another period or the *métayer* would be dismissed if the lessor saw fit to do so. In fact, most agreements gave the right to the lessor to dismiss the *métayer* at any time during the agreement, provided six months' notice were given. If dismissed, the *métayer* was to leave behind seed for the next season and all capital equipment in the condition in which it had come to him.

To most observers, *métayage* appeared abhorrent. When Arthur Young traveled through the region in 1789, he was struck by the living conditions of the *métayers*. "The tenants are in the lowest state of poverty, and some of them in misery. . . . There is not one word to be said in favor of the practice, and a thousand arguments that might be used against it."[8] Dupin called it "a miserable form of agriculture which holds the *colon* in a dependency differing little from serfdom."[9] In 1847 Jean-Baptist Avril, a leading member of the *département*'s *Société d'agriculture,* demonstrated that a day-laborer with a wife and three children who worked for two hundred and fifty days of the year at 1.50 francs a day was in a better financial position than the *métayers* employed on the *Société*'s model farms.[10] Later in the century Antoine Desforges wrote that the situation of many *métayers* was so desperate that even the life of a farm servant appeared enviable. "It's the *bellemain* that kills them," he explained. "A sharecropper recently said to me that, after all his accounts had been settled with 'le Moussieu,' he had seventeen francs left to show for all his pains."[11]

Such judgments were well justified. *Métayage* acted to ensure that few benefits of farm production would accrue to the sharecropper and his family. With the farm methods then employed in the Morvan, which relied heavily on fallows to maintain soil fertility, an average *domaine* of sixty hectares would have only fifteen or so hectares planted in cereals. With returns of about four for one, such a *domaine* would produce something like one hundred sixty-four hectoliters of grain annually. From this would be deducted seed for the following year as well as the lessor's share of the crop. This left the *métayer* with only sixty-one hectoliters of grain, roughly the consumption requirements of a share-cropping household of six adults and nine children. If anything above subsistence was to be earned, it would have to be derived from the other areas of farm production, principally cattle sales. Because of the light soils of the Morvan, plow teams were composed of only four oxen, occasionally six. Each year the oldest pair would be sold off and replaced by two younger head which were broken into the team. During the first decade of the nineteenth century, a team of oxen would bring about 370 francs on the local market.[12] The sharecropper's share thus would be 185 francs which, with other sales of calves and sheep, would be just enough to cover the *bellemain* and taxes. The system of *métayage* thus left little or no room for profits for the direct producers, and indeed scant margin to cover losses from harvest failures or loss of cattle from disease.

The autobiography of Etienne Bertin, a sharecropper in the Bourbonnais born in 1823, provides stark testimony to the problems faced by families trying to turn a profit under *métayage*. One of the constant themes of *Life of a Simple Man* is the obsession of Bertin's family to try to make ends meet each year. His often unscrupulous landlords would frequently take advantage of their tenants' illiteracy and fear of dismissal to cheat the family out of even the smallest sums. Bertin recalled the slow, pained efforts of his parents as they attempted to determine their share in the farm profits. After several evenings of often confused calculations, their efforts were simply ignored by the landlord.

> With his paper in his hand, he would say: "The purchases come to so much—sales to so much; returns to you, Berot."
>
> In bad seasons our share was nothing; we were even behind. Sometimes it came to two or three hundred francs, never more. Sometimes, when my father had hoped for more, he would venture to say: "But, sir, I did think I should have had more than that."
>
> Then the master's face would wear its worst frown: "How more than that? Do you take me for a thief, Berot? If that is so, I beg you will find another master, who won't rob you."
>
> My father would hasten to stammer very humbly: "I'm sure I don't mean that, sir."
>
> "That's just as well, for you know *laboureurs* are not scarce; after you another."[13]

Not all families were subjected to such circumstances. A large proportion of the inhabitants of Larochemillay were independent landowners. In fact, the commune encompasses two distinct geographic regions in which property relations differed greatly. Sharecropping dominated the southeastern sections of the commune, where the terrain is generally less broken. In this part of the commune, lying at about 300 meters above sea level, peasant proprietorship was limited to the area immediately surrounding the hamlet of Larochemillay. North and west of this lowland area, the mountains of the Morvan begin to rise abruptly to 600 meters. The terrain is more rugged and steep, woodland is more extensive and farmland restricted to fairly narrow valleys. Unlike the southeast, where the settlement patterns are characterized by scattered farmsteads surrounded by large enclosed fields, in the northwest there are fewer *domaines*, more hamlets and smaller fields. Indeed, to a traveler descending from the Morvan, the abrupt change in settlement

Map 3. The commune of Larochemillay

communal boundary

—400— meters above
sea level

Chef-lieu of the commune ⊙

Châteaux ▬

Hamlets ○

Domaines ●

and field patterns is striking. This hilly northwestern section of Larochemillay constitutes the southernmost extension of the Upper Morvan and is dominated by peasant proprietorship. Thus, in the southernmost cadastral section of Larochemillay, one proprietor owned fifty-five percent of the land. In contrast, no single proprietor owned more than twenty percent of the land in the northeastern section of the commune.

Under the Old Regime, this part of the commune was a separate parish, that of Saint-Jean-Goux. Numerous *terriers* and *dénombrements* from the eighteenth century indicate that most of the land of the parish was held under *bordelage*.[14] It is possible that the hamlets in this section of the commune, and many hamlets throughout the Upper Morvan as well, were created by the successive partition of land once held by one or more *communautés*. The progressive division of property may well account for the unique residence patterns of the region, which are not found in any other part of the province. In many hamlets the majority of families recorded in tax and census lists have the same last name, often the same as the hamlet in which they reside. Thus, of eleven families residing in the hamlet of Le Marceaux, eight were surnamed Marceaux. All twenty families residing in three neighboring hamlets were surnamed Martin.

Peasant Succession Strategy and Household Structure

These differences between the two sections of Larochemillay make the commune a kind of microcosm of property relations in the Nivernais as a whole. The combination of *métayage* and peasant proprietorship there offers an excellent opportunity to compare the household structure and kinship ties of sharecroppers and peasant landowners within a single locality. The primary source for this examination will be marriage contracts and *acts de communauté* drawn up by the residents between 1775 and 1835. When available, the actual notary minutes themselves were consulted. Unfortunately, few such minutes are available. However, this does not cause a serious problem, since other sources on contracts do exist. These are the *livres d'enregistrement* containing a detailed summary of all civil acts either passed before a notary or under private signature.[15] The registers have an important advantage over notary minutes. Entries were made on a day-to-day basis, each entry noting the most important aspects of the contract, including the names, relations, and residences of the principals involved in the original act. Unlike notary minutes, which contain only the contracts passed before an individual *notaire,* the registers contain summaries of all written

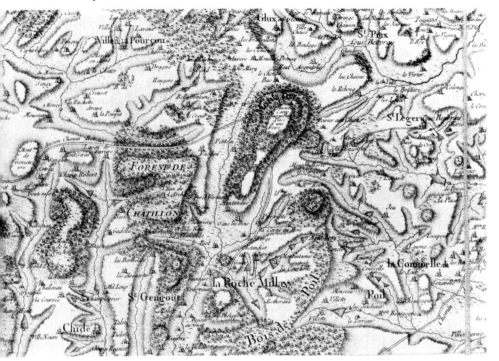

1. Larochemillay. The present commune was formed from the Old Regime parishes of Larochemillay and St. Gengoux, shown here on a map drawn up in 1782. The territory of the commune covers a triangular area extending north and west from the road leading to Mont Beuvron to the old Roman Road.

contracts involving property sales, transfers, leases, donations, testaments, marriage contracts, and so forth, that were passed within the territory of the registry bureau. These *bureaux de contrôle des acts des notaires* were first established in 1693. Larochemillay has a further advantage in that, up until 1791, it was the seat of one such bureau. After that date, the bureau was suppressed and registry incorporated into the bureau at Luzy, the new cantonal seat.

One problem in using such registers concerns the differences between the provisions laid down before and after 1791 regarding which acts were to be recorded at which bureau. Under the Old Regime, the bureau at which acts were to be recorded depended upon the residence of the notary before whom the act was passed, rather than that of the principals or the location of the property involved in the contract.[16] After the reorganization of the registries in 1791, these provisions were changed. Henceforth all acts were to be registered at the bureau in which

2. Hamlet of Montjouan, commune of Larochemillay, circa 1880. The hamlet is located in the north-west section of the commune, an area dominated by small peasant-owned farms.

the property covered by the act was situated. These differences in regulations could cause severe problems since, prior to 1791, contracts involving individuals who went to a notary residing outside of the territory of the bureau under study would not be included in that bureau's registry. Fortunately, Larochemillay was not only a *bureau de contrôle* under the Old Regime but also the residence of the only two notaries for the area. After 1737 the nearest other notary was in Luzy, fifteen miles away. It is unlikely that the inhabitants would travel that far to have their contracts drawn up with notaries so nearby. A check of the surrounding bureaus revealed only three instances in which residents of Larochemillay went to other notaries living outside the village. It is fairly certain, then, that the registries examined contain all the contracts drawn up by the inhabitants of Larochemillay.

Table 9. Proportion of marriages regulated by contract (1775–1835)

Years	Number of Marriages Recorded at Larochemillay	Marriages by Children of Proprietaires or Métayers	Marriage Contracts	Acts of Association	Percent
1775–1793	147	–	42	5	32.0%
1794–1814	183	131	43	52	53.0
1815–1835	167	108	35	12	28.0
Totals	497		120	69	38.0

*Registers prior to 1792 too often omitted occupation of parents.

3.   Hamlet of Petition, commune of Larochemillay. Only the narrow valley bottom is suitable for agriculture, the steep hillsides are left in forest.

The use of contracts to examine family structure and kin ties presents at least one other important problem: How representative of the general population were those families who drew up such contracts? Since acts of association were generally written when an individual married, one way to test this is to compare the number of contracts with the number of marriages that took place in the commune during the same period. In Table 9 the numbers of marriage contracts and acts of association are compared to the total number of marriages recorded in the parish registers and *état civil* for Larochemillay.[17] For the entire period between 1775 and 1835, thirty-eight percent of all marriages were regulated by a contract. However, as the table clearly indicates, the number of contracts jumped considerably during the decades after 1793, when over half of all marriages were accompanied by a written contract. Both prior to and following that period, less than a third of the marriages were so regulated. This increase in the number of contracts after 1793 was due largely to legal changes affecting the formation of the *communauté*. Whereas customary law recognized the existence of a *communauté* after the coresidence of its members for a year and a day, under

64

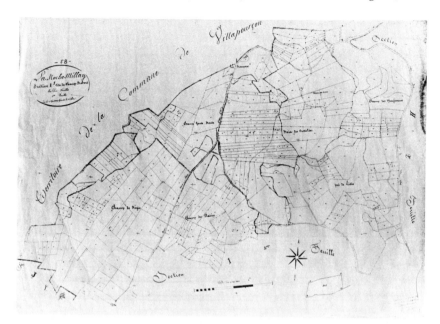

4. Cadastral maps for Larochemillay, 1845. Above are small peasant holdings in the most northwestern section of the commune. On the following page are the large enclosed fields of the domaines of Goulots and Bas Rivière in the south. Separated only by about a mile, the differences in field sizes are striking.

the Napoleonic Code, the *communauté* (or *sociéte,* in the new legal jargon) required a written contract. The increase in the percentage of marriages regulated by written contracts was thus due largely to changes in the laws governing associations.

As the figures show, however, most marriages at Larochemillay took place without the formality of a written contract. This was due to several factors. First, most contracts were drawn up by proprietors and sharecroppers rather than landless peasants. Second, many marriage contracts contained clauses stipulating the dowries and inheritances not only of the bride and groom but of their brothers and sisters as well. This was a convenient means of providing for other heirs without having to make a separate contract for each. Finally, in various *quittances* and *cessions* made before 1793, there are references to verbal contracts made by parents, a practice that almost certainly was continued in the nineteenth century. All these combined to reduce considerably the number of formal contracts which the villagers drew up. Nevertheless, given the proportion of marriages among proprietors and sharecroppers that were regulated by formal agreements, as well as the remarkable

65

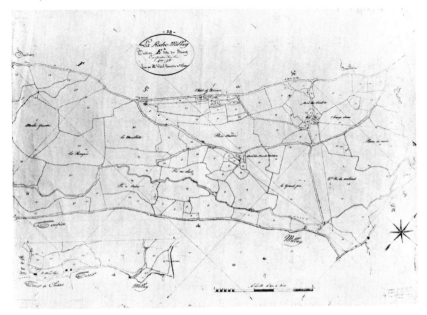

5.   Cadastral map for Larochemillay, 1845.

similarities between the contracts themselves, there is no reason to doubt that the sample is representative.

Of the one hundred and twenty marriage contracts passed during the period, sixty-three contained clauses of association. Together with the acts of association, this gives a total of one hundred and twenty-one *acts de communauté.* Fifty-two contracts can be identified as having been drawn up by proprietors, either because the principals were so designated or because some land was mentioned in the contract. Sixty-nine contracts were drawn up by sharecroppers, identification again based on occupation or residence at one of the *domaines* of the commune. For three contracts, no positive identification could be determined, and so they were omitted from the analysis.

It should be noted that contracts of *communauté* cannot be unequivocally equated with household structure. Their purpose was to specify those persons who would share property, income, and expenses. Even though coresidence was invariably stated as a condition for entry into the *communauté,* at times families excluded certain individuals who resided with them. Because common residence, under customary law, was synonymous in the eyes of most persons with the establishment of a *communauté,* it was necessary to specify explicitly those relatives who

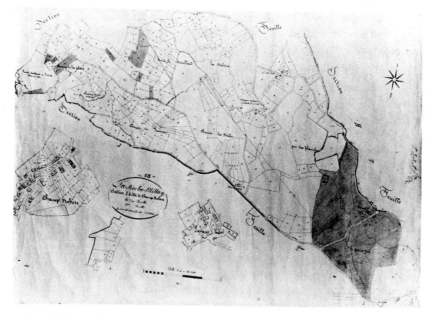

6. In this section of Larochemillay, small peasant holdings and large domaine farming exist side by side. The shaded fields in the lower right are seventeen hectares of the domaine of Bequin; in the upper left, the scattered properties of Jean Cloix totaling about two hectares.

were to be excluded. Usually, these were either older widows no longer able to contribute financially or physically to the family enterprise, or relatives hired as servants (a common practice) who might otherwise have been able to lay claim to rights in the *communauté*. As long as the law demanded that families specify who was and who was not to participate in the *communauté,* such contracts were virtually mandatory. The problem is that, as long as contracts of *non-communauté* were legally necessary, one can gain a more or less accurate picture of household structure. Under the Napoleonic Code, however, the connection between coresidence and co-ownership was abolished. The possibility therefore increases that the *communautés* specified by notary acts may not reflect the full complexity of the households to which they pertain. The problem is somewhat mitigated by the fact that as late as 1830, contracts of *non-communauté* continued to be drawn up by families even though the civil code rendered such acts unnecessary. Presumably, joint ownership of property by persons living together continued to be associated in most people's minds and this concern led them to make sure that no unwarranted claims would be made against their *communauté*. If anything, then, contracts of association passed after 1804 would probably underestimate the actual degree of household complexity.

Keeping this in mind, *acts de communauté* and marriage contracts containing clauses of association were used to reconstruct the household structures and kin ties of proprietors and sharecroppers at Larochemillay. The results, presented in Table 10, show a remarkable difference between the two groups. The large, joint household appears to have been widespread among sharecroppers but formed only sporadically by landed peasants. Moreover, this contrast was as true for the period prior to 1793 when both *bordelage* and customary law remained in effect, as it was for the subsequent period.[18] In Larochemillay, at least, long before its abolition, *bordelage* had ceased to contribute significantly to the formation of large, complex domestic groups. Instead, the joint household had become synonymous with a class of peasants for whom *bordelage* restrictions were of little concern.

This decline in joint households among landed peasants was due to the increased control exercised by this class over the disposition of inheritance settlements gained during the fifteenth and sixteenth centuries. The result had been a progressive division of holdings over the centuries. By the end of the Old Regime, the process had been carried to such an extent that the inhabitants of Château-Chinon had complained in 1789 that "the properties of the Morvan are extremely small and divided to infinity."[19] As holdings continued to shrink, there were fewer and fewer families with enough land to support large multiple households. Significantly, in the former parish of Saint-Jean-Goux, where

Table 10. Household structure, Larochemillay (Contracts of *communauté* 1775–1835)

	STEM	JOINT				
	2	3	4	5	6	TOTAL
Owners:						
1775–1794	13	2				15
1795–1814	21	1				22
1815–1835	14	1				15
	48	4				52
Sharecroppers:						
1775–1794	–	4	1	1	1	6
1795–1814	4	17	17	4	2	44
1815–1835	4	8	5	1	–	18
	8	28	23	6	3	69

Number of Marital Units Forming a Communauté

peasant proprietorship was most heavily concentrated, the number of households steadily increased in the century prior to the Revolution. Numbering thirty-eight in 1686, they grew to forty-eight in 1709, fifty-nine in 1760, and to seventy-one by 1789. In contrast, the number of households in the parish of Larochemillay, where sharecropping predominated, remained stable. Numbering forty-three in both 1686 and 1760, by 1789 they had increased to only forty-seven.[20]

Ironically, the division of peasant holdings was brought about by the very demand for adults needed to work them. To fully understand why this was so, we must examine more closely the strategies employed by landed peasants when settling their successions. In all contracts drawn up by proprietors prior to 1794, the parents would donate all the real and personal property they owned to the new couple. The donation would take effect either immediately upon the marriage of their children or at the death of the parents. If property was donated outright, the parents would usually retain usufruct over it or would retire, claiming only a *pension viager,* that is, a specified sum of money or goods that the new couple would pay them annually. Both parties would also enter into a *communauté,* thereby ensuring that all acquisitions made by either party would remain in control of all parties. Invariably, parents would charge the new couple to pay off the dowries of their other children who had been apanaged in return for their renunciation of any further claims to inheritance. Parents often went to great lengths to ensure that apanaged heirs would cause no future problems for their *communautés.* Many added clauses to the contract threatening to reduce the dowries of apanaged children to their *légitime* if any future claims on the succession were made.

When a single heir was designated to succeed to control of the holding, there would be no threat to its division. However, the preservation of the holding was not the only factor weighed by parents when deciding the settlements of their children. It must be recalled that in peasant societies, the passing on of property from one generation to the next involves two related, yet distant, events. For the younger generation, it marks the point in life when control over the means of production is at last attained. One's marriage and, to a great extent, one's independence from parental authority depend on this transfer. For the older generation, loss of control over the farm also means loss of control over one's own security. In societies lacking the benefits of social security or savings accounts, one's livelihood in old age depends directly upon one's kin. To ensure that such security would be forthcoming, parents invariably specified in the marriage contracts of their heirs the exact amount of cash and farm products they were to receive upon retirement, which rooms they were to occupy, and what furniture and clothes they would keep. These clauses were added for very good reason. In his commentaries on the customs and manners of the Morvan, Emil Blin observed in the nineteenth century that "parents who live too long are often considered as a burden, even as less than strangers, by their shameless sons. Their meager pensions are sullenly furnished with utmost parsimony, and often only after threats from the court baillif."[21] Many parents were to learn this first-hand. Ten years after Jean Aurousseau retired in 1780, he had to go to court to recover three years' arrears in the pension that his son-in-law was supposed to furnish. In another case, Leonard Bouillot also had to resort to court action to force his similarly negligent son-in-law to pay him the pension due by a contract signed less than two years earlier. Similar cases are scattered through the minutes of notaries, stark testimony to the transience of filial devotion.

One way to avoid such threats to retirement was to make sure that the farm that passed to succeeding generations would be able to support not only the younger family but one's pension as well. With small- and medium-sized farms, this was accomplished by passing the holding intact to a single heir. However, with large farms of thirty and forty hectares, such a strategy could actually undermine the economic viability of the farm. Holdings of this size required a considerable labor force, particularly in a region such as the Morvan where fallows were a crucial means of maintaining soil fertility. Preparation of the fallow for planting was the most demanding of all farm operations. A thirty-five-hectare farm would usually have anywhere from twelve to fifteen hectares of fallow each year. These were plowed three times each season: in the summer, early autumn, and again just prior to planting in mid-October. With plow teams able to work about a third of a hectare per day, such a farm would require anywhere from one hundred and twenty to one hundred and fifty workdays just to prepare the seedbed.[22] In addition to plowing, soil preparation involved the spreading of manure prior to the *semaille,* or fall plowing, a time-consuming and laborious task because of the difficulties of transporting the heavily laden carts across the open fields. Even with the assistance of women and children, the operation would take some two to three weeks to perform. A farm of this size, then, would require at least two full plow teams.

Because these tasks were carried out for extended periods of time, such teams had to reside on the farm for most of the year. Ordinarily, the work force would be composed of a father and his grown sons. The problem came when the father retired and control of the farm passed to a single heir. This virtually assured that the successor would have to employ hired labor until his own sons were old enough to shoulder these burdens. In the last decades of the eighteenth century, however, the cost of a team of plowmen was about eighty *livres,* plus food and lodging.[23] *Vingtième* lists from the Morvan during this period indicate that a farm of approximately thirty-five hectares produced an annual revenue of only between five hundred and five hundred and fifty *livres.*[24] By forcing one's successor to resort to employing paid plowmen, the parent was placing a considerable strain on the farm's resources, a strain that might ultimately threaten his own pension if it became too great.

The most obvious means by which such costs could be avoided would be to rely on the labor of the adult family members. The problem was how to keep such kin on the farm. One way would be to retain younger sons as farm servants. We may assume, however, that with no stake in the farm or its operation, there would be little incentive for such individuals to remain with their families for very long. A more certain strategy would be to simply incorporate two or more children into a *communauté* in which all property was held jointly. With both heirs sharing an interest in the farm, the preservation of a labor force would be assured.

While such a strategy secured an adequate work force, it also sowed the seeds for the eventual break up of the farm. Strong pressures for division would eventually arise since even a farm that required the labor of two or three adults had an absolute limit on the number of persons it could support. As grandchildren grew to adulthood, the steadily increasing pressures on family resources would develop into open conflict between the family members. Eventually, the *communauté* would be forced to dissolve and divide the property. This occurred most often after the death of the father, whose authority was usually the only source acting to suppress internal disputes. Of the twenty acts formally dissolving *communautés* drawn up between 1775 and 1835, ten were carried out by households composed of married siblings and six others of married siblings living with their widowed mother.

The history of one family at Larochemillay as depicted in the notary records illustrates how the strategy worked in practice as well as its affects on family holdings. In 1784 Pierrette Tixier married Leonnard Godard. At that time Pierrette's widowed mother Emée and her other children lived in a *communauté* with her brother, Pierre Lambert. Based on information from various other contracts, the *communauté* owned approximately thirty hectors. Pierrette's marriage posed no problem for the *communauté*, for she was apanaged into another family in the neighboring village of Chiddes. However, a disagreement over the terms of the marriage contract ended with Pierrette's return in 1787 to her mother's household. In 1790 Pierre Lambert's son married and, along with another daughter, received by donation all of Pierre's land. In return, they were to pay off the marriage portions of their younger brothers and sisters and were to provide their parents with an annual pension upon their retirement. Significantly, while the two children were incorporated into their parents' *communauté*, they were excluded from the *communauté* of Emée and her children, even though both families continued to reside together. Clearly, Pierre and Emée did not intend to continue the association. Indeed, in a contract drawn up three months later, they divided the real estate held in common. Their farm at one time had not only been able to support both families but had required the labor of several adults. Yet it could not withstand the pressures exerted by additional families as their own children were married.

The strategy of incorporating two or more heirs into a *communauté* at first appears somewhat contradictory. Parents must certainly have been aware of the inevitable consequences of joint-ownership between their children. The paradox arises only when one views peasant strategy as aiming solely to preserve the integrity of the family holding. However, avoiding its division was not an end in itself but only a means to an end. The ultimate goal was to maintain the economic viability of the farm. Both generations had a direct interest in doing so, children because the future well-being of their own families would be based upon the farm, and parents because the security of their retirement pension depended on it. Between these two related yet separate concerns, that of the parent's took precedent, simply because customary law granted them the power to manipulate successions as they saw fit. It was in their interest not to burden the farm with added costs of hired hands because pensions would be all the more secure if the farm income remained within the family. Incorporating more than one heir not only achieved this goal, but at the same time increased their own security by extending the obligation of maintaining their pensions to several kin. In this sense, the *communauté* acted as a kind of insurance policy in which investments were made in relatives rather than savings or stock.

For sharecroppers, the *communauté* represented something quite different. The purpose of their associations was not to provide care for the aged but centered instead on the strict necessity of procuring an adequate workforce for the large *domaines* they leased. Few acts of associations drawn up by this group contain clauses related to the pensions of members. The stipulations regarding property specified only the items to be held in common and those which were to be excluded from the *communauté*. Farm tools and equipment, farm products, profits, and income were the usual items entered into the common fund. Goods not held in common included personal property such as clothes, furniture, dowries, and any inheritances to which a member might succeed. If these latter, known as *propres,* were mixed into the common fund, their owners always retained the right to withdraw them prior to any partition of the *communauté*.

Parents' security after they were too old to contribute their labor to the farm operation depended solely on their own *propres* and the goodwill of their relatives. Several contracts reveal that the aged members of a *communauté,* once they retired, were entirely without rights to the association and totally dependent on their children for their care. A declaration drawn up in 1825 by Jean Granger, his son and daughter-in-law, stated that it was only out of "filial piety" that they allowed Granger's widowed sister to reside with them, and that she would have no rights in their *communauté*. A further clause specified each item that his sister had brought with her and to which her brother and his children renounced any claim. The property she was so careful to itemize? A wooden chest, the clothes she wore, and her linen, all valued at a total of seventy-five francs. Another contract drawn up in 1828 by the children of Catherine Petit, the widow of Jean Talbotier, stated that the eldest would lodge, feed and provide food and fuel for their mother in exchange for one hundred francs a year, which his brothers and sisters would pay to him.

The fact that families felt obliged to resort to notarized contracts indicates how little such actions were brought about by a natural and spontaneous desire on the part of children to provide for their aged parents. Even in the closest of families, the necessity of caring for persons who contributed little towards the family income must have been viewed at times as a regretted drain on limited resources. These kinds of attitudes about the aged are strikingly revealed in *Life of a Simple Man,* the autobiography of Etienne Bertin. In one memorable passage, Bertin described the death of his grandmother. Over eighty, she had suffered a heart attack and had remained paralyzed for several months.

> I often heard people say to my mother or to one of my sisters-in-law: "Do you think she is likely to last long?"

To which they would reply:

"It is to be hoped not."

I neither liked nor disliked the old woman. I was rather indifferent about her. But in spite of that I was pained by the remarks in which the desire for her death showed itself.

At the beginning of winter she had a second attack and died after a day of the most acute suffering. This death made no difference in our daily routine. The usual work was done; meals took place at the ordinary hours in front of that bed whose closed curtains concealed a corpse. . . . My godfather was sent to the clerk at the Town Hall to declare the death and to arrange with the priest the hours of the burial. . . . When my godfather returned, he busied himself fixing a new plough and I had to help him. The task finished, he said to me with a satisfied air:

"How many times I have wanted to see the end of that job! I just needed a day like this!"

Such an expression of calm selfishness hurt me. One is easily touched when one is young. Later, when I was as old as my godfather was at that time, I became quite as practical as he.[26]

Bertin's own mother was virtually abandoned by her children. When he went to visit her one Christmas, she openly vented her bitterness toward his two brothers and sister. "I shall die here alone. One fine morning they'll find me dead from sorrow and suffering and cold and hunger. The Scamps! That Slut!" Only after Bertin's constant urgings did her other children agree to provide for her.

Kinship Ties in the Communautes

Prior to the abolition of customary law in 1793, coresidence between generations and landholding families was intrinsically linked to the transmission of property. This transfer was itself governed by the principle of male preference in succession. While the patrimony as a whole devolved on both sons and daughters, males were favored with the family's real estate while daughters generally received only cash or removals. Daughters at times inherited land, but for the most part this occurred only in the absence of a direct male heir. The basis for such male preference is not fully understood by anthropologists, although it characterizes nearly all landed peasant societies in Europe and Asia.[27] In the Nivernais, this principle was epitomized in the customary laws of the province. Article 24 of Chapter 23 declared that "daughters who are married and apanaged by their parents . . . cannot return to their parent's succession so long as there exists a male heir or descendants of a male heir." In other words, apanage, in the eyes of the law, was synonymous with female exclusion. This principle was further extended in the customs to collateral succession, where females and their descendants were barred entirely from inheriting from collaterals who died without heirs in the direct line.[28]

Jean Lucien Gay, whose study of notarial practice in the Nivernais during the Old Regime was based on several thousand marriage contracts drawn up between the fourteenth and eighteenth centuries, stated that in the vast majority of the cases, couples who entered into *communautés* did so with those of the groom's parents; the association of sons-in-law was relatively rare.[29] Although Gay gives no figures, it is clear from his remarks that, since the Middle Ages when records become available, the *communautés* in the Nivernais were essentially patrilineal and patrilocal; that is, inheritance passed down to sons who, when they married, cohabited with their parents. Daughters were usually provided with only linen, a few pieces of furniture and perhaps some money. They were otherwise excluded from the inheritance.

An examination of notary contracts for Larochemillay, however, shows that the selection of kin incorporated into the *communauté* was far more complex than Gay indicates. At least fifteen of the *communautés* established by contract were formed by the association of female kin (married daughters, sisters, or other female relatives) and another thirty-five by the association of both male and female kin. Only sixty-three *communautés*—a little over half—were characterized by strict male preference in the selection of coparcenors. A closer examination of these contracts indicates that male preference was largely a function of land ownership. Table 11 distinguishes between *communautés* formed by landowning peasants and those formed by sharecroppers. Among peasant proprietors, kin ties between male coparcenors accounted for seventy percent of all associations. Indeed, virtually all of these *communautés* were established by the association of parents and their married sons. Kin ties within sharecropper *communautés* tended to be far more complex. Not only were there a greater number of female kin incorporated into the *communautés*, but twenty of these were formed by married siblings joining together into an association.

These differences between sharecroppers and proprietors open the way for some tantalizing speculations. Was the tendency toward male preference described by Gay for the early modern period discarded by peasants as a result of the transformation of property relations within the province during the seventeenth century? Did the spread of *métayage* dampen the principle of male preference so firmly rooted in the

Table 11. Proprietors and sharecroppers kinship ties within communautés at Larochemillay (1775-1836)

Kinship tie to head of household through	Proprietors	Sharecroppers
Males	36	32
Females	10	5
Both males and females	3	32
	49	69

landowning peasantry? Again, because Gay fails to give specific figures, it is difficult to compare his findings with those for Larochemillay. It is possible that he arrived at his conclusions because he relied solely on marriage contracts for his study. At Larochemillay, most of the *communautés* among proprietors were formed by marriage contract, while sharecroppers tended to draw up acts of association. Thus, the nature of Gay's sources undoubtedly biased his conclusions by omitting those kinds of contracts utilized by nonlandowning families. In fact, it appears that male preference existed to some extent even among sharecroppers. Closer examination of individual kin ties within their *communautés* reveals that, while many involved links through females, the majority of ties were agnatic. Of one hundred and thirty-seven ties between parents and married children,[30] ninety-three were with married sons compared to forty-seven with married daughters. Of fifty-one lateral ties among the heads of sibling-headed households, forty-five were between brothers while only six involved married sisters. Taken as a whole, then, the cognatic nature of kin ties among sharecroppers reveals a marked preference for the male principle.

Breaking down sharecropper's *communautés* by residential pattern and household size indicates that the male preferences of this group were tempered by the needs for additional labor to farm the large *domaines*. Daughters and their husbands tended to be incorporated into a *communauté* only after the association of a son or brother. Table 12 reflects this. In the early stages of household formation—those *communautés* with two or three marital units—agnatic ties predominated. In the later stages of household development, daughters and their hus-

Table 12. Sharecroppers only

| Kinship tie to head of household through: | Number of Marital Units | | | | | |
	2	3	4	5	6	Total
Males	7	16	7	2		32
Females	1	2	2			32
Both males and females	2	11	13	4	2	5
	10	29	22	6	2	69

bands, as well as more distant kin, were brought into the association. It is likely that this preference for sons was based on the father's concern with maintaining his authority within the domestic group. Presumably, this could be more easily exercised over his own sons than over in-laws. Such preferences ultimately had to give way to the demands imposed by *domaine* farming. This is best indicated by the degree to which families sought out kin to incorporate into their *communautés* in order to meet the heavy labor demands of the *domaine*. Many *communautés* included among their coparceners the kin of their in-laws, such as a daughter-in-law's parents or married brothers. In at least one case, a kind of fictive kin tie was established. Less than a year after Pierre Gautheron and his son Jean leased out the *domaine* of Vanoise, Jean abandoned the farm, taking with him his movables and other personal property. In apparent desperation, his father concluded an agreement four days later with Antoine Cloix and his wife by which they would replace his son in the *communauté*.

Labor demand not only affected kin ties within the household, but served to strengthen ties between sharecropping households as well. *Métayage* placed heavy burdens on individual families, particularly during the summer months when crops were harvested and had to be transported to the landlord's granaries. Sharecroppers relied a great deal on their neighbors for such seasonal work. Bertin, for example, described the women of three neighboring *domaines* as working together to feed the threshers employed by their families.[31] Most leases contained clauses stipulating that the sharecropper would be responsible for all cartings necessary for the maintenance, repair, and construction of farm buildings. Because roads were virtually impassable during winter months, such cartings had to be carried out during the spring and summer, thereby increasing the burden on the farm's wagons and teams. In order to meet these demands, families often pooled their resources and shared their wagons and oxen. "These *communautés*," wrote one observer, "never refuse a wagon and team to those who ask, and, between families, lend each other mutual support. . . . The *maître de communauté* need worry little. His neighboring *communautés* are informed and on the stipulated day, eighty to one hundred oxen or more, plus carts and drivers, are at his disposition."[32]

Such mutual assistance between sharecroppers was reinforced by the establishment of kinship ties between families who worked neighboring *domaines*. Marriage within one's own social stratum was of course quite common.[33] Economic interest as well as a certain prejudice against families with fewer resources encouraged selection of husbands and wives from families of similar means. In *Life of a Simple Man*, Bertin relates how he had become enamored of a servant girl. Marriage, however, couldn't have been further from his thoughts. "It would have been condescending to marry a servant; only the daughters of *métayers* were of my rank."[34] Prejudices of this sort were based on an economic reality that turned marriages into veritable property transactions. The dowries provided newlyweds by their respective families were of matching sums of money or movables of near-equal value. Since the share of the family patrimony to which an individual was entitled and the dowry received at the time of one's marriage were usually of equivalent value, the size of the dowry depended on the wealth of the family. Dowries, then, determined that marriages would take place between families on the same economic level.

This did not mean, however, that marriages were necessarily alliances between families. One's family may have had the last word on whom one married, but such decisions did not mean that permanent ties between the groom's and bride's families were being consciously sought out. On the other hand, there is substantial evidence that the children of sharecroppers were exchanged between families as part of a strategy to establish bonds with neighboring farms. In this way, the burdens of farming could be alleviated by creating a reserve of kin upon whom one could call in times of need.

There are numerous instances of sons or daughters marrying the offspring of families working contiguous *domaines*, and it was invariably these children who were incorporated into the *communautés* of each family. If, as was often the case, the families remained on the same farms for long periods, such arrangements would be repeated in succeeding generations. Thus, the bonds established between two families by the marriage of their children would be reestablished by the marriage of their grandchildren. These arrangements become clear when portrayed graphically. In the following charts, the genealogies of several sharecropping families working contiguous *domaines* have been depicted in order to show how the process operated.

The first example concerns four *communautés* residing at the four *domaines* dependent on the Château d'Ettevaux: the Lauroys, the Dureux, the Dudragnes, and the Roys. Each family, through a number of marriage alliances, established a kin link with its neighbor. In 1792 Dominique Dudragne married Marie Lauroy and was incorporated into the *communauté* of Marie's brothers. The Lauroys then quickly formed a series of alliances with its other neighbors, the Roys at the *domaine* of Montanteaume and the Dureux at the *domaine* of Cheptendiau. In

Figure 1. Kinship ties beyond the household

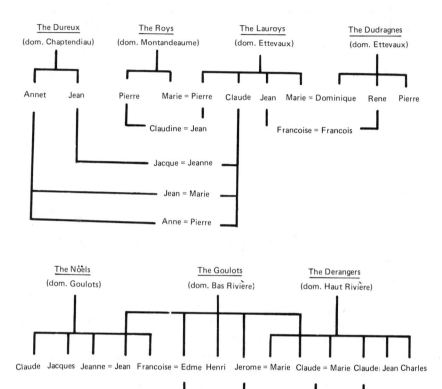

November of the same year, two of Claude Lauroy's daughters entered the Dureux's *communauté* while his brother's son married one of the Roy girls, who was brought into their *communauté*. This last marriage had succeeded an earlier tie between the Lauroys and the Roys that had been established when Pierre Lauroy married Marie Roy. In 1808 a further link with the Dudragnes was created when Jean Lauroy's daughter married François Dudragne and was admitted to his father's *communauté*.

A similar pattern can be seen with the Derangers, Goulots, and Noëls at the *domaines* dependent on the Château de Rivière. Jerome and Henri Goulot took up the lease of Bas Rivière in the late 1780s. It was shortly

79

after this that ties were established by two double marriages with the Noëls and the Derangers. Two girls from the Deranger family and one from the Noëls entered into the Goulot *communauté*, while Jean Goulot married into the *communauté* of Claude and Jacques Noël. In 1818 the ties between the Derangers and the Goulots were strengthened by the marriage of Claude Deranger's daughter to Jean Goulot's son.

Marriage ties between neighbors are one thing, but to what extent were such bonds maintained after children were exchanged? The fact that such arrangements were repeated in succeeding generations indicates that something more than mere chance was involved in the selection of mates. Perhaps the most significant indication that these marriages were a conscious reinforcement of kin ties between families is the fact that the leases for these *domaines* were often shared by the *communautés*. In 1806 the Dudragnes and the Lauroys joined together to lease the two *domaines* at Ettevaux, stipulating in a separate agreement between themselves as to who would work which *domaine*. The same kinds of arrangements were made between the Goulots and the Dudragnes on three occasions between 1811 and 1818. In this way the equipment and resources of each farm could be more easily shared between each family.

The traditions and customs surrounding marriage in the Morvan reveal a tendency to avoid or at least soften the transfer of membership from one's family of origin to that of one's in-laws. Marriage feasts were held in the homes of both families, with breakfast at the bride's home and supper at that of the groom. Fifteen days after the marriage, the bride's family made a formal visit to their daughter's new home, there to celebrate *le beau dimanche*.[35] While the new wife may have renounced all rights to her parents' inheritance, she nonetheless continued to maintain close ties with her family of birth. Sundays were traditionally reserved for wives who had married into other families to return to their parents' home to spend the day.[36] Ties were maintained in other ways as well. The *poêlée*, or harvest feast, was an occasion in which related *communautés* and neighboring families gathered to share in the feast. The *maître* of each *communauté* would designate members to represent their household at the feasts of their neighbors.[37] Celebrations accompanying the slaughtering of a pig were shared with relatives of nearby farms, with portions of the animal sent as gifts to nonrelated neighbors.[38]

Were similar strategies carried out by landowning peasants? If so, it appears they did so with far less deliberateness or calculation. In the first place, the children of proprietors married into the families of immediate neighbors less frequently than did the children of sharecroppers. Only twenty-five percent of the sons and daughters of landowners selected mates from families living in the same hamlet, compared to thirty-three percent of the children of sharecroppers who chose their husbands or wives from families living on contiguous *domaines*. Village endogamy was also less frequently practiced by proprietors. Forty-two percent of the spouses of landowning peasants came from outside the commune, compared to twenty-seven percent for sharecroppers.[39]

When writing about mutual assistance among neighbors, nineteenth century observers of rural traditions indicated that such practices were carried out primarily among the large *communautés*. However, the absence of any literary evidence for such practices among proprietors should not be taken as proof that they did not exist among proprietors as well. Bourgeois observers were rather prone to attribute any kind of mutual aid to the influence of the extended family, which they saw as a bastion of rural morality. Certainly, as residents of a community, proprietors were subject to the innumerable unwritten rules of conduct governing relations among neighbors. These countless mutual obligations, or *politesses,* bound all members of the village to prescribed forms of behavior. Each family was expected, in its turn, to receive their neighbors for *veilles,* which not only provided opportunities for story-telling and gossip but afforded a means by which costly fuel and lighting could be saved. Assistance was expected, too, in times of crisis. "Even among his enemies," reported one observer, "a peasant would not refuse to assist someone or their endangered animal, after which normal relations could be resumed."[40] Above all, it was the community that sanctioned what was considered moral or appropriate behavior, and transgressors could expect to be visited with *charivaris* or other forms of punishment.

Yet relations between neighboring landowners at times seem to have been subject to considerable strain and often to have degenerated into open conflict. Reports by contemporaries are littered with references to such antagonisms. The Morvan proprietor, it seems, had a propensity to sue his neighbors. "The slightest offense, the course of a rivulet, the borders of a field or meadow, an injury suffered in the heat of an argument, almost always becomes the cause of a lawsuit and a source of misfortune for families."[41] Dupin, who laid much of the blame on lawyers eager for fees, claimed that it was not rare to see the costs occasioned by such lawsuits soar far beyond the amount of the damages sought in the original suit.[42] Even Vauban had been shocked by the number of lawsuits and damage claims brought on by the inhabitants of the Morvan.[43] One writer even declared that the fear of being sued by one's neighbors was the main reason for the dispersed settlement patterns of the Morvan. "Each tries to isolate himself as much as possible from his neighbor. The peasant builds his house in the middle of his property in order to avoid any contact with his neighbor so that he may live peaceably by himself."[44]

For contemporaries, at least, the very fact that one owned land meant that one had to be constantly on guard against threats to his fields from neighbors who might usurp a bit of land by moving boundary markers or interfere with irrigation rights by altering the course of a small stream or creek. Part of the problem was certainly brought about by the excessive division of holdings. The mayor of Fretoy, where peasant proprietorship was more concentrated than in any other part of the Morvan, urged in 1883 that the cadastre be redrawn because the confusion generated by successive divisions of fields was resulting in an explosion of court cases over boundaries.[45] Almost a century earlier, a similar plea had been made by the inhabitants of Château-Chinon.[46] Continued litigation of this sort would certainly have put a strain on one's relations with the neighbors, no matter how strong the kin tie.

Differences between proprietors and sharecroppers in the strength of the bond tying related households probably ought not to be exaggerated. Proprietors certainly depended upon kin and neighbors in many ways. Yet the two groups did differ in a number of important respects, and it is fair to say that these dissimilarities were more evident than their similarities. Indeed, the gulf separating *métayers* and *proprietaires* went far deeper than the number of married children with whom the parents of each group shared property and labor. Both faced different problems and were subject to different demands. When, after 1794, the legal framework in which owners and tenants operated was transformed, these differences would become even greater.

CHAPTER FIVE

Revolutionary Civil Legislation and the *Communauté*

The Transformation of Succession Law

> Provence is divided into two classes: the despoilers and the despoiled. These latter, without property and forming the vast majority, have been reduced to a precarious existence and expunged from the list of citizens.

Such was the complaint in an anonymous petition to the Third Estate of Provence in 1789, demanding the abolition of testamentary rights which parents held under Roman law.[1] The "despoiled" were those heirs who had been excluded from their inheritance by their parents. The remarks reflect the social ideals of the legislators of the Convention who were to remodel succession law for France. Their views were based on the conception that political inequality was due to extremes in wealth. Never aiming to abolish private property, they sought rather to prevent its concentration by organizing and regulating its existence. The most forceful attempts to give these ideals a political reality came in the years 1793 and 1794, with such laws as that ordering the sale of *emigré* properties in small lots and the division of common lands among all members of the commune. The *Maximum* itself was as much an attempt to implement these ideals as it was to deal with inflation. Few of these met with success; most were fairly short-lived. Perhaps the most successful effort to achieve these aims was the law establishing forced equality of inheritances. Although set forth as a principle as early as 1791, it was not until 1793 that it became a reality. And though tempered by the Thermidorian reaction and later by Napoleon, it survived with sufficient force to become an established principle in French law, the consequences of which continue to be discussed even today.

The remaking of succession laws presupposed the consolidation of

French civil law into a single, national code. The rationalization of France's myriad customary laws was an ideal with roots already centuries old by the time of the Revolution. It had been the dream of Louis XI and been advocated by such leading jurists as Loysel, Daguesseau, and DuMoulin, not to mention most of the eighteenth century *philosophes*—Montesquieu excepted. Coquille himself, enamoured by the unity of Roman law, had sought to establish a commonality among the various bodies of French customary law which would serve as a basis for interpreting particular customs.[2] However, it was only with the Constituent Assembly that the first efforts toward this goal were realized. The law of April 16, 1790, which reorganized the nation's judicial system, declared unequivocally that there would be a uniform civil code "common to all the kingdom."

The principle of a national civil code was established with relative ease. The victory of the principle of equality between heirs in successions was anything but immediate. It was established only with hesitation and in the face of considerable opposition. The law of March 15, 1790, abolished male preference and primogeniture, but only for the nobility. The extension of this law to nonnobles came only a year later and after a desperate struggle waged by deputies of Normandy and Bearn to prevent its adoption.[3] Yet, equality between heirs remained a dead letter because the law of April 15, 1791 applied only to *ab intestat* successions. Testamentary rights remained intact. As long as parents retained the power to favor any of their heirs through donations or wills, inequality would continue to exist.

Opposition to the abolition of testamentary rights was considerable, and both the National Assembly and the Legislative Assembly failed to resolve the question. The ability to favor an heir, it was argued, responded to the necessities of agriculture. Forced equality would result in the excessive division of properties and despoil eldest sons of their rights to a unified holding. The state, it was said, had no right to interfere in the disposition of one's property because property was a right rooted in nature and was not a gift of society. Those who demanded the abolition of testamentary rights countered that property was instead a creation of society, and as such society had a direct interest in regulating its organization in accord with "natural law." Moreover, the concentration of property into fewer and fewer hands resulted in political inequality by excluding the vast majority of the population from the rights of citizenship.[4]

In fact, the attack on testamentary rights succeeded only when the arguments against it were linked directly to the politics of the Revolution. The first months of 1793 marked a major turning point in the course of the Revolution. In January despite the efforts of the Girondins, the king was tried and executed for treason. Already faced with economic crisis and counterrevolution, within a month the country was at war with all Europe. In March these combined external and internal crises came to a head. The French invasion of the Netherlands was routed and Belgium lost. During the same month, the revolt in the Vendée broke out while, in Paris, the Sections were putting increased pressure on the Convention to enact price controls. Faced with the combined threats from within and without France, and with the Girondins unable or unwilling to take those measures deemed necessary to meet the crisis, the Montagnards began to adopt the political program demanded by the Sections and the popular militants.

It was against this background that the Convention voted the law of March 17, 1793, abolishing testamentary rights. The debate surrounding the measure clearly shows that its adoption was a direct response to the political and social crisis then in progress.[5] Discussion opened on March 7 with the declaration by several deputies that testaments were being used by fathers who opposed the Revolution as a means of punishing revolutionary patriots. "It is certain," declared Mailhe, a member of the Legislative Committee, "that aristocratic fathers are avenging themselves for not having been able to draw their children away from their parties by making testaments which are unfavorable to them." Another deputy proposed that the Convention pass a law declaring null and void all testaments which had been made as a means of attacking the Revolution. Mailhe countered that "it is necessary to attack the heart of the abuse. The right to make testaments must be abolished." Another deputy argued that testaments in the collateral line ought to be preserved in favor of those parents without children. This provision was accepted and the final law abolished only testaments made in the direct line.

Manipulation of laws governing succession for political purposes was intensified after the consolidation of the Montagnards' position toward the end of 1793. In December of that year, the English, Prussians, and Austrians were driven from French territory and the Vendeans defeated. In the same month, all constituted bodies and public officials were placed directly under the authority of the Committee of Public Safety. It was in this atmosphere that the Convention established a single uniform law governing succession. The law of 17 Nivôse Year II reiterated the principle of equality with a vengeance. Equality of inheritance was assured by limiting donations to a tenth of one's property if immediate heirs were still living, and to a sixth if no children survived. Moreover, donations could not be made to heirs, thereby eliminating any possibility of favoring a child in the slightest way. That these provisions aimed at preventing any concentration of property is underlined in Article 34, which forbade the amount of property disposable by donations to exceed 10,000 *livres*. If the donee already possessed an equivalent fortune, he or she was forbidden to accept it.

The most radical aspect of the new law was contained in its first article, which declared that the provisions of the law would be retroactive to all successions opened on or after July 14, 1789. By this measure, all donations, testaments, and renunciations dated before January 6, 1794, and made by individuals who had died after July 1789 were null and void. Such successions would be subject to the rules laid down in the new law. This in fact directly opposed the principle of the illegality of retroactive laws proclaimed in the Declaration of the Rights of Man. The pretense for its adoption was that, the principle of equality having been established from that date onwards, to act otherwise would be to fail all patriots who had supported and fought for the principle since that date.

Reaction was immediate. A flood of protests literally inundated the Legislative Committee. "I can't believe that learned and just republicans could give their citizens such a law. Terrible! We shall be victims of our own respect for the law!" "To give a retroactive effect to this law will sow confusion and disorder in countless families that have already regulated their interests!" "The retroactive provision is absolutely without any advantage to the Republic. It will divide families and rob many of the fortunes they have possessed for several years."[6]

The Convention remained adamant. Article 1 of the law continued in effect for two years, until nullified by the Thermidorian reaction in 1795.[7] This was the first in a series of acts aimed at softening the militant ideals of strict equality pushed forth by the Montagnards. The law of 17 Nivôse had been a tool of the Terror and the Thermidorians viewed it as such. All other provisions of the law, however, were retained, and it was not until Napoleon that forced equality itself came to be eroded. In 1800 the amount of property disposable by donation was increased to a fourth if there were three children, with the amount declining with each additional child. Most important, such donations could be granted to any heir, thereby allowing parents to favor a single child over the others.[8] The Napoleonic Code expanded these rights somewhat by allowing parents freely to dispose of half their property if they left one heir, a third if they left two heirs, and a fourth if they left three or more heirs.[9] While weakened, the principle of equality among heirs nonetheless remained firmly established. The extent to which parents could favor a single heir had been drastically reduced. Under customary law in the Nivernais, for example, parents with three heirs had possessed the right freely to dispose of four-fifths of their property. Under the new Civil Code, this proportion was limited to a fourth.

These provisions reflect only one aspect of the transformations in civil law brought about by the Revolution. The entire thrust of the new laws governing succession was to increase the rights of individuals by transferring control over the disposition of succession from parents to their heirs. Thus, the right to apanage children was abolished entirely. No longer would parents be able to reduce the inheritances of their sons and daughters to their *légitime;* their children now possessed clear title to an equal share in the succession. Moreover, the intent of the Code regarding the composition of this share was clearly expressed in Article 832: Each portion must contain, as much as possible, equivalent amounts of real and personal property.

There were, in fact, measures by which the partition of landed property could be avoided. Heirs could renounce their inheritances in favor of one or several of their coheirs, or they could cede their portion for its equivalent cash value. However, no heir could be forced to do so against his will.[10] Another means of preserving the integrity of the family holding was through joint ownership. This could be accomplished in two ways. Either the property itself could remain undivided after the succession had been settled, or the coheirs could form a *société* by mixing their property and sharing its profits. In each instance, the decision to do so depended not on the parents but on their heirs. Article 815 of the Code declared that no heir could be forced to remain in indivision; further, an heir could demand a *partage* at any time. Joint ownership in such cases would always be threatened by a disgruntled coheir or his descendents.

A more effective strategy would be to form a *société*. This was in fact the legal successor to the *communauté* of customary law, but with one important difference. Under the Napoleonic Code, the link between joint ownership of property and coresidence was abolished. Even before the Revolution, the *communauté taisible* had been attacked by jurists because of the alleged disruptions within families caused by confusion over property owned in common by the coparceners and property held separately by each member.[11] In 1803, Bouteville, a member of the *Commission du Tribunat* charged with preparing preliminary reports for the Legislative Committee, wrote that "the associations known to our ancestors under the name *communautés taisibles,* and which were formed solely on the basis of cohabitation, have for some time been contrary to the needs of our time." His associate, Gillet, concurred, adding that while the *communauté taisible* was an "interesting souvenir" of France's patriarchal past, it could "no longer be permitted in our more mature civilization."[12] Most of the remaining provisions of customary law governing the *communauté* were incorporated into the articles regulating the *société*, except that the *société* could be established only by written contract and not by verbal agreement. The importance of the *société* was that, if no length for its existence was specified in the contract, then the *société* would last for the life of the parties and could be dissolved only by the death of one of the members. The coparceners could stipulate that, in this event, the *société* would be maintained either between the survivors or between the survivors and the deceased's heirs.[13] While any member could withdraw, he could not do so in any way that might jeopardize the *société*. If, on the other hand, a specific length had been assigned to the *société*, then no member could withdraw before that time had elapsed.[14]

There were, therefore, any number of ways in which partition of family property could be avoided, or at least curtailed. But the decision as to which of these strategies, if any, would be adopted rested with the heirs, not the parents. This is what is meant by control over the disposition of the succession passing to children. Secure in their rights to an equal share in the inheritance, each heir now had to be consulted before any of these alternatives to partition could be adopted. The effects of Revolutionary civil legislation on the household organization of rural families must be viewed in the context of these changes. As we have seen, the existence of extended family structure in the Nivernais depended on whether property was divided or concentrated at the succession. Both landowning and sharecropping families adopted strategies aimed at preserving the integrity of the patrimony, although for quite different reasons: sharecroppers because of the labor demands imposed by the *domaines*, proprietors largely to ensure parents' security after their retirement. In each case, it had been the parents who had manipulated inheritances to achieve these goals under customary law. Would these strategies continue after control over succession passed to their children? This question ultimately revolves around how each generation within the family regarded the role and function of the patrimony. Did a young couple just establishing their own family view property in quite the same way as an elderly couple just entering into retirement?

Economic security in peasant societies depends largely on the possession of land, and a family's livelihood depended on its ability to gain access to it. Parental strategies aimed at achieving this goal by concentrating property as much as possible in a single heir. In this way, they could more easily maintain their control over it while at the same time preserving it at its greatest productive potential. Concentration of the patrimony, however, meant the exclusion of other heirs from inheritance. If these could not "marry land," their economic position would be precarious. In this way the goals of parents and children conflicted with one another. Yet such strategies had been employed by families for countless generations. Had their persistence established a kind of cultural bias uniting the conceptions of both parents and their children regarding the function of property in the family economy? Could tradition, reinforced by socialization processes, mitigate this built-in conflict between parents and children? Or did the Revolution provide the means whereby this conflict was given full vent, eliminating the economic ties that had united parents and children and thereby destroying the basis of the extended family?

Bourgeoisie Sociology and the Communauté in the Nineteenth Century

Capitalist development in nineteenth century France provoked a variety of responses among intellectual and politicians, ranging from enthusiastic acceptance of economic progress to outright revulsion at the dislocations accompanying industrialization and the commercialization of agriculture. French conservatives in particular were repulsed by the effects of social change on family life, for in their view the family was the prime source of social stability. Their greatest criticisms were therefore leveled at the new Civil Code, which they saw as the principal factor contributing to the disintegration of the family and thus the growth of immorality among the peasantry and working classes.

Interest in the *communauté* in the Nivernais grew precisely because French conservatives viewed its survival well into the nineteenth century as a unique example of how the traditional patriarchal family could withstand the onslaught of modern values. In their initial reports, Frederic LePlay and his followers concluded that the families they had occasion to visit and observe appeared to them to have been governed by the same spirit of familial solidarity and respect for parental authority that had regulated their personal relations and household organization for centuries. Victor de Cheverry, an associate of LePlay, studied several *communautés* in the Morvan during the 1860s. It was his opinion that their survival was due in large part to the region's isolation from "modern ideas." "Their lively existence," he asserted, "so eminently patriarchal, makes a strange contrast to the kinds of rural lives being led all around them . . . Defying any new ideas, they have faithfully conserved the traditions of their race, their religion and their family."[15] According to de Cheverry, the *communautés* of the Morvan, enveloped in a kind of cultural backwater, even continued to govern property relations according to old customary law, completely ignoring the provisions of the Civil Code.

Yet the more they studied the families, the less certain they became of the ability of the *communauté* to survive the impact of modern ideas and values instituted by the Revolution. The penetration of the Morvan by markets and roads was accompanied by an invasion of modern values of individualism and personal ambition, values which proved deadly to the *communauté*. When de Cheverry revisited the Pervys, he was shocked to learn that the *communauté* was dissolving and doing so on terms that were less than amicable. The breakup of the *communauté* resulted when one of its members, the son-in-law of the *maître*, repeatedly clashed with his father-in-law over the administration of the household and the farm. When their constant fighting became unbearable, it was decided to dissolve the association. De Cheverry clearly laid the blame for the dissolution on the insubordination and self-interest of the son-in-law. De Cheverry claimed that in the past, the *communauté* had divided numerous times, but these had always been undertaken by common accord, with the main branch of the family lending it financial and moral support to the newly formed cadet branch. After 1789, however, "the separations were almost always violent and always with recourse to the court."[16]

This last point is important for understanding the framework in which de Cheverry and others viewed the development of the *communauté* in the nineteenth century. Markets and roads may have been the vehicle by which individualism and self-interest penetrated the *communautés*, but ultimate responsibility for their decline lay with the legal regime instituted by the Revolution. Lawyers, judges, and Republican politicians who adhered to the principles first invoked during the Reign of Terror were the main instruments that supported and even encouraged the new values to wreak havoc on the cultural traditions which the *communautés* themselves were trying desperately to preserve.

The most celebrated example of this process was that of the Jault family, a wealthy landowning *communauté* residing in the commune of Saint-Benin-des-Bois. Their reputation was widespread, so much so that Louis Phillipe and his sister, the Princess Adelaide, saw fit to honor the family with a medal as an acknowledgement of their adherence to the spirit of association and family solidarity.[17] When Dupin, the deputy from the Nièvre, visited the Jaults in 1840, he was amazed at the degree to which the members had remained faithful to pre-Revolutionary traditions of regulating property relations within the household. The coparceners owned over one hundred hectares of land valued at 300,000 francs. The integrity of this fortune was preserved by apanaging those members who married out of the *communauté* with a dowry of 1,350 francs. "How astonishing," exclaimed Dupin, "that such an extraordinary regime, so oblivious to the present laws, has been able to resist the laws of 1789 and 1790 and that of the Year II concerning successions! Yet such is the force of customs when they are well-founded. This association has maintained its family spirit and traditions despite all the suggestions of those who are so enamoured of divisions and litigations."[18]

By divisions and litigations Dupin was referring to a series of court cases brought against the *communauté* by the children and grandchildren of those members who had been apanaged after 1793. These descendents claimed that, since their parents' and grandparents' renunciations of their inheritances had not been formally declared before a clerk of the court, as required by the Napoleonic Code, they were invalid. As the heirs of these individuals, they demanded that the *communauté* be divided so that they could obtain their rightful inheritances. In most cases, the Jaults were able to buy off the claimants with cash payments in exchange for their shares, although in one case the issue had gone all the way to the high court at Bourges before being settled in 1835. It was obvious that further claims would be forthcoming as long as members continued to be apanaged. The final blow came in 1843. François Lejault, the son of a male member of the *communauté* who had been apanaged in 1812, brought a suit for the division of the *communauté*. Reportedly, François, who was then living in Paris, had been urged to pursue the case by the radical Ledru-Rolin. Unlike his predecessors, François refused to be bought off, and in 1845 the tribunal at Nevers ruled in his favor. The Jaults immediately appealed. By this time, however, some thirty-four different claimants had appeared, all demanding their inheritance rights as descendents of apanaged coparceners. The assault on the Jaults was overwhelming, and in 1847 they were forced to dissolve.[19]

To LePlay and his followers, the demise of the Jaults was a classic instance of a centuries-old tradition of family cohesiveness that had been sacrificed to a misguided legal system based on principles of individual

91

7.   ''The last of the Jaults'', Pierre Lejault and his wife Pierrette in 1930. Pierre was the son of Francois Lejault, *the maître de communauté* at the time of its dissolution in 1846. The author visited the Jault farmstead in 1977 and found it to still be owned and operated by the Jaults.

self-interest. The fact that the claimant whose suit struck the final blow had been counseled by a radical republican, and that the breakup occurred on the eve of the 1848 revolution, only reinforced their contentions. If the *communautés* had only been left alone, they argued, they would have easily resolved any internal disputes which might have arisen, basing their decisions on age-old cultural traditions. "Experience has proven," wrote de Cheverry, "that recourse to the courts only brings about the dispersion of the *communauté.*"[20]

The monographs on the *communautés* in the Nivernais produced by this group reveal only too clearly the romanticist conceptions of peasant family life. According to one writer, the strength of the Jaults was their "indefatigable attachment to the traditions of their ancestors: a sincere and intimate sense of solidarity and a rigorous adherence to domestic virtues and divine law."[21] All this was being destroyed by what LePlay called "the radical vice of the Napoleonic Code." The laws left to France by the Revolution were seen as the institutionalized expression of modern values which were steadily infiltrating rural society, instilling the youth with misdirected demands for personal emancipation from the constraints of paternal discipline. This interpretation of social change continues to be propounded even today, although with considerably greater sophistication. The view that family organization and social relations in general are products of fairly resilient cultural traditions which are destroyed only under the impact of modernization continues to attract social scientists.[22] The question that must be dealt with, then, is whether there existed any basis for the arguments advanced by LePlay and his associates, or whether their entire schema was nothing less than a wholesale romance.

Peasant Adaptation to the Civil Code

As described by LePlay's followers, the transition from cultural traditions emphasizing family cohesiveness and paternal authority to self-interest and personal gain took place over several decades. The Jault *communauté*, which broke up in 1847, was often described as the last vestige of traditional family values. The survival of the *communauté* in the Morvan up to the 1860s, according to de Cheverry, was due to the region's isolation from the corrupting influence of modern values. Cultural transformation, it was argued, took place over two or three generations. Does the evidence support such a view? Hardly.

According to the available sources, the effect of Revolutionary civil legislation on the relations between family members was immediate.

Evidence for this conclusion comes from the proceedings of countless *tribunaux de famille*. The purpose of this judicial institution, established in 1790 and lasting until 1796, was to arbitrate any disputes arising within families over marriage contracts, inheritance claims, divorces, and so forth. Each party in the dispute would name two or three arbitrators who, after listening to the facts of the case, would render their opinion on the matter. The arbitrators were sometimes relatives, sometimes neighbors, but often lawyers, notaries, priests or wealthy landowners, whose views carried considerable weight. The decision arrived at by the arbitrators was considered binding.

The proceedings of the *tribunaux de famille* for the Nièvre are yet to be classified,[23] so that a systematic analysis of their contents is impossible. However, the following sample of cases involving family disputes in the Morvan shows how quickly individuals there moved to take advantage of the succession laws passed by the Convention, in particular that of 17 Nivôse Year II. Less than a week after this law was passed, Jean Lepere and his wife, Louise Bonnot, brought suit against Françoise Bourgoin, the widow of Louise's uncle, Jean Bonnot. When her uncle had married in 1772, his father had endowed him with all his property at Saint-Honoré, charging them to pay off his other children with four hundred and twenty *livres* each as their marriage portions and apanages. Because her grandfather had died after 1789, Louise demanded the division of Bourgoin's property among all other heirs. The arbitrators determined that Louise Bonnot was within her rights and ordered the division to be carried out.

In a similar suit a few months later, the *communauté* of Jean and François Bondoux, brothers living at Villapourçon, was dissolved by a claim brought against them by their aunt, Françoise Bondoux, and her husband. Françoise had been apanaged by her father, who had bequeathed all his real estate to the brothers' father. Françoise and her husband demanded half of her nephews' property, basing their claim on the fact that Françoise's father had died after 1789, which nullified both her apanage and her renunciation of her father's inheritance. In order to meet their aunt's demands, Jean and François Bondoux were forced to alienate real estate valued at five thousand francs. Shortly thereafter, they dissolved the *communauté* that had existed between them.

Another case: On 15 Ventose Year II, Louis and Leonard Berger demanded the division of the *communauté* existing between their brothers Jacques and François. By a marriage contract drawn up in 1787, Jacques and François had been given all their parents' real estate at Chiddes while their brothers had been apanaged with eighteen hundred *livres* each. Their father had sought to ensure the renunciations made by Louis and Leonard by stipulating that, should they bring forth any further claims against his succession, he would reduce their shares to their *légitime*. He had not counted on the National Convention. Louis and Leonard invoked the law of 17 Nivôse and demanded equal shares in their brothers' *communauté*. Jacques and François, however, were able to show proof that their father had died before July 14, 1789, and so were able to keep their property.

Numerous cases such as these are scattered throughout the *tribunaux de famille*. Relatives, it appears, were all too ready to overturn the wishes of their parents regarding inheritance settlements at the first opportunity. They did so because they felt they had a right to an equal share in the family patrimony. If this right could be obtained only at the expense of the *communautés* of their relatives, they did not hesitate in the least. Little regard was paid to the wishes of their parents and no concern whatsoever was shown for the *communauté* as an institution—unless it was their *communauté* that was threatened!

The extent to which Revolutionary legislation was utilized to overturn the system of preferential inheritance is made evident by the abrupt increase in the number of property divisions recorded after 1793. The vast majority of *partages* carried out involved family inheritances divided between heirs. The following graph displays the number of such divisions registered between 1750 and 1824 at the bureaus of Château-Chinon, Moulins-Engilbert, and Luzy, all in the Morvan.[24] The increase after 1793 is both immediate and striking. Although leveling off after a few years, the number of *partages* began to increase once again after 1800, accelerating rapidly until reaching a peak just after the adoption of the Napoleonic Code in 1804.

This increase in property divisions cannot be interpreted as anything but a complete rejection of the legal system allowing parents to favor one or more children in their succession. Equal division of inheritances was not imposed by the state on an unwilling population; it was readily, even eagerly, accepted. There is little evidence that family solidarity or respect for paternal authority was a widely held cultural value in the pre-Revolutionary Morvan. Ample provisions existed after 1800 by which heirs could either renounce or cede their inheritances in favor of their brothers or sisters, yet few persons opted to do so when given the choice. Because of this, the new Civil Code forced families, especially landowning families, to alter their strategies regarding the disposition of inheritances. The goals remained the same as before; only the means of attaining those goals changed.

Figure 2. Partages registered in the Morvan, 1750-1824

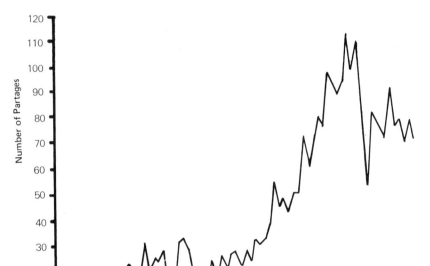

Table 13. Peasant Succession Strategy at Larochemillay (1775-1860)

	Number of contracts in which			
Years	Real estate divided between heirs	Single heir favored over other children	Heir(s) renounced succession	Heir(s) cede rights to coheirs
1775-1793	6	26	26	1
1800-1820*	33	6	1	3
1821-1840	28	6	–	8
1841-1860	43	13	–	4
Totals	110	51	27	16

*Because of the strict limitations imposed by the law of January 6, 1794, contracts drawn up during the time when this law was still enforced were omitted from the analysis.

 The degree to which the new Civil Code altered inheritance strategies among proprietors at Larochemillay can be seen in Table 13. Here, all contracts pertaining to the disposition of inheritances passed before and after 1793 have been grouped into four categories: *partages,* in which real estate deriving from a succession was divided equally among heirs; donations, in which a single heir was favored over other children;

cessions, in which heirs forfeited their share of real estate in exchange for cash payments; and renunciations by heirs to succession.[25] The figures clearly show that the adoption of the new Civil Code marked a complete break with the pre-Revolutionary strategy in which heirs were favored with the bulk of family property. The number of *partages* in the twenty years after 1800 was five times that recorded during the last two decades of the Old Regime, while the number of donations favoring heirs dropped by a similar proportion. There was only a single case in which an heir renounced a claim to inheritance after 1800, and few heirs chose to cede their rights to their parents' landed property in exchange for money. In fact, only seven of the cessions recorded after 1800 were for paternal successions. Most involved collateral successions or successions to more distant relatives. Of the few which did involve paternal succession, in only two cases was a single heir able to retain all the land left by the parents. The rest were cases in which individuals made cessions to their coheirs because they had moved out of the commune and no longer had a direct interest in the property itself.

The consequences of repeatedly dividing inheritances are reflected in the dwindling size of peasant holdings at Larochemillay. The cadastral survey for the commune was completed only in 1845, unfortunately well after the adoption of the Civil Code.[26] Tax lists for 1835, however, list two hundred and forty-four *côtes* for Larochemillay, compared to two hundred and eighty at the time the cadastre was completed in 1845.[27] After that date, the size of properties continued to shrink at a fairly constant rate. This can be shown by tracing individual proprietors over the course of the century. All property transfers in the commune were carefully noted and dated in the cadastre, and by subtracting alienations and adding acquisitions made by each proprietor, the size of each *côte* can be determined for any year during the century. The results of this procedure are displayed in Table 14. Overall, the number of proprietors at Larochemillay continued to increase after 1845, an increase due

Table 14. Property size at Larochemillay according to the communal cadastre (1845-1875)

Size of Property	All Proprietors			
	1845	1855	1865	1875
under 1 hectare	105	119	149	163
1 to 5	103	128	126	140
5 to 10	22	24	38	47
10 to 20	23	23	20	16
20 to 50	8	10	10	11
50 to 100	10	10	10	10
over 100	9	9	9	9
Totals	280	323	362	396

almost entirely to the division of holdings of under twenty hectares in size.

It is entirely possible, however, that many of these new proprietors were owners only in the legal sense of the word. While farms may have been divided among heirs, only one heir may have actually remained on the farm while paying rent to his or her coheirs. Although there are no instances of arrangements of this type stipulated in any formal contract, verbal agreements could easily have been made. Such a possibility can be controlled for by including only those persons listed in both the cadastre *and* the census lists for 1846, 1856, 1866 and 1875.

The assumption here is that individuals who resided on or near the land they owned would more than likely exercise direct control over it as well. When nonresident landowners are excluded, as in Table 15, the number of proprietors does, in fact, decline. The decline, however, is only slight and the number of *côtes* under ten hectares continues to show a rapid increase up to 1875.

Table 15. Property size at Larochemillay according to the communal cadastre (1845-1875)

	Residents Only			
Size of Property	1845	1855	1865	1875
under 1 hectare	94	111	134	147
1 to 5	89	117	116	126
5 to 10	22	24	34	40
10 to 20	18	13	17	13
20 to 50	8	10	9	8
50 to 100	9	6	4	5
over 100	5	6	6	6
Totals	245	287	320	345

Heirs quite clearly preferred their share in the family farm to a cash payment of equal value. Yet parents only occasionally attempted to mitigate the consequences of equal partition of inheritances by exercising their right to favor one heir with a quarter of their property. Only in the years after 1840 was this faculty invoked with greater frequency. By then there were also more proprietors in the commune, so the rate of such donations may well have remained constant. If parental succession strategy was linked to providing security for their own retirement, then why did so few take advantage of those provisions of the Code allowing them to temper the headlong rush towards a society of microfundia? Certainly, by favoring a single heir, parents would have created a more economically sound basis upon which they could draw their retirement pensions.

Most parents chose not to do so because the Code provided them with a far more effective means of preserving the integrity of the family holding, at least for as long as they were alive. A husband and wife would donate to one another the usufruct of all real and personal property they left after their deaths, thereby circumventing the problems posed by a basic demographic fact: husbands and wives do not usually die at the same time. This was a problem because, under the Code, a widow or widower could claim only half of his or her spouse's inheritance. The rest was divided equally among their children. If any or all of these chose to claim their shares, the surviving parent would lose control over that much of the family patrimony. However, if they held the usufruct of their spouse's property they retained complete control over all the family property until their own death, after which their children were free to divide their inheritances if they so desired.

Parents had not followed this strategy during the Old Regime because customary law in the Nivernais strictly limited a widow's claim to her husband's inheritance. Their children had immediate claim to half of their father's inheritance, which had to be delivered to them within forty days after his death.[28] As long as parents were free to endow an heir with the bulk of their property in return for their pensions, this limitation presented no problem. While the Code had restricted this right, it had also extended widows' rights to their husbands' inheritance, opening the way for mutual donations between spouses. In effect, parents no longer settled their succession with the marriages of their heirs, but delayed the settlement until their deaths, thereby allowing them to retain control of the family property. This change in strategy can be seen by examining the relationships of persons receiving donations both before the new Civil Code and after it, as shown in Table 16. Under customary law, donations were mostly in favor of children. After 1800, however, the greatest number were to husbands and wives.

Table 16. Donations at Larochemillay (1775-1860)

Years*	Donations in favor of			
	Spouse	Children	Heirs in direct line	Collaterals
1775-1793	2	26	–	3
1800-1820	44	6	3	14
1821-1840	41	6	2	6
1841-1860	43	13	1	12
Totals	130	51	6	35

*Because of the strict limitations imposed by the law of January 6, 1794, contracts drawn up during the time when the law was still in force are omitted from the analysis.

There were other means by which parents secured their retirements. One was to make up a contract in which the shares of each heir were specified. These were then formally donated by the parents, who stipulated that, in exchange for this "gift," they would receive an annual pension, to be paid by the heirs. Another strategy was to form a *société* with one heir and the heir's spouse. Both couples would mix their property into the common fund, as well as any acquisitions, *propres* excluded. By this means, both parents not only retained rights over their child's inheritance but extended their rights to the property of their son- or daughter-in-law as well. However, this strategy came to be employed with less and less frequency by proprietors in the course of the nineteenth century. Between 1815 and 1835, fifteen such contracts were drawn up; after 1835, only three were recorded.

These various strategies were aimed solely at ensuring parent's security after they retired. All achieved the same goal: maintenance of control over the family property until one's death. Parents showed little concern over the increasing division of holdings and their children even less. In some families, children actually refused to allow their parents to favor one of them above the others. When, for example, Jean Michon and his wife, Catherine Gendriau, attempted to favor their son, Pierre, their other children reacted vigorously. In 1820, Michon's widow was forced to draw up a contract revoking their gift to Pierre. "In order to establish equality between all her children," read the agreement, "and to maintain peace within the family, said Gendriau, by means of good faith and intelligence, declares that she formally forbids herself from favoring one or several of her children at the expense of the others." Until the last decades of the century, when improved roads and the penetration of the Morvan by the railroad gave the inhabitants an opportunity to seek other means of securing a livelihood beyond their own *pays,* the ability to gain access to land provided the best basis for economic security. For this reason, children were only too eager to demand their share in the family holding. Thus, between 1835 and 1852, the number of *côtes* in the Morvan increased by forty-six percent, higher than in any other region of the *département.*[29] This progressive division of peasant holdings served to accelerate the process which, even before the Revolution, was eroding the economic base of landowning joint households. The Napoleonic Code did not destroy the landowning *communautés* in the Nivernais, but it did hasten their disappearance. After mid-century, they would be all but extinct in the province.

The same cannot be said of sharecroppers, who simply formed *sociétés* in much the same way that they had formed *communautés* under customary law. The only difference was that, because such associations could be established only by formal contract rather than by simple cohabitation, more frequent trips to the *notaire* were now necessary. Indeed, a number of families, perhaps concerned about their legal situation after 1804, drew up *acts de société*, stating that they had been living in *communauté* for several years, sometimes even decades, and wished to formalize the arrangement. Most *sociétés*, or *communautés*, as they were still sometimes called, were without specific time limits, and were therefore intended to last for the lifetimes of the members. Some, however, did state that the association would last only for the time they leased such-and-such a *domaine*. Occasionally, individuals would be incorporated into existing *sociétés* for a limited time. When Jean Durand married the daughter of Jean Comte in 1807, their marriage contract stipulated that he would be incorporated into his father-in-law's association only until Comte's own son returned from the army. Generally, the members mixed farm stock and equipment, profits and income from the farm, while personal property such as clothes, furniture, and property received by inheritance was excluded. When members married into the association, they were required to mix a specific sum into the common fund in order to acquire the *droits de communauté*. Thus, the associations contracted by sharecroppers in the nineteenth century differed little from those of the Old Regime.

These associations continued to thrive because the *domaines* they leased were in no way affected by the Revolution or the Civil Code. Many were confiscated and auctioned off during the Revolution. Perhaps as much as ten percent of the total farmland of the *département* of the Nièvre was expropriated from the Church and from *emigrés*, yet only in rare instances were *domaines* broken up and sold by parcels. In the vast majority of cases, they were auctioned as single properties, usually to local *fermiers, régisseurs,* or merchants.[30] For these persons, the Revolution provided a fairly cheap means of quickly increasing their fortunes at the expense of the local nobility. In the words of one historian of the period, "The properties of the clergy and *emigrés* changed hands rather than dimensions."[31] It was from this class of *fermiers* and merchants that most of the local political offices in the *département* were filled during the Revolution, and it was not uncommon to see the names of such individuals regularly repeated on the lists of purchasers of national properties.[32] It was clearly in their interest to preserve the *domaines* intact.

Wealthy owners of these large farms, whatever their origins, considered their *domaines* as distinct units of property and so these *domaines* were never broken up when inheritances were settled.[33] Individual parcels may have from time to time been sold or added to a particular *domaine*, but in general they retained their basic configurations throughout most of the nineteenth century. The only record of *domaines* being broken up at Larochemillay was when they were sold to peasants, usually to several families who had pooled their resources to make the purchase. The *domaine* at Petition, for example, was purchased in 1806 by five families and divided between them a year later. On the whole, *domaine* farming at Larochemillay preserved a remarkable stability during the century following the Revolution. Tax records for 1789 state that some fifty *domaines* existed in the parish at that time; the agricultural inquiry of 1892 listed forty-six farms of thirty hectares or more.[34] Because *domaines* retained their basic structure, the labor demands around which the sharecropper's *communauté* was organized continued well into the nineteenth century.

Both the survival of the joint household among sharecroppers, and its decline among propertied peasants, can be documented by census lists for Larochemillay.[35] In Table 17, the household structure of both groups is compared for the decades between 1846 and 1876. In order to assure accuracy, the names of individuals in the census were checked against resident property owners listed in the cadastre. This way, landowners who had been listed in the census as *journaliers* or artisans rather than *proprietaries* would be included in the analysis. As the figures show, the nuclear family overwhelmingly predominated among proprietors, with three-fourths of all households containing a single marital unit. In 1845 only three landowning families were organized in joint households; by

Table 17. Household structure at Larochemillay (1846-1876)

	1846		1856		1866		1876	
	N	%	N	%	N	%	N	%
Proprietors								
No Family	13	9.8	11	8.2	5	3.3	11	6.1
Nuclear	102	76.7	100	74.1	118	78.1	139	76.8
Stem	15	11.3	23	8.2	27	17.9	31	17.1
Joint	3	2.2	1	.7	1	.7	–	–
	133	100.0	135	100.0	151	100.0	181	100.0
Tenants*	N	%	N	%	N	%	N	%
No Family	–	–	–	–	–	–	–	–
Nuclear	12	27.9	15	32.6	16	35.6	19	43.2
Stem	7	16.3	14	30.4	15	33.3	6	13.6
Joint	24	55.8	17	37.0	14	31.1	19	43.2
	43	100.0	46	100.0	45	100.0	44	100.0

*Includes leaseholders as well as sharecroppers.

1876 there were none. At the same time the number and proportion of stem families increased. In fact by this last date there was a greater percentage of extended families among proprietors than in 1845. What had changed was the nature of the extended family, which had become less complex as fewer joint households were formed. Sharecroppers' households, on the other hand, were decidedly more complex than those of landowning families and remained so throughout the period. Over half the households of this group were joint in 1845, about a third in 1866, and over forty percent in 1876. The Napoleonic Code, which accelerated the decline of landowning households, had little effect on the large extended families of sharecroppers.

This is not to say that the Civil Code had no effect whatsoever on sharecropper families. Far from it. The new laws governing inheritance placed added burdens on their already precarious financial position. Before 1793 sharecroppers, like proprietors, had apanaged those children who married out of the *communauté*. While no real estate was involved in these transactions, the provisions of the customs had enabled parents to retain within the *communauté* as much of the family's property as they could by leaving the bulk of their property to those children who stayed to share the work of the *domaine*. Once the law demanded that all heirs receive an equal share of their succession, this strategy could no longer be used. Henceforth, all children, whether they remained within the *communauté* or not, would have to be provided with an equal share.

Just how much of a drain on a family's resources this could create can be shown by comparing the provisions made by one family for children married under customary law with those married under the Code. In 1789 Annet Dureux, *maître et chef de sa communauté,* provided his daughter Jeanne with a dowry of one hundred and fifty *livres* at the time of her marriage. Jeanne, in turn, renounced any further claims to inheritance and went to live in the *communauté* of her husband. Two years later, Annet's son Jean was married and incorporated into his father's *communauté*. This time, however, the marriage portion provided by Annet was three hundred *livres,* twice that given to his daughter. After 1793, however, Annet had to forego this strategy. Thus, when Marie, another daughter, married and left her father's *communauté* in 1794, she was provided with a dowry equal to that given her brother. The same was true for a third daughter who married a year later. This drain on the Dureux's resources was partly mitigated by the dowries brought into the *communauté* by the husbands and wives of children who married into the association. Yet the only way such a family could fully recoup the losses suffered as a result of the Code was by keeping more children within the *communauté* and marrying fewer out. This, on the other hand, had to be weighed against the added drain on farm income produced by another family.

While equal inheritance never threatened the *communautés* of share-croppers, it did place them under greater financial stress. In the early decades of the nineteenth century, one sees an increasing number of contracts drawn up by *métayers* declaring that so-and-so had received his full share of his parents' inheritance and therefore had no further claims on their succession. Thus, when Pierre Alexandre formed a *société* with his son in 1828, he had his two sisters draw up separate statements declaring that the succession of their father had been settled some twenty years ago and, in consequence, "They had nothing more to say or do concerning this subject." He was obviously concerned about any claims they may have pretended to have held against his association.

On the whole, however, the advent of Revolutionary civil legislation had little effect on the households of sharecroppers. Because land never entered the common fund of their *communautés*, family fission did not result in land fragmentation. Organized upon an economic base, the joint families of *métayers* would begin to disappear only when economic change transformed that foundation. That, however, would not occur until many decades after 1804. More deeply affected by the Code were the households of landed peasants. Joint family ties among this group, already rare by the time of the Revolution, would become less and less frequent as the division of inheritances continued to reduce the number of holdings which needed or could support several related families. By replacing a system of impartible inheritance with one of partibility, the Code completely transformed peasant succession strategies. These changes were not the result of an evolution in cultural values. Changing circumstances dictated that families employ new strategies, yet the strategies which were adopted ultimately sought to achieve the same goals as before.

CHAPTER SIX

The Geographic Distribution
of the Joint Family
in the Nivernais

An examination of the impact of Revolutionary civil legislation on household organization shows little support for the argument that changes in family structure were a result of the intrusion of "modern values." Change occurred, to be sure. Yet the introduction of the new Civil Code tended rather to accentuate processes already inherent in landowning families prior to the Revolution and had very little affect on the organization of sharecropper households. There exists further evidence that household organization in the Nivernais was a product of distinct economic and social relations, rather than specific cultural traditions or biases. This evidence is derived from a comparison of household structure both within and between culturally distinct regions of the Nivernais. As has already been noted, the Nivernais is by no means a unified geographic or cultural entity. Indeed, regional diversity within the province has been one of its most characteristic features. The province of the Nivernais and its successor, the department of the Nièvre, are administrative units encompassing several separate *pays*, each with its own geography, field systems, settlement patterns, and history (see maps, page 114). Coquille himself recognized this, arguing that while the Nivernais was distinguished from surrounding provinces by its adherence to its own legal system, it was nonetheless composed of a number of "contrées principals."[1] Broadly speaking, the main regions of the Nivernais are the Morvan, occupying the eastern third of the province; the Nivernais proper, extending west and south from the Morvan to the Loire; the Yonne Valley in the North; and the Donziais in the Northwest.

More than any other part of the Nivernais, the Morvan has sparked the imagination of writers and travelers fascinated by this "Scotland of France." The natural beauty of its forest-covered mountains explains much of its charm, but it is above all the distinctiveness of its inhabitants that accounts for its reputation and makes the Morvan a country apart. Dupin called the Morvan a kind of bugbear for any traveler, not simply because of the cold, snow, and rugged terrain, but because of the "savagery" of its people. It was, he claimed, a true *pays de loup*.[2] To most observers, the peculiarities of the Morvandeau seem to have outweighed any similarities with the people of the *plat pays,* a quality that guidebooks continued to emphasize well into the twentieth century.[3] Ethnographers in the late nineteen hundreds even attributed distinct physical characteristics to the inhabitants of the Morvan, who supposedly had retained the racial features of their Celtic ancestors.[4]

For as long as men have written about the Morvan, it has been described as an isolated backwater, a *pays noir* separated both physically and culturally from surrounding provinces. In the fourth century Fortunatus called it a country of demons and beasts; Saint Germain is said to have performed a miracle there when he drove out the evil spirits inhabiting the region. Christian parishes penetrated the region only in the fifteenth century, a tardy arrival that may explain the inhabitants' attachment to pagan rituals and superstitions even as late as the nineteenth century.[5] The cultural isolation of the Morvan was reinforced by its language. Late into the nineteenth century, writers cautioned that full comprehension of the Morvan patois could be attained only after many months in the country.[6] Thus the Morvan, while legally and politically a part of the Nivernais, was in fact a culturally distinct region.

The Nivernais proper is, in fact, a part of the Loire Plain. Its topography ranges from rolling, forested hills in the central areas of the *département* to the broad lowlands bordering the Loire. Like the Morvan, this part of the Nivernais is characterized by dispersed settlements and isolated farmsteads surrounded by fairly large, enclosed fields reminiscent of the Brittany bocage. From the town of Decize in the south to La-Charité in the north, the proportion of the rural population living in small hamlets and farms ranges from eighty to almost one hundred percent of a commune's total population. The liassic soils of this region make it one of the most fertile in the *département*. Since the Middle Ages winegrowing has been an important part of the economy, with the Loire providing a direct outlet for marketing wines. However, the wines of the region have never been noted for their quality and production has remained limited to the area around the towns of Pougues and La-Charité-sur-Loire.

The Yonne Valley in the north is also a region of lowland plains and gently rolling hills. However, any similarity between the Yonne and the rest of the Nivernais ceases there. Characterized by nuclear villages and open-field farming, the Yonne is geographically more like northern France than the rest of the province, with between sixty and eighty percent of the communal populations listed as *agglomerée*. Unlike the Loire Plains and the lower reaches of the Morvan, where large *domaines* predominate, in the Yonne tenancy is far less extensive and *domaine* farms fewer and much smaller in size. In 1815 the prefect reported that while *domaines* in the *arrondissements* of Château-Chinon and Nevers, encompassing the Morvan and the Loire Plains averaged between fifty and seventy-five hectares, those in the Yonne Valley averaged only twenty-five hectares.[7] Moreover, *domaine* farming in the Yonne was hampered by the nature of open-field farming there. The subprefect for the *arrondissement* complained that, "The morcellement of property considerably hinders the progress of agriculture . . . all the cultivators are proprietors, which explains the division of the land."[8]

The last region, the Donziais, occupies the northwest quarter of the *département* and is roughly contiguous with the *arrondissement* of Cosne. Geographically, the Donziais holds an intermediate position between the Yonne and the Loire Plains. Isolated farmsteads and large enclosed fields are scattered throughout the region but are interspersed within a pattern that is essentially one of open-field farming and nucleated settlements. There are numerous *domaines* of considerable size, particularly in the western half of the region, near the town of Donzy. Yet most holdings are fairly small or medium-sized farms of between ten and fifty hectares. Technically, the Donziais is not a part of the Nivernais at all. The Comte de Donziais was acquired by the counts of Nevers in the twelfth century and has remained tied to the Nivernais ever since. However, the counts—later dukes—of Nevers appear to have considered the Donziais a separate entity.[9] What most clearly distinguished the Donziais from the rest of the Nivernais was the fact that under the Old Regime it had been governed by the customery law of Auxerre rather than that of the Nivernais.[10] This is especially important, for the Auxerre customs differed in two crucial respects. They recognized neither *bordelage* nor the existence of a *communauté taisible* beyond that of a husband and wife.[11] Thus, the Donziais lacked the kind of legal tradition supporting joint family ties that existed in the Nivernais.

What effects did cultural, legal, and economic variations have on family structure in the Nivernais? To answer this question, a sample of

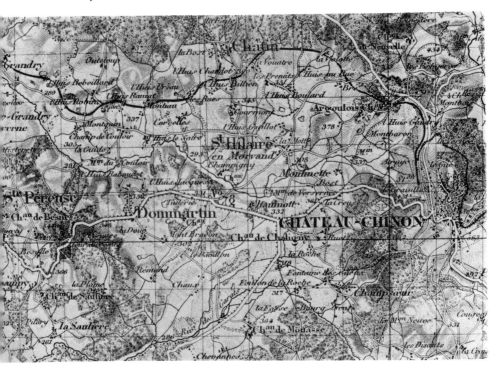

8. Dispersed settlement in the Morvan near Château-Chinon. (Service géographique de l'armée, 1889)

households was drawn from the 1820 census schedules for the *département*.[12] This census is the earliest one for which lists have survived for most of the three hundred and twenty or so communes. It has the disadvantage, however, of not being nominative. Only the name and occupation of the head of household were recorded, along with the number of single, married, and widowed males and females residing in the household. Only two lists gave ages and only a few noted kinship ties within the households. While lacking in detail, the 1820 census does allow one to examine the number of marital units per household and to create from this a typology of household structure. Household types are based on the number of marital units living in the household, with each couple and each widowed person counting as a single marital unit. If there was only one marital unit, the household was termed "nuclear"; if there were two, "stem," and, if three or more, "joint." These categories do not correspond precisely to actual family types. Some stem families may in fact have been nuclear families employing a married or widowed

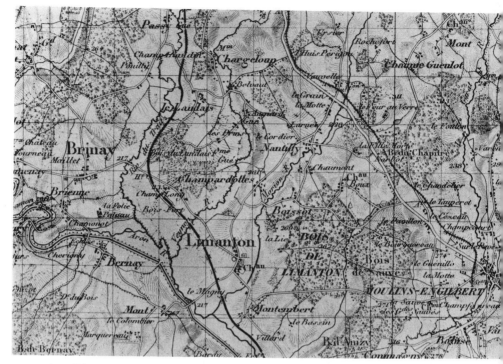

9.   Dispersed settlement in the Loire Plain. Commune of Limanton.

servant, while others may in fact have been joint families composed of two married siblings. The figures derived from the categories should be taken as rough approximations of actual household complexity.

The sample itself was arrived at by selecting every third commune from a list in which all communes were listed alphabetically by canton. Cities and large towns were omitted. In some cases the census proved to be inadequate, either because it failed to note occupations or was incomplete. When such lists were encountered, the commune appearing next on the list was selected. For the cantons of Nevers and Decize, only a few censuses survived and so all were included in the survey. In all the sample covered one hundred and fourteen communes and 16,135 households, or about thirty percent of all households recorded in 1820.

In Table 18 the households are broken down by type and by the occupation of the head of household. While extended families existed among all classes, they were clearly most concentrated among peasant proprietors and tenant farmers (*métayers, fermiers* and *locataires*), with thirty-seven percent of all tenant households containing two or more

10. Grouped settlement in the Yonne Valley near Clamecy.

marital units. Joint households—those with three or more marital units—existed almost exclusively among tenants, most of whom were sharecroppers. These differences in household complexity confirm for the *département* as a whole the findings derived from the contracts of association passed at Larochemillay.

In Table 19 the distribution of households is shown for each region. Distinct variations in household complexity are clearly evident, with the

Table 18. Percentage of households by occupation
Département of Nièvre (1820)

Occupation	Stem (2MU)	Joint (3 + MU)	Both (2 + MU)	N
Rural laborer	12.0%	.8%	12.8%	6,526
Artisan	13.7	.4	14.1	2,008
Winegrower	15.4	.6	16.0	1,241
Peasant proprietor	19.8	2.8	22.6	2,193
Peasant tenant	26.0	11.2	37.2	3,034
Bourgeois	11.7	1.7	13.4	727

(MU = marital unit)

Table 19. Percentage of households by region
Département of Nièvre (1820)

Household Category	Regions			
	Yonne	Donziais	Loire	Morvan
Nuclear (1 MU)	87.8%	83.3%	82.1%	71.4%
Stem (2 MU)	11.7	14.6	15.4	21.8
Joint (3 + MU)	.5	2.1	2.3	6.8
N =	2,746	2,831	6,713	3,443

(MU = marital unit)

percentage of stem households ranging from twelve percent in the
Yonne to twenty-two percent in the Morvan. Likewise, the percentage
of joint households ranges from less than one percent in the Yonne to
almost seven percent in the Morvan. Differing occupational structures
had little to do with regional variations in household type. When
occupation is controlled for, as in Table 20, the marked regional
variations in household complexity remain. Only seventeen percent of
all tenant households were extended in the Yonne, whereas over a third
were extended in the Loire Plains and almost half in the Morvan. Joint
families, rare among both proprietors and tenants in the Yonne, somewhat more common in the Donziais, were most widespread in the
Morvan.

Table 20. Regional distribution of household types (tenants and proprietors)

Tenants	Regions			
Household types	Yonne	Donziais	Loire	Morvan
Nuclear	82.4%	63.8%	65.0%	53.3%
Stem	16.4	26.5	24.6	30.0
Joint	1.1	9.7	10.5	16.6
N =	627	412	886	1,109

Proprietors				
Household types	Yonne	Donziais	Loire	Morvan
Nuclear	86.1%	80.3%	79.2%	69.1%
Stem	13.5	18.0	18.3	26.1
Joint	.3	1.8	2.5	4.8
N =	339	167	1,062	625

How can such regional variation in family structure be accounted for?
Legal traditions inherited from the Old Regime appear to have had little,
if any, effect on household organization in the early nineteenth century.
The most striking aspect of these figures is that the variations in family
structure do not correspond with areas where customary law favored

the *communauté*. Although the Yonne, Morvan, and Loire Plain were all governed by the Nivernais customs, households in the Yonne were predominantly nuclear, while complex households were widespread in the rest of the Nivernais. Even more significant, in the Donziais, where customary law had severely restricted the *communauté*, there was a greater degree of household complexity than in the Yonne Valley. Obviously, legal traditions alone cannot explain family structure or the existence of joint households.

Farm size and tenancy had a far greater effect on household structure than legal traditions inherited from the Old Regime. Information on farm size is provided by the government's agricultural inquiries taken every ten years after 1852. Unfortunately, data derived from the earliest survey for the Nièvre is far too unreliable to be of any use. In many cases, only farms worked by *fermiers* were included in the original communal reports, omitting owner-operated farms and those worked by sharecroppers. In other cases, the figures given are obviously *côtes* rather than individual farms.[13] The 1862 survey, on the other hand, failed to count holdings of less than a hectare, thereby omitting half the farms of the *département*. The earliest data on farm size that can be employed with any reasonable assurance of accuracy is that from 1872. While there are some serious problems even with this inquiry—data for one canton is missing, for example—the communal reports appear to have been compiled with greater care than those of either 1852 or 1862.[14]

Table 21. Property distribution in the Département of the Nièvre (Côtes de propriété)

Amount of taxes paid in francs	1817	1835	1842	1858	1894
under 20	60,000	68,940	75,572	99,513	124,996
20 to 300	14,000	13,691	14,887	14,144	14,528
300 to 1,000	750	986	1,021	1,003	1,041
over 1,000	250	244	285	268	371
	75,000	83,861	91,765	114,928	140,936

Although data on farm size is separated from the 1820 census by half a century, little significant change seems to have occurred among the large farms during that time. This can be inferred from data on property size obtained from tax returns. Between 1817 and 1858 the number of large proprietors in the Nièvre—those paying over three hundred francs in land taxes—never surpassed two percent of all landowners in the *département*. During the same period, the proportion of the total land tax for the Nièvre paid by this group remained stable at forty-three percent. Between 1817 and 1894 the number of *côtes* paying three hundred francs or more in taxes remained remarkably stable, and actually increased between 1817 and 1842[15] (Table 21). Up to that year the average amount of tax paid per hectare of taxable land in the *département* actually decreased slightly, so the increase in large properties was, in fact, somewhat greater than the figures in Table 19 indicate.[16] Given the stability of large properties and the fact that few *domaines* were ever divided by their owners, it is unlikely that the situation with respect to large farms had altered appreciably over the century.

Table 22. Farm size and land tenure (1872)

Region	Percent farms by size (hectares)				Percent land farmed by tenants
	(5)	(5-10)	(10-20)	(20+)	
Yonne	90%	6%	2%	2%	27%
Donziais	80	11	6	5	45
Loire	79	9	5	7	68
Morvan	63	18	10	10	50

Table 22 displays data on farm size and tenure for the four *arrondissements* of the Nièvre, each of which corresponds roughly to the four regions under study. Both the Loire Plains and the Morvan were characterized by a greater percentage of large farms than either the Yonne or the Donziais, and in both regions over half the farmland was either rented or sharecopped. These conditions—large consolidated farms worked by tenants—explain the existence of the joint family in the southern half of the Nivernais. The Donziais, where legal tradition did not favor the *communauté,* nevertheless had a greater percentage of both joint and extended households than did the Yonne Valley. This was because farms in the Donziais tended to be larger than those in the Yonne, where peasant ownership of small holdings predominated and where few large *domaines* existed.

The relationship between farm size, tenancy, and household structure becomes even more graphic when viewed at the cantonal level. The following series of maps were constructed using data from the 1820 census schedules and the 1872 agricultural survey. The connections between farm size, tenure, and family organization are even more striking when presented this way. Generally, where farms were small, family structure tended to be least complex. This was especially true for the northcentral cantons of the *département* comprising the Yonne Valley. This was also the case in those cantons lying along the Loire in the northwest, where winegrowing predominated. Joint households, on the other hand, were widespread in the southern half of the *départe-*

Map 4.

Regions of the Nivernais

open fields, nuclear villages

open fields, some bocage

bocage

enclosed fields, scattered
hamlets, and farmsteads

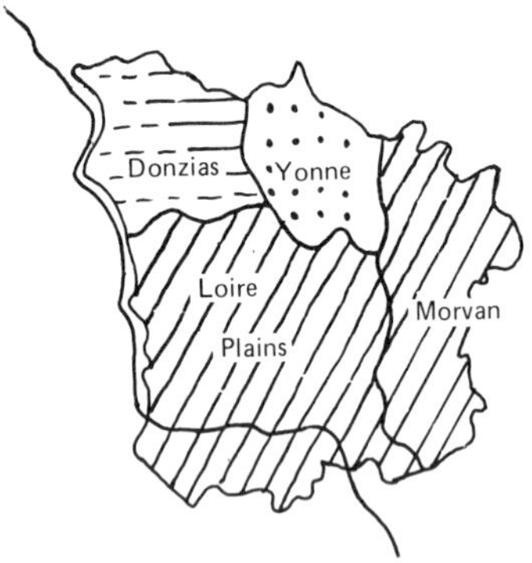

Map 5.

Administrative divisions of
the departement of the Nièvre

arrondissements

cantons

Map 6.

Administrative divisions of the
province of the Nivernais

provincial boundaries

éléction boundaries

present départemental boundaries

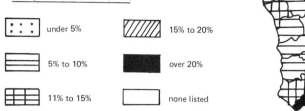

Percentage of joint families
among tenant households (1820)

· · · under 5%	⬛ 15% to 20%	
☰ 5% to 10%	■ over 20%	
▦ 11% to 15%	☐ none listed	

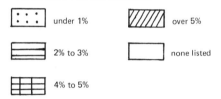

Percentage of joint families
among proprietor households (1820)

· · · under 1%	⬛ over 5%
☰ 2% to 3%	☐ none listed
▦ 4% to 5%	

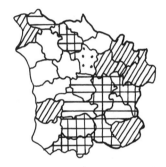

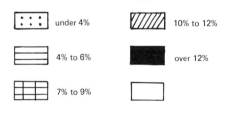

Percentage of joint families among
all tenant and proprietor households

· · · under 4%	⬛ 10% to 12%
☰ 4% to 6%	■ over 12%
▦ 7% to 9%	☐

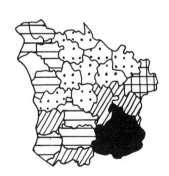

Map 7. Distribution of Household types in the Nièvre

115

Percentage of nuclear families
among tenant and proprietor households

 45% to 54%

 55% to 64%

65% to 74%

75% to 84%

over 85%

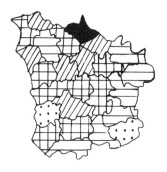

Percentage of stem families among
tenant and proprietor households

 10% to 14%

 15% to 19%

20% to 24%

25% to 29%

over 30%

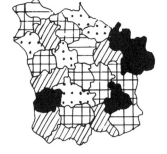

Percentage of extended families among
tenant and proprietor households

 10% to 17%

 18% to 28%

29% to 31%

32% to 37%

over 38%

Map 7. Distribution of Household types in the Nièvre (continued)

Percentage of farms over 50 hectares

 under 3%

 7% to 10%

 3% to 5%

over 10%

 5% to 7%

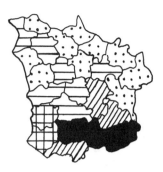

Percentage of farms between
10 and 50 hectares

 2% to 4%

 10 to 13%

 4% to 7%

 over 13%

 7% to 10%

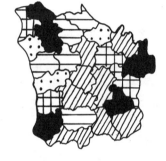

Percentage of farms under 10 hectares

 70% to 75%

 88% to 93%

 76% to 81%

 over 94%

 82% to 87%

Map 8. Distribution of Farm size in the Nièvre

117

Percentage of total farmland
worked directly by owner

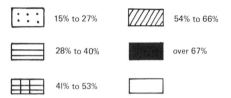

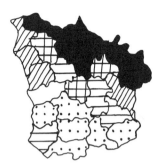

Percentage of total farmland worked
by fermiers or métayers

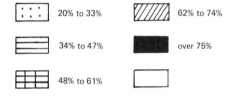

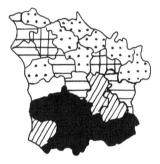

Map 9. Distribution of Tenant-held farms in the Nièvre

ment, particularly in the southeast. This was also the region dominated by tenancy and large farms of over fifty hectares.

It is noteworthy that this relationship cut across culturally distinct regions. In the Morvan household complexity was greatest in the south, where large farms were most concentrated. In the northern Morvan most farms were of moderate size, between ten and fifteen hectares. In this region, extended families were common, yet most were stem rather than joint families.

Regional variations in farm size and tenancy in the Nivernais may well have been the result of developments dating back to the engrossing movement of the seventeenth century. In the Old Regime the province was divided between five different generalities. The *élections* of Nevers and Château-Chinon, encompassing the southern half of the present-day *département,* were part of the Generality of Moulins. Most of the Yonne Valley was administered by the *élection* of Clamecy and attached to the Generality of Orleans. The Donziais was divided between the Generalities of Orleans and Bourges. The Morvan was also divided, with the south administered by the Generality of Moulins, the north by the Generality of Paris as the *élection* of Vézelay, and the extreme northeast by the province of Burgundy (see map, p. 114).

These administrative divisions had important consequences for the development of property distribution in the Nivernais because each *élection* during the seventeenth century was subject to different rates of direct taxation. The inhabitants of the southern Nivernais suffered a far greater burden of taxation than did their neighbors to the north. This can be seen by comparing the variations in the average amount of the *taille* paid per household for each election in 1696.[17] The population of the Loire Plains and the southern Morvan paid almost three times the amont of taxes owed by the inhabitants of the northern half of the province. Landowners were acutely aware of the inequities of such tax assessments. In 1696 Vauban wrote that many Morvan proprietors in the *élection* of Château-Chinon whose lands lay near administrative boundaries were outraged to find themselves shouldering far greater tax burdens than their neighbors in nearby parishes administered by the Generality of Paris.[18]

Because of the differences in the burden of state taxation, growing peasant indebtedness, which in the south led to property consolidation and the spread of *métayage,* was inhibited in the north. The crisis of peasant proprietorship, which ravaged landholders in the south, was far less severe in the Yonne Valley and in the Donziais. Only in the central Morvan was this pattern broken. Here, despite heavy taxation during

Table 23. Variations in rate of Taille in 1696

Élection	Généralité	Regions	Feux	Taille	Taille per feux
Gien	Orleans	Donziais	11,904	139,606 livres	11.7 livres
La-Charité	Bourges	Donziais	6,610	69,629 livres	10.5 livres
Clamecy	Orleans	Yonne	7,350	82,845 livres	11.3 livres
Vezelay	Paris	North Morvan	5,328	40,656 livres	7.6 livres
Château-Chinon	Moulins	South Morvan	15,584		30.5 livres*
Nevers	Moulins	Loire Plain	2,387		

*Rate for Générality of Moulins.
Figures for éléctions not given.

the seventeenth century, peasant landowners were able to retain ownership of their properties. As suggested earlier, this exception was likely a result of the poverty of the region, its rugged terrain, and the sterility of its soils. All combined to protect the Morvan peasant from noble and bourgeois engrossers.

Regional variation in agrarian development during the seventeenth century led in turn to regional differences in household structure as revealed by the 1820 census schedules. Once the joint household, which had been threatened during the sixteenth century by legal changes in the status of *bordelage* tenure, was adopted to *domaine* farming and *métayage,* its persistence into the nineteenth century was assured. Changes in inheritance practices ushered in by the Napoleonic Code had little affect on the household organization of landless tenants. Because real estate seldom entered into the common fund, family fission did not lead to land fragmentation.

How then do we account for the persistent alarms of bourgeois contemporaries that the *communauté* was everywhere in decline? To be sure, many of these individuals, including LePlay himself, only frequented the province for a short period of time. Their reports did not therefore benefit from the advantage of prolonged observation over time. Yet others, such as Joseph Imbart de la Tour, the Count Saint-Benin d'Azy and Dupin himself, owned substantial tracts of land in the Nièvre and resided on their estates for considerable periods of time. Given their keen eye for detailed observation, it is difficult to dismiss their conclusions regarding the decline of the large joint household as simply an attempt to mold evidence to fit their theoretical constructs.

The fact is that the large, multi-family *communauté* was disappearing from the Nivernais, and after the mid-nineteenth century at an exceedingly rapid rate. The problem with LePlay and his followers was not their conclusion that the *communauté* was declining in the Nivernais, but rather their explanation for its decline. Ironically, we shall see that the decline of the joint family was brought about by another development in which these men held a keen interest and nurtured with wholehearted enthusiasm: the improvement of agricultural production. For it was the advent of the agricultural revolution and its attendant transformation of farm techniques that spelled the demise of the *communauté*.

CHAPTER SEVEN

The Agricultural Revolution in the Nivernais

By the early nineteenth century, the continued formation of joint households among Nivernais farmers came to depend almost entirely on the heavy labor demands of the large *domaine* farms, as well as a system of tenure that compelled tenants to rely on the labor of their adult kin rather than on paid employees. The French Revolution, by abolishing both feudal tenure and customary law, eliminated the last purely legal restraints contributing to shared residence by coparceners. Indeed, these legal restraints were themselves so weakened by the time of the Revolution that their effect on peasant household organization had diminished considerably. By 1820, at any rate, only a small fraction of peasant proprietors coresided with more than one married relative. The joint household in the Nivernais had become virtually synonymous with sharecropping and *domaine* farming.

Because of the continued existence of large, complex households centered on the labor demands imposed by the *domaine*, any reductions in that demand would necessarily alter family structure. This is precisely what occurred during the nineteenth century as a result of technical changes in farming brought about by the agricultural revolution. During the decades after 1840, the nature of the region's agrarian economy was dramatically altered. The Nivernais, hitherto a *pays jaune* concentrating on wheat and rye production, was transformed into a *pays vert*, a region of meadows and pastureland devoted to cattle raising and fattening.

The consequences of these changes for the families of *domaine* farmers were profound. The grinding poverty to which *métayers* had been subjected for centuries was at last alleviated as tenants were able to appropriate a greater and greater share of the increased wealth brought about by economic development. At the same time, household organization was simplified as labor allocation on farms was adjusted to meet the needs of the new husbandry. As clovers and alfalfa replaced fallow, and pasture replaced arable land, the necessity of maintaining a large year-round labor force disappeared and, with it, the basis for the household organization designed to supply it. The decline of the joint household in the nineteenth century was the result of technical developments associated with the nature of agrarian change, not of a weakening in paternal authority, custom, or agnatic kin ties.

The technical changes associated with the Agricultural Revolution were first developed in the Low Countries during the seventeenth century. The principal characteristics of these changes were: (1) The improvement of farm implements, allowing deeper, more effective cultivation of the seed bed; (2) The elimination of fallow and its replacement by continuous crop rotations involving nitrogen-fixing plants such as clover, alfalfa, or lucerne, or root crops such as turnips or sugar beets; (3) An increase in the available supplies of fodder crops, thereby allowing farmers to maintain larger numbers of farm animals, which in turn made possible: (4) An increase in animal manure, serving to increase yields per acre of land. The new agriculture was thus a mixture of cereal farming and animal husbandry. Increased yields were made possible only by increasing the number of stock animals per farm beyond the minimum required for actual farm operations. At the same time, increased grain output was accompanied by increased production of farm animals.

By the early decades of the nineteenth century, most of these techniques had yet to be adopted by Nivernais farmers. In fact farm techniques in the province were so primitive that the Nivernais relied regularly on grain imports from the Berry. In years of poor harvests, supplies were sought from as far away as the Beauce and the Brie.[1] Throughout the first decades of the century, local officials estimated that the Nièvre imported each year between fifteen and twenty percent of all grain consumed in the *département*. In 1817 an unusually harsh winter made worse by the requisitions of Allied occupation troops, almost a third of the *département*'s needs were met by imports.[2] With a population that was almost entirely rural and an economy almost entirely agrarian, this inability of the Nivernais to feed itself was due not to a lack of resources but to a reliance on farming methods that can only be described as primitive.

The Deficiencies of Petite Culture

In his article for the *Encyclopédie* entitled "Fermiers,"[3] François Quesnay distinguished between two dominant forms of agriculture practiced in France. *Grande culture,* as he termed it, employed a triennial crop rotation of wheat, spring grains for feed, and fallow or artificial meadows. This system encompassed most of northern and northeastern France, with the Loire River as its southernmost boundary. The system employed in most of central and southwestern France Quesnay called *petite culture.* Only a small fraction of total farmland was subsumed under production, usually relying on a biennial crop rotation. Most farmland was left uncultivated for several years and served as pasture for oxen and cattle, during which time it would regain its fertility. It would then be cropped for a year or two, after which it was returned to fallow and the cycle repeated. Except for the open fields of the Yonne Valley, such an infield-outfield method of farming was practiced throughout the Nivernais and was largely responsible for the region's limited agricultural production. Most farms were operated on a two-course rotation of cereals and fallow, with as much as one-half of total arable land left in fallow each year. In the Morvan, the situation was even worse. The subprefect for the region reported in 1815 that only a sixth of the arable land was planted in rye, a sixth in oats or barley, with the rest left fallow.[4] Not only was most of the potential farmland left unused under such a system, but the small proportion that was cropped in any year lacked sufficient manure, since cattle were grazed on outlying fields, with no attempt made to conserve manure for fertilizer. Moreover, the poor quality of these pastures, sprouting only broom, scrub grasses and thistles, together with the limited area reserved for meadow, severely restricted the number of cattle that a farm could support. As cattle were virtually the sole source of fertilizer, farms operating under such a system were seriously deficient in their ability to maintain soil fertility.

Because fallow provided the main source of feed for farm animals, even the largest *domaines* possessed only a few hectares of meadowland. Cattle were left in pasture as long as the weather permitted, often well into the winter, before they were put to stable and fed on the precious little winter feed provided by meadows. Excessively long winters or scorching summers periodically destroyed much of the meager supply of winter hay available, forcing farmers to run their animals in woodlands to search for whatever scrubs and grasses they could find. It is not surprising that oxen were small, thin, and usually too weak to provide sufficient draft power to effectively cultivate the soil.

Once put to harness, wrote one observer in 1801, such oxen, always overworked and always undernourished in pastures of the poorest grasses, are given a respite only at the beginning of autumn when they are put to stable and fed on the hay reserved for them from the meadows. . . . Cows are small and so their calves' growth is retarded, so that they are unable to provide enough strength for working difficult terrain.[5]

When, after several years of work, oxen became too old and too weak for further labor, they were fattened as much as possible and sold to butchers or cattle merchants who exported their purchases to Paris. Because oxen, rather than horses, were the principal draft animals in the region, agriculture generated a sizable number of cattle for market each year. However, the meat obtained from such aged and overworked cattle was tough and stringy, and whatever lean meat they had acquired during the spring was quickly turned into tough muscle by the long drives to the markets of Paris or Lyon. While cattle had been exported from central France since the seventeenth century,[6] they had never been anything more than a mere by-product of *petite culture*.

Extensive use of fallow to maintain soil fertility, limited fodder for cattle, and the inefficient allocation of manure combined to make the Nivernais, in the words of Arthur Young, "the worst cultivated in the kingdom." Young did not limit his criticisms to farm methods. Indeed, his harshest judgments were reserved for *métayage*, which he saw as the principal cause of the "wretched and despicable" husbandry practiced in the province. A tenurial regime that sought to squeeze profits from a poverty-stricken mass of tenants, rather than attempt to improve production and thereby to expand overall farm income, seemed to Young the very height of shortsighted folly.

> Nothing can hardly be poorer than the *métayer* . . . and the landlords feel the effects of their poverty in a manner that one would think sufficient to open their eyes to their real situation. . . . It is in vain to expect any improvements from [the *métayers*]. If in such a situation gentlemen will not take their lands into their own hands, at least enough to prove that the country might yield far other crops, they must be as torpid as their *métayers*, and receive from their poverty the just reward of prejudice and indolence.[7]

The exorbitant rents levied on sharecroppers dictated that direct producers would not likely accumulate sufficient capital to invest in improvements. The half-share of the harvest allotted the *métayer* was usually only enough for the subsistence needs of his own family and domestic servants as well as several laborers hired in the summer months. The tenant's share in cattle sales provided him with enough cash to pay state taxes and the *bellemain,* but little more. If the *métayer* was able to make even modest improvements, the result was often an increase in rent, as Etienne Bertin discovered, to his chagrin. When, after years of backbreaking efforts to improve the *domaine* he leased, he succeeded in increasing his own profits, his landlord responded by jacking up his rent by three hundred francs. "I was over-whelmed. . . . If the products of the farm were increased, it was because I, the farmer, had improved it by my toil. . . . The injustice made me sick at heart." Bertin protested and was given an ultimatum: submit or leave. His master's rule of thumb in such matters was quite simple. "*Métayers* are like domestic servants: in time they become too bold; one has to change them every so often."[8]

Tenurial relations could be an even greater hindrance to progress if estates were not directly managed by their owners but instead leased to an agent, or *fermier,* who then oversaw the *métayers.* Indeed, the *fermiers'* attitude toward their tenants differed little from their tenants' own harsh treatment of their cattle. Jean-Claude Flamare d'Assigny, a local notable and first republican mayor of Nevers, complained, "The *métayers* who depend on *fermiers* are generally worse off than those who depend on proprietors. The *fermiers* are monopolers who leave their *métayers* only that which they can't steal. . . . The *fermiers* squeeze their *métayers,* ruining them by working them as much as possible and then sacking them when their youth and strength is exhausted."[9]

It is little wonder that during the Revolution it was against such *fermiers* that sharecroppers vented their rage. In 1790 several parish assemblies in the central Nivernais attempted to limit the amount of land an agent could lease to a single *domaine.*[10] Four years later the *Société populaire* of Moulins-Engilbert charged that *fermiers* who were also speculating in small rural iron foundries and in logging were destroying agriculture in the region. The profits they derived from farming were invested in their industrial operations rather than agriculture, while their *métayers* were ordered to haul lumber and charcoal. This, they complained, led to the early exhaustion of their plow teams. Yet it was this very class of agents that controlled local government posts throughout the Revolution and was thus able to thwart such protests.

Nevertheless, the leasing of estates to such middlemen was clearly preferred by absentee landlords residing in Paris. Direct management ran the risk, in a year of poor harvests, of reduced income. By leasing their *domaines* to *fermiers* for nine, twelve or eighteen years, a steady income was assured, especially when the property of the *fermier* served as a guarantee.[12] On the other hand, proprietors ran a very real risk of seeing their farms deteriorate in their absence, since it was in the interest of the *fermier* to exact as much as possible from the land during the period of the lease. Overcropping of the soil, by not allowing sufficient time for fields to regain fertility, led to declining yields and ultimately to soil exhaustion.[13] Proprietors tried to prevent such abuses by stipulating in their leases the extent of arable to be sown and the number of seasons land should be left in fallow. Abuses nonetheless occurred, often followed by lengthy and expensive court battles.[14] The subprefect for the *arrondissement* of Nevers claimed in 1815 that such fears of proprietors actually hindered the spread of artificial meadows. "The proprietors will not permit even the smallest change in existing crop rotations. The *fermiers* want only to harvest several crops and without interval of fallows or hay, which is the worst of all systems and ruins the soil in a few years."[15]

To an agronomist such as Arthur Young, conditions in the Nivernais were all the more lamentable since, to his trained eye, they appeared so unnecessary. However miserable the agrarian regime of the province, the land itself possessed great potential for development. "One of the most improvable I have seen anywhere. . . . All from Autun to the Loire is a noble field for improvement." Young was right. From the Morvan to the Loire and beyond, the rich liassic soils of the Nivernais were capable of producing abundant crops. Even the poorer granites of the Morvan could be made productive with marling and lime. And the potential of the Nivernais was enhanced even more by the organization of farming into large *domaines*. "If I had a large tract in this country," declared Young, "I think I should not be long in making a fortune."[16]

Within the Nièvre itself there were those who shared both Young's condemnations of existing conditions and his recognition of the region's potential. Flamare d'Assigny was one of the rare landowners who attempted to introduce improved farm methods. His memoirs record not only the results of his efforts but his disgust with his neighbors' practices of leasing their *domaines* to capital-deficient agents. "The *fermiers* of the canton are not rich enough to create a vigorous and prosperous agriculture. They abandon all to their *métayers* whose methods are governed by ignorance, routine and poverty. . . . Artificial meadows or clover are regarded as dangerous. . . . Alfalfa occupies the land for too long a time to please our cultivators who want only to have wheat at any price." As frustrated as d'Assigny was at such practices, he never lost faith in the possibilities of eventual success. "Ah, never lose courage! Without hope, all would be lost in the darkness of chaos."[17]

D'Assigny's remarks reveal a crucial factor operating against the

adoption of more productive farming techniques: resistance on the part
of landowners and *fermiers* themselves. This was an obstacle which
local officials exhausted considerable energy trying to overcome,
usually without success. The prefect in 1814, Joseph Fièvèe, threw up
his hands in disgust at the inertia of local landowners. "Their only
interest is to oversee their *métayers,* to preside at the harvest, to
maintain their farm buildings, to follow local markets. They come to
pass a few months in town during the winter, yet so discretely that their
presence can hardly be noticed. Such is their existence, and one that is
reflected in all classes: apathy, with few passions even for gain,
preferring the benefits made through economizing to those which could
be made by speculating."[18] Fièvèe's remarks were echoed five years
later in a report on agriculture by the subprefect for Nevers. "None of
the cattle-owners give the least care to stock-breeding to improve their
herds. The neglect of such matters is the result of damnable indifference
to the benefits they could obtain if they acted otherwise."[19]

Resistance to improvement did not stem from lack of technical
knowledge on the part of landowners, who were usually well aware of
the benefits possible therefrom. The decision to adopt new methods of
farming, however, depended on whether or not the innovations could
increase profits. The nature of the new husbandry dictated that this
decision, in turn, hinge on the market demand for meat. Initially,
suppression of fallowland resulted in a fall in crop yields due to a lag in
the time between which extra manuring of fields could compensate for
the decline in fertility resulting from the abandonment of the fallow.[20]
Eventually, the benefits of improved soils would be realized in increased
yields. In the meantime, farmers who increased the sizes of their herds
would depend heavily on the earnings gained from the sale of animals to
offset short-term declines in cereal production. Without a sufficient
increase in the demand for meat, the introduction of new farm methods
would remain limited.[21]

Information available on meat consumption in the Nivernais and in
France in general indicates that there was little incentive to increase
animal production prior to the 1840s. In the early nineteenth century the
city of Nevers, together with the larger towns in the *département,*
constituted the principal market for meat in the region. Peasants,
whether tenant farmers, proprietors, or day-laborers, seldom ate meat,
even as late as the 1890s. Per capita consumption of meat (beef, lamb
and pork) increased only slightly during the early decades of the
century, from 35.7 kilos in 1816 to 37.9 kilos in 1833.[22] While the urban
population of the Nièvre did increase during the first half of the century,

from some 26,900 in 1801 to 31,490 in 1836, the limited size of this population precluded the development of a vigorous local demand on a scale large enough to spark major innovations in farming. Without such a demand, the costly investments necessary to transform production— new crops, new equipment, new farm buildings, and an expansion of livestock—could not be covered by sales of animal products. This rather basic fact of economics was discovered by the Comte de Pracomtal in 1815 when he attempted to introduce the new husbandry on his *domaines* near Châtillon-en-Bazois. When sales failed to cover Pracomtal's investments during the next few years, his neighbors carefully noted the fact and declined to follow his lead.[23]

The Agricultural Revolution in the Nivernais

Improvements in agriculture could be brought about only with greater demand for meat and other animal products from the major urban centers of France, and increased demand for such products in turn depended on higher incomes and more rapid urbanization. Recent studies indicate that per capita consumption of beef in France as a whole failed to increase appreciably from the late eighteenth century to the mid-1840s, hovering at about twenty kilograms per person. Total consumption of beef between the years 1815-1824 and 1835-1844 grew by only twenty-five percent.[24] Large regional differences in meat consumption existed, with the highest per capita consumption of beef (about thirty kilograms) in the Paris Basin, Normandy, and northeast France. In the rest of the country, meat consumption ranged between twelve and twenty kilograms per person.[25]

From the 1840s on, however, the market for beef began to improve rapidly. According to Jean-Claude Toutain's figures, by the decade 1855 to 1864 average per capita beef consumption had risen to thirty kilograms and would rise to over forty-four by the end of the century. Total beef consumption likewise rose, by one hundred percent between the 1840s and the 1890s.[26] In the urban centers of France, where meat-eating had always been more pronounced than in the countryside, both per capita and total consumption expanded rapidly, a result of the increase in the size of cities and in urban incomes. Between 1840 and 1882, the total amount of beef consumed in cities of ten thousand or more increased from 250,000 to 636,000 tons; Paris, which alone accounted for ten percent of all meat eaten in France in 1840, accounted for fourteen percent by 1882.[27]

This growth in the demand for beef after 1840 created the necessary economic incentive for agricultural improvement. Demand was one thing. Transforming Paris' demand for beef into an incentive strong enough to affect a farmer living two hundred kilometers to the south was something else again. Before demand could affect production, access to markets had to be achieved. A crucial aspect of the agricultural revolution in the Nivernais was the role played by the improvements in transportation, improvements that transformed production geared essentially for local markets into production for national and even international markets. Improvements in land and water transport during the first half of the nineteenth century vastly increased the volume of products that could be moved to markets. At the same time, transport costs were lowered, allowing farm products from the Nièvre to compete successfully with those of northern France.

Before 1789 the only major road linking the province with Paris and Lyon was the old royal route that followed the right bank of the Loire. This left the interior of the Nivernais with no means of transport or communication. The royal route itself left much to be desired. Just beyond the town of Pougues, the road simply disappeared in the marshes along the river, emerging again only near Pouilly, ten kilometers away.[28] In the interior, the narrow, unpaved local roads were little more than trails or paths. Impassable during the winter, such roads made even summer travel hazardous. Travelers and carts were frequently impeded by fallen trees or by creeks which cut across the hedge-lined roads every few miles.[29] Many of the parish *cahiers de doleances* in 1789 contained bitter complaints about the inability of farmers to move their products even to local markets because of inadequate or nonexistent roads. The inhabitants of Langy declared that they had great difficulty even driving cattle to local fairs because roads were too narrow or impassable. At Mingot the people complained that in the absence of any discernible roads through the village, teamsters hauling lumber from the Morvan simply chose their own routes, usually through the villagers' fields and gardens. "Whenever we complain they gather together and threaten us!"[30]

Plans for improving the road system in the Nivernais had been advanced as early as the seventeenth century but little had been accomplished. The first tangible effort to improve transport facilities was initiated in 1784 when construction began on the Nivernais Canal. The canal was intended to link the Loire with the rivers of northern France by cutting directly across the center of the Nivernais. The outbreak of the Revolution and the Napoleonic wars delayed the work so that progress was slow. The first Section, linking the interior of the

Nivernais with the Loire itself, was opened only in 1838; the entire system was not completed until mid-century.

During the 1830s rapid progress was made in improving and extending the network of roads of the Nièvre as the national and *départemental* governments allocated increasing sums of money for road building, maintenance, and bridge construction. From a paltry 880 francs spent on roads and bridges in 1816, total annual investment in the Nièvre grew to 81,000 francs in 1822, to 153,000 in 1829 and to 337,000 francs in 1838. As a result, by the 1840s the *département* was crisscrossed by seven national and twelve secondary roads, linking all major towns of the lowland interior. Most Sections were paved by the MacMahon method, thereby providing year-round access.[31] The Morvan, however, with its difficult terrain, was not penetrated by a major road until 1858, when the road to Château-Chinon was completed. Even then, a system of secondary roads was not even begun until the 1870s.

The creation of a network of roads within the Nièvre allowed farm products to circulate at substantially reduced costs. In the 1820s, the transport costs for a hectoliter of grain were estimated at about five centimes for every kilometer. By the 1860s, costs had been reduced to between two and three centimes.[32] The completion of the Nivernais Canal in 1846 provided farmers with access to the markets of Paris and the Midi, both of which became principal export regions for Nivernais grain and other farm products. By far, however, the most important achievement in transportation came in 1851, with the completion of the first rail line linking Nevers to the main line between Paris and Clermont-Ferrand. A more direct line running through the Nièvre, linking Paris and Lyon, was opened in 1861. By 1866 another line, across the southern part of the *département* to Dijon, was completed. Railway construction was especially important because it eliminated the long and exhausting cattle drives during which animals lost any fat they may have acquired during spring fattening. With the railroad, not only could the effects of spring fattening be preserved, but younger animals, previously unable to survive the cattle drives, could now be shipped to Paris. This was an important development because young cattle could be more easily fattened than could older animals.

Agriculture in the Nièvre responded readily to the pull of the market. Overall production increased dramatically, first by expanding the total area of farmland and second, by transforming production itself. In the early years of the century, it could be asserted with some justification that, next to logging, agriculture was only the second most important industry in the Nièvre. Perhaps half the *département* was covered with

131

forest, making it the most heavily wooded region in France. "Ten leagues from Nevers," claimed one traveler in the 1820s, "and one is presented with virgin forests as thick and primtive as the banks of the Mississippi."[33] Lumber and charcoal had been the principal exports of the Nivernais since the sixteenth century. After the second decade of the nineteenth century, however, growing use of coal for heating and iron manufacturing made logging in the Nièvre less and less profitable. At the same time, the value of farmland was increasing. By the 1880s, some 60,000 hectares of woodland had been cleared and turned into arable and pasture. Wasteland was also turned to more productive uses; by 1862, the extent of waste had been reduced to a third of the area estimated in 1815.

Some of the prodigious efforts exerted by individual farmers who cleared forest and waste have been preserved in their memoirs. Those of Pierre Boisseau, a *métayer* born at Cessy-les-Bois in 1805, attest to the often frenzied efforts undertaken by farmers to take advantage of increased demand for agricultural products by expanding farmland. Ambitious and hard-working, Boisseau seems to have spent the better part of his life transforming forest and waste into profitable arable and pastureland. In 1836 he acquired ten hectares of *"mauvais bois"* near Saint-Mâlo, which he cleared and converted into "bonne culture." Ten years later he purchased two hectares of *chaume* from the commune; this he cleared, drained, marled and turned into meadowland. In 1850 another ten hectares of waste and scrub fell to Boisseau's axe. His advice to his readers: "Any tenant or proprietor who has poor land, whatever its nature, can improve it."[34]

More significant than the expansion of farmland were the changes in farm methods introduced in the 1830s and 1840s. Each season saw more and more farmers replacing the traditional two-course rotation with three-and four-course rotations, utilizing a variety of new crops. The new rotations, which increased the amount of arable planted each year, could not be undertaken without providing some means of maintaining soil fertility. Increased cropping required greater amounts of fertilizer, and that meant greater numbers of farm animals; more animals meant more forage crops. The key indicator of change was thus the amount of land reserved for animal feed. Of all the improvements realized during this period, certainly the most significant was the increasing use of clover, alfalfa, and lucerne to replace the fallow. Such artificial meadows increased available forage while at the same time replenishing the soil with their nitrogen-fixing root systems. Increased forage allowed farmers to maintain larger herds, thereby increasing available stocks of animal fertilizers. All these changes were thus intimately linked to one another, and all combined to dramatically increase grain yields. Wheat yields in the Nivernais, which had averaged about three or four for one since the seventeenth century, rose to six for one in the 1840s, seven for one in the 1860s and to nine for one by 1882.

The extent of these changes can be appreciated when comparing the various government surveys of agriculture in the Nièvre between 1803 and 1882.[35] It should be noted, however, that such inquiries were subject to considerable inaccuracies and even outright falsification. At the time of the 1837 survey, ten of the *département's* twenty-five cantons had yet to be surveyed for the cadastre, making accurate reporting simply impossible. Many communal returns for that year frankly admitted that the figures reported were mere estimations of conditions and should be taken as such. For example, at Chitry-les-Mines, where a three-course rotation was employed, and which, according to a later cadastre, possessed some 595 hectares of arable land, the 1837 survey reported 120 hectares planted in wheat, 60 in barley, 60 in oats and 120 in fallow—obvious estimations based on the rotation system used in the commune rather than the results of careful data-gathering. Even in 1882 returns were not complete as many communes failed to complete the surveys. By that year the government's questionnaire had become rather intricate, requiring considerable effort on the part of local officials for the forms to be filled out properly. The mayor of Sully-Latour solved the problem by copying, figure for figure, the report submitted by his neighbor, the mayor of Saint-Martin-sur-Nohain! (Or was it the latter who arrived at this solution?) To be sure, the government did its best to rectify errors, and many reports were repeatedly returned to mayors to be redone; yet such controls were effective only when errors were strikingly blatant. Given such problems, the figures in Table 24 should be taken as suggestive trends in agriculture rather than as precise indications of the extent of land given over to a particular crop.

And, indeed, the trends are suggestive. Between 1815 and 1852, the total area planted in cereals and other crops increased by some 65,000 hectares. During the same period, wheat steadily supplanted rye as the principal grain sown in the Nièvre. Fallows, which had constituted over half the total arable land in the *département* at the beginning of the century, were reduced to a third by 1862 and to a sixth by 1882. Artificial meadows, virtually unknown in the second decade of the century, covered some 19,000 hectares by 1837, 34,000 by mid-century, and nearly 57,000 by 1882. When the extent of artificial meadows is combined with the total area given to pasture and natural meadows, the

Table 24. Distribution of crops in the Nièvre, 1803-1882 (hectares)

	1803	1815	1837	1852	1862	1872***	1882
Cereals		121,075	146,090	170,000	172,262	220,383	192,171
Root crops		–	9,495	10,367	12,593		31,163
Other*		1,182	6,321	6,541	7,000	8,578	6,446
Fallows		140,000	92,184	101,593	93,924		45,604
Total arable	218,582	262,257	254,090	288,601	285,779		275,384
Artificial meadows	–	400	19,096	34,002	37,668	44,190	56,811
Pasture and meadows	55,388	68,765	52,851**	99,934	95,519	105,160	102,023
Herbages	–	–	–	–	1,436	5,492	3,252
Total fodder crops	55,388	69,165	71,947	133,936	134,623	155,186	162,086
Waste	11,113	15,076	52,513**	10,794	7,920		5,078
Woodland	192,513	205,099	258,896	244,690	237,713		200,426
Vines	7,889	14,057	10,325	9,856	10,362	10,915	11,270
Total	485,584	565,654	647,771	677,083	668,477		654,244

*Vegetable, gardens and industrial crops.
**Pasture included with waste in survey.
***Returns for this year did not include figures on extent of fallows, waste, or woodland.

total number of hectares providing forage more than doubled between 1815 and 1852, and by 1882 had tripled.

The key to the successful introduction of new crops and farm methods was the expansion of cattle production for urban markets. Until a demand for meat and other animal products developed with growing urbanization, higher incomes and better transport facilities after 1840, cattle production in the Nivernais remained only a by-product of cereal farming. The number of farm animals was kept at the absolute minimum needed for plowing and hauling; animals were sold to the butcher only when too old for these tasks. In fact, a limited cattle-raising industry, geared solely for the meat market, had existed in the Nivernais since the 1770s. It was at that time that a new breed of cattle was introduced into the region, the white-coated charolais. Tradition accords this distinction to one Claude Mathieu d'Oye, an *emboucheur,* or cattle fattener, from the Charolles. In 1773 Mathieu, then a *fermier* at Anlezy in the central Nivernais, introduced the breed onto his *domaines.* The importance of the charolais lay in its ability to fatten quickly and at an early age. The indigenous breed, the morvandelle, while a sure-footed and sturdy animal able to work well on steep inclines, could not be fattened easily. Able to withstand long periods of heavy labor with only meager forage, the morvandelle was well suited to the traditional agrarian regime of the Nivernais. The charolais, on the other hand, consumed enormous amounts of feed, some fifteen kilograms of hay each day.

Without sufficient market incentive, few farmers were willing to invest in the creation of meadowland and new barns and stables needed to maintain the new breed. Local officials clearly recognized the problem. In 1819 the subprefect of Château-Chinon complained that while some *emboucheurs* had been importing charolais oxen for several years, this was limited to the small river valley known as the Bazois where abundant forage was provided by natural meadows and extensive pastureland. In three-fourths of the *arrondissement*, however, lack of sufficient meadowland made such operations impossible.[36]

With growing demand for meat and other animal products after 1840, together with the steady improvement in transport facilities, landowners throughout the *département* increased the size of their herds with purchases of charolais cattle and expanded pasture and meadowland. A government census of cattle in 1815 reported a total of 96,959 head in the Nièvre; by 1862 this figure had doubled to 182,875 head.[37] An integrated economy of *élévage* and *embouche* quickly developed. Farmers engaged in a mixed enterprise of cereal growing and animal husbandry would select from their stock those oxen that had been worked for three or four years. These were then sold in the spring to cattle fatteners who grazed the animals for three months on rich meadows, or *herbages*. During this period a mature ox would increase its weight by as much as one hundred kilograms, and it was from this increase that the *emboucheur* realized his profits.[38]

The intensification of cattle raising is reflected in several changes that took place in this sector of the Nivernais economy. First, after 1840, there occurred a steady drop in the age at which cattle were sold to butchers at Nevers and Paris. In the early decades of the century, cattle had been sold only after their strength had been exhausted in a decade of heavy labor. By 1862 cattle were being fattened at five or six years of age, thereby taking advantage of the ability of younger animals to fatten more quickly. The size of oxen increased as well, due to the increased forage now available to them. In 1815 the average weight of an ox in the Nièvre was a mere 208 kg. By 1862 this had risen to 513 kg.[39] Yet the most dramatic indication of the intensification of cattle production in the Nièvre was the growing number of oxen exported to urban markets, particularly Paris. In 1822 it was estimated that the Nièvre exported some 5,000 head of cattle annually, including those sold in neighboring *départements*. By mid-century some 10,000 head were being shipped to Paris alone, with an additional 3,000 head to markets in the Midi. Exports of cattle continued to increase, especially after the introduction of the railway. By the 1880s the Nièvre shipped some 24,000 head of cattle to Paris each year, making the *département* one of the leading sources of meat for the capital.[40]

The rapidity with which agriculture in the Nièvre responded to the growing demand for beef and other animal products is evident from other sources, particularly prices for beef in the *département's mercuriales*.[41] A careful examination of these shows the point at which cattle production for urban markets outside the Nièvre itself began to influence prices in the local markets of the region. Prior to the exportation of cattle on a large scale, beef prices in the Nièvre were determined largely by local conditions such as the number of cattle sold to butchers and by weather conditions affecting cattle raising. The supply of cattle in any year depended to a great extent on one's ability to fatten animals during the spring. In good years, when meadows provided sufficient feed and stocks of hay, there would be little problem. Excessively long winters, however, or rains that failed to materialize in the spring, could prevent adequate fattening of animals and might even induce farmers to withhold cattle from the market, in the hope that conditions might improve the following season.[42] The price of beef was thus, in a very real sense, pegged to the availability of feed as reflected in the price of hay.

This relationship between hay and beef prices can be seen in the following graph, which shows the average price of both commodities for the *département* as a whole between 1813 and 1890. In general, the years 1813 to 1840 were characterized by a kind of symbiotic relationship between the two series. That is, as the price of hay rose, so too did that of meat. The exceptions to this pattern, such as the years 1826 and 1830, when beef prices continued to rise after a substantial drop in the price of hay, reflect the losses of cattle suffered from the outbreaks of anthrax in 1825 and in the 1830s.

In 1839 drought throughout much of central and southern France drove up hay prices and with them the price of beef. However, during the early 1840s, as hay prices began to fall substantially, the price of beef at Nevers and other markets in the Nièvre remained high and remarkably stable. It was at this time that large numbers of cattle began to be exported from the *département*, causing beef prices within the Nièvre to remain high. Indeed, it appears that cattle raisers were selling their best head to buyers from outside the *département*. While the average weight of oxen sold in the Nièvre had increased by seventy-five kilograms between the 1830s and 1840s, the average weight of oxen sold at Nevers actually *dropped* by fifty kilograms. The heavier animals were being exported to Paris, leaving the smaller head for the local market.[43]

136

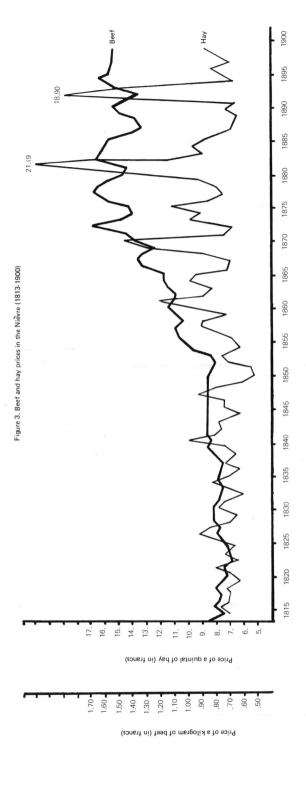

Figure 3. Beef and hay prices in the Nièvre (1813-1900)

After a long, steady decline in the price of beef during the late 1840s (the result of the depression throughout Europe), beef prices literally skyrocketed after 1853, the year the Nièvre was first linked to Paris by rail. A further jump in prices was registered after 1866, when the direct line between Nevers and the capital was completed.

Other significant changes began to take place after mid-century. Unlike the early decades of the century, when an increase in the price of hay caused beef prices to rise, after 1853 dramatic jumps in hay prices caused substantial declines in the price of beef. By that time cattle raising was no longer a mere by-product of cereal farming but an essential part of the economy of the region. Farmers specializing in cattle raising or fattening were now widespread. Severe droughts or floods which destroyed winter feed forced growers to cut their herds, thereby flooding the market with beef. Beef prices would climb steadily in the following years as cattle raisers concentrated on rebuilding their herds.

Based on the evidence provided by the *mercuriales*, it appears that the new husbandry came to be adopted on a large scale in the 1840s and spread quickly in the succeeding decades. This is not to say that individual farmers had not begun to implement improvements prior to this period. Evidence clearly indicates that many progressive farmers had made significant changes in farm organization and techniques as early as the 1820s.[45] However, it was only after 1840 that these began to make themselves felt on a scale large enough to influence the regional economy as a whole. By the 1850s, with the penetration of the Nivernais by more efficient means of transport, the transformation of the region's agrarian economy accelerated, gaining a momentum it would never lose.

Changes in the Allocation of Farm Labor

The transformation of agriculture in the Nièvre provoked major alterations in farm methods, the most important of which occurred in the seasonal allocation of labor. The most intense period of labor demand, for any farmer, occurred during the summer months when crops had to be harvested, threshed, and stored. The mowing of hayfields had to take place within a few days; if cut too early the hay would lack sufficient nutrients, and if cut too late it would contain excess moisture that would harm livestock by producing digestive diseases or even abortions. An unexpected downpour could easily ruin an entire year's efforts. It is not without some significance that peasants in the Nivernais forsook Christian practices by making supplications during the *fenaison* to the forces controlling wind and rain.[46]

Even the largest of *métayer* households lacked a sufficient work force during these months. Most families employed seasonal workers during the harvest to supplement their own family labor, paying such help in kind or occasionally in money. The colder climate of the Morvan, as compared to the rest of the Nivernais, provided a ready seasonal labor force, during the early spring and summer. Crops ripened as much as one month later in the high mountains of the Morvan, releasing large numbers of men and women who traveled in teams to the *pays bas* each summer seeking employment during the harvest.

Sharecroppers' reliance on adult kin served only partially to alleviate the concentration of labor demand in the summer months. The main function of the large tenant *communautés* was to provide a permanent work force that could carry out the year-round tasks necessary to farm the *domaine*. Of all these tasks, preparation of the seed bed for sowing created the greatest demand for labor. Fallows first had to be plowed, before winter or in early March. This plowing, known locally as *somber*, was performed to break up existing stubble and weeds. It was followed by a second plowing, or *biner*, in June. A final plowing, the *semaille*, was carried out just prior to the sowing of the fields. The *semaille* served to loosen the soil and to turn under whatever manure could be distributed over the fields. After the crops were sown, each field had to be hersed in order to destroy any large dirt clods left from the *semaille*.

Plowing was a particularly laborious task requiring considerable strength on the part of the plowman, as well as years of experience, in order to assure the proper cultivation of the soil. Indeed, the age at which a boy was able to shoulder the heavy burdens of plowing was treated almost as a kind of rite of passage into manhood. If becoming a plowman was equated by peasants with manhood, it was only because of the enormous efforts it demanded of an individual. No better example of this can be found than Etienne Bertin's description of his initiation into the world of adult labor.

> When the weather was good, the time passed with the least amount of weariness, but on bad days it seemed endless. I remember one March when we were plowing in the chestnut field, the most distant of our fields. A strong wind was blowing all the time from Souvigny, that is, right out of the northeast, with cold rain, hail and sometimes snow. This soaked through my clothes, enveloping me in an icy shroud; my hands were purple-red, speckled with violet.[49]

It is only after reading such passages that one begins to appreciate the French word for work: *travaille*.

In the heavier clays of the lowland Nivernais, a plow team would be composed of six to eight oxen and two males. A good team could cultivate a little less than a third of a hectare in one day; most were able to work between a quarter and a third, depending on the nature of the soil.[50] The *somber* had to be accomplished within at least one month's time before winter rains inundated the fields, making cultivation impossible. An average *domaine* of seventy-five hectares, employing a biennial crop rotation, would probably have anywhere from thirty to forty hectares in fallow each year, which translates into between 105 and 120 man-days of labor. Only by employing three plow teams could such a farm be adequately cultivated. Indeed the size of *domaines* in the Nivernais was usually reckoned by the number of plow teams it supported, and leases often stipulated that the tenant had to furnish at least one adult male for every ten hectares.[51] Thus, household structure and *domaine* size were intimately linked to one another.

Both the expansion of meadowland and the introduction of artificial meadows substantially reduced the size of the year-round labor force needed on the *domaines* of the Nivernais, either by eliminating the necessity of plowing altogether or by reducing the amount of cultivation required for soil preparation. While the transformation of waste and arable to pasture involved considerable inputs of labor, once established, pastures required little work outside of the occasional repair of irrigation ditches.[52] By replacing fallow with clover or lucerne, the number of plowings necessary for soil preparation for the next season's wheat crop were reduced from three to one. Cover crops such as these accomplished naturally the same tasks performed by plowing. Clover, when introduced into crop rotations, controlled weeds by smothering them in the early stages of their growth. Those weeds that did survive were cut down before their seeds could germinate when the meadows were mown in June. The roots of plants such as clover, lucerne and especially alfalfa also acted to loosen the soil, further eliminating the need for plowing. After these grasses were cut in June, fields needed only a single plowing to prepare the seed bed for the sowing of cereal crops.[53] For many agronomists, this reduction in necessary plow-time was the principal advantage to be derived from the introduction of artificial meadows. "What every intelligent farmer ought to desire," declared one such writer in 1865, "is to have to execute only as many plowings as are strictly necessary. We can achieve this goal easily by the creation of artificial meadows."[54]

The French government's agricultural survey of 1852 provides an excellent basis for calculating the actual reduction in labor-time result-

11.   Plow teams working a field in the Bazois, circa 1880. Note the exclusive use of the Charolis breed.

12.   Plow team in the Morvan, late nineteenth century.

13. Watering down the farm herd. Note the wooden shoes, or *sabots,* still worn by older peasants in the Morvan today.

ing from the substitution of artificial meadows for fallow and the replacement of arable with pasture. One aim of the inquiry was to determine net revenues per hectare of agricultural land and thus detailed information on both labor requirements and costs was required. Production costs were determined by the local commissions charged with carrying out the survey for all types of cereals, root crops, fallows, artificial meadows, and pasture. Dividing these costs by the average daily wage of rural day-laborers will thus give the total man-days of labor required for each crop. In the following tables, these calculations were made for fallowland, artificial meadows, arable land planted in wheat, and pasture in each of the four *arrondissements* of the Nièvre. Table 25 compares labor input for fallow and artificial meadows, omitting costs of sowing and harvesting of cereal crops (The figures on costs for artificial meadows include expenditures for mowing). According to these figures, a thirty percent reduction in man-days per hectare could be achieved simply by employing clover to replace fallow. In Table 26, the cost of one hectare of land planted in wheat (including the cultivation of the fallow) is compared with the costs of a hectare of pasture. Here the reduction in labor input is even more striking. When pasture replaced arable land, the number of man-days per hectare dropped by eighty percent!

However, increasing meadow and forage crops at the expense of fallow had the result of sharply increasing labor demand during the summer months. Now, with more hayfields to be mown and more crops to be harvested, a larger number of hired hands was needed to get the

14.   *Le Labourage nivernais* by Rosa Bonheur 1849. Musée Rosa Bonheir, Château de Fontainebleau, Paris.

Table 25. Fallow and artificial meadows labor-input per hectare by type of crop

	Arrondissements				
	Château-Chinon	Nevers	Cosne	Clamecy	Average for the departement
Day-wages for a *Journalier* (francs)	1.26f	1.38f	1.40f	1.15f	1.30f
Fallows					
Total labor costs for a ha. of fallow	36f	44f	60f	44f	46f
Man-days per ha. of fallow	28.6	31.9	42.9	38.3	35.4
Artificial Meadows					
Total labor costs for a ha. of clover	25f	41f	31f	29f	32f
Man-days per ha. of Clover	19.8	29.7	22.1	25.2	24.6
Man-days saved by supplanting fallow with clover	8.8	2.2	20.8	13.1	10.8
Percentage reduction in labor input	30.8%	6.9%	48.5%	34.2%	30.5%

crops in. The peak of labor demand therefore shifted to the summer as the need for plowmen declined and the need for temporary labor increased. For tenant families, this meant that fewer kin were needed to work the farm while more hired hands were needed for seasonal work.

It is important to note that this reallocation of labor did not entail an

Table 26. Wheat and pastureland

	Arrondissements				
	Château-Chinon	Nevers	Cosne	Clamecy	Average for the departement
Wheat					
Total labor costs for a ha. of wheat*	134f	142f	148f	139f	141f
Man-days per ha. of wheat	106.3	102.9	105.7	120.9	108.5
Pasture					
Total labor costs for a ha. of pasture	23f	37f	25f	28f	28f
Man-days per ha. of pasture	18.3	26.8	17.9	24.3	21.5
Man-days saved by supplanting arable with pasture	88.0	76.1	87.8	96.6	87.0
Percentage reduction in labor input	82.8%	74.0%	83.1%	79.9%	80.2%

*Includes preparation of the fallow.

overall reduction in labor demand. Nonetheless, a large year-round work force was no longer needed to operate *domaine* farms. This shift in the seasonal nature of labor input provoked a complete reorganization of domestic production units in order to adjust to the changing demands of farming methods, one that streamlined household organization by eliminating family units that were now superfluous. The changes in the nature of farm production in the Nivernais were achieved within a single generation, indeed within a decade or so of their initial introduction. The adjustments by tenant farmers to these changes were equally swift.

CHAPTER EIGHT

The Transformation of Tenant Household Structure, 1840-1875

The transformation of agriculture in the Nièvre during the nineteenth century was by no means a uniform process. Some regions of the *département* underwent early and rapid change while in others farming techniques preserved their centuries-old characteristics well into the second half of the century. *Départemental* figures on agriculture showing a steady increase in productivity and the expansion of artificial meadows and pasture mask important regional variations in the pace with which new crop rotations were introduced. Even as late as 1882, communes in the Morvan continued to rely on extensive fallows to maintain soil fertility. At Ouroux half the arable was left uncultivated each year; At Gien-sur-Cure cattle continued to graze on broom and thistles that grew in fields left fallow for five years or more. As late as 1906 the morvandelle remained the principal draft animal for farmers in the Upper Morvan.[1]

The following series of maps provide a readily visible portrait of the uneven pace of agricultural change in the Nièvre.[2] Here two indicators of progress in agriculture, the percentage of arable left in fallow and the percentage covered in artificial meadows, are shown for each of the twenty-five cantons of the Nièvre. Even as early as 1836 the eastern half of the *département* was distinguished by its lack of cover crops and its heavy reliance on fallows. Indeed, in most of the Morvan over forty percent of the arable was left uncultivated. By 1852 the use of artificial meadows to replace fallows had not significantly increased in the Morvan. In the canton of Luzy over fifty percent of the arable was reported to be in fallow that year. Even as late as 1872, when most of the farms of the Nivernais had adopted four- and five-course rotations, biennial rotations continued to be widespread throughout the Morvan.

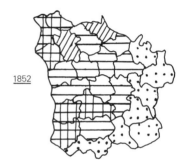

Percentage of arable planted
in artificial meadows

`· · ·`	under 5%
☰	5% to 10%
⊞	11% to 15%
▨	16% to 20%
■	over 20%
☐	no information

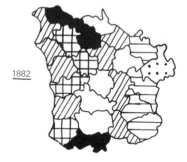

Map 10. Distribution of crops in the Nièvre

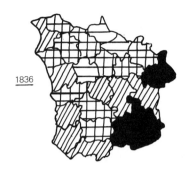

Percentage of arable left in fallow

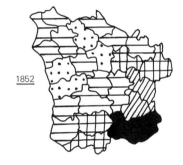

Map 10. Distribution of Crops in the Nièvre (continued)

To some extent the adoption of more productive crop rotations was impeded by the existence of a substantial number of minuscule farms, a problem underlined in 1853 by the subprefect for Château-Chinon. "What the Morvan lacks is capital, which cannot be procured because of the division of properties."[3] Even in the lowland Nivernais, smaller peasant-owned farms proved slow to adopt the new husbandry. At Biches, in the fertile valley of the Bazois, the mayor reported in 1882 that larger farms had maximized production by utilizing four- and five-course rotations of wheat, spring grains, root crops and clover, thereby providing ample forage for livestock. Small producers, however, for whom wheat was as much a subsistence as a cash crop, employed only a three-course rotation of wheat, oats and clover.[4] The subprefect of Clamecy repeatedly decried the impediments to progress posed by the excessive division of property in the open fields of the Yonne Valley. He contrasted the achievements made in communes such as Saint-Pierre-du-Mont, where "the lands are not divided," with communes such as Cuncy-les-Varzy where "the *morcellement* of property considerably hinders the progress of agriculture," or Beuvron where "property is extremely divided and worked by peasants who have little desire to initiate improvements."[5]

Isolation caused by the absence of roads continued to hinder the development of agriculture in the Morvan. The first national route through the region, begun in 1838, was completed only in 1858. By that year the total length of both national and *départemental* roads in the Morvan, which covered over a third of the surface area of the Nièvre was a mere 86 kilometers, compared to almost 400 kilometers in the rest of the *département*.[6] The problem posed by lack of roads was doubly acute for the Morvan because of the nature of its soils. Grasses such as clover and sainfoin were effective only on soils with sufficient lime, an ingredient that the sandy granites of the Morvan lacked entirely. Before cover crops could be introduced, fields had to be marled with deposits brought from outside the region, yet lack of adequate roads made transport costs prohibitive.

The completion of national routes by the early 1860s only partially alleviated the problem, for without a network of local roads linking each commune high transport costs would continue to hamper farming. The subprefect pleaded for more attention to the problem. "The point upon which the government ought to concentrate its attention is the system of smaller local roads. For a long time nearly all resources have been spent on major and secondary communications. This system has produced good results and has permitted us to establish a complete network of excellent routes, but to continue this would be to fall into a fatal excess. It is crucial to render to local roads a part of these resources."[7] Efforts to improve local roads in the Morvan were undertaken in the second half of the century, yet the steep terrain of the region inhibited rapid progress. As late as 1902 Emil Blin warned potential travelers to the Morvan that its roads were at best inadequate; during the rainy season communal roads turned into "veritable rivers."[8]

The agricultural revolution thus proceeded at a far slower pace in the Morvan than in the rest of the Nivernais. This retarded nature of agrarian change in the Morvan only heightened the distinctiveness that had characterized the region for centuries: an isolated backwater impervious to change where traditions and practices survived long after they had been discarded elsewhere. The patois, superstitions, and domestic customs of the Morvandiau would provide a wealth of material for eager folklorists in the nineteenth century as well as myriad anecdotes for a score of guidebook writers.

The retarded nature of agrarian change in the Morvan had even more important consequences for peasant household organization in the region. The continued reliance on fallows to ensure soil fertility meant that farms in the Morvan would require a large work force for their operation. Because agricultural methods remained unchanged for much of the century, even on the large *domaines* of the region, tenant households continued to be organized in such a way as to provide the labor needed to work the farms they held. Throughout the lowlands, however, the transformation of agriculture brought with it the need to totally restructure household organization in order to adapt it to the new demands posed by modern farm techniques.

In order to demonstrate the effects of the agricultural revolution on tenant households in the lowland Nivernais, and to contrast these with households in the Morvan where household organization remained virtually unchanged, two communes were selected from each region. The reader is already familiar with Larochemillay, situated in the canton of Luzy in the southern Morvan. Throughout this canton traditional farming practices survived longer than in any other part of the Nièvre. In 1852 fallows were reported to have covered over half the arable land in the canton; three-course rotations appear to have been introduced only in the 1870s, becoming widespread a decade later. The use of artificial meadows, even as late as the 1880s, was extremely limited. Rye remained the principal cereal grown at Larochemillay throughout most of the century, and it was not until 1882 that the area sown in wheat exceeded that sown in rye. Grain yields were the lowest in the

149

département, reported at about three for one in 1852 and four for one in 1867.

Until 1850 no paved roads linked Larochemillay to the outside world. Communication with neighboring communes was by footpath or wagon track, both impassable during the rainy season. Without roads, transport of lime needed to improve soils so that clovers could be introduced was impossible. In place of clovers, by the 1850s farmers had begun to introduce potatoes into their crop rotations as a means of controlling weeds and aerating the soil. More of a garden crop in the early decades of the century, the potato thrived on the thin sandy soils of the Morvan; by the 1850s most *domaines* were planting several hectares of potatoes each season. Unlike clovers, however, cultivation of the potato required enormous expenditures of labor. Fields had to be plowed before each planting and, as the plants began to sprout, had to be hersed and weeded by hand. When mature, the plants were harvested by hand as well. In all potatoes required between eighty and ninety man-days per hectare of labor, an increase of 150 percent over the thirty-five man-days of labor for cultivation of a hectare of land planted in cereals.[9]

The commune of Limanton, only fifteen kilometers from Larochemillay, remarkably resembled both the social structure and economy of its neighbor. Located in the fertile lowlands immediately west of the Morvan, both communes were characterized by large dispersed *domaine* farms and scattered small hamlets. Like Larochemillay, the economy of Limanton was almost entirely agrarian, with over three-quarters of its population in the nineteenth century directly engaged in agriculture, either as landowners, tenants, or as day-laborers. The remainder of Limanton's population was comprised of artisans whose incomes were obtained by serving the needs of the farming community. A comparison of the occupational distributions of Larochemillay and Limanton in 1820 reveals how closely the two communes resembled one another.[10] Peasant proprietors and tenant farmers, accounting for almost half the households in both localities, dominated the social structure of each commune. In fact, the number of tenants in the two communes was very nearly equal, between forty and forty-five for each.

Although the 1820 census listed twice as many proprietors in Limanton as in Larochemillay, the cadastral survey (completed in 1845 for both communes) shows that property was in fact more heavily concentrated at Limanton. At Larochemillay nineteen proprietors owned fifty or more hectares of land, totaling seventy-four percent of all land in the commune. At Limanton, twenty-one proprietors owned fifty hectares or more, totaling eighty-one percent of the commune's land. Unlike

Table 27. Occupational structure Larochemillay and Limanton (1820)

Households headed by:	Larochemillay (pop. 841)		Limanton (pop. 777)	
	N	%	N	%
Tenants	37	32.2	36	23.5
Proprietors	18	15.7	39	25.5
Artisans	21	18.2	17	11.1
Day-laborers	26	22.6	50	32.7
Indigents	7	6.1	11	7.2
Other*	6	5.2	–	–
	115	100.0	153	100.0

*Watchmen and gardeners

Table 28. Distribution of landholdings Larochemillay and Limanton (1845)

Limanton

Hectares	Number of proprietors	Percentage of proprietors	Total area	Percentage of area
under 1	98	40.8%	42.2 ha	.9%
1 to 5	79	32.9	190.4	4.2
5 to 10	24	10.0	145.5	3.2
10 to 20	6	2.5	73.3	1.6
20 to 50	12	5.0	414.3	9.1
50 to 100	14	5.8	840.2	18.4
over 100	7	2.9	2,850.8	62.6
Totals	240	100.0	4,556.7	100.0

Larochemillay

Hectares	Number of proprietors	Percentage of proprietors	Total area	Percentage of area
under 1	105	37.5%	45.2 ha	1.2%
1 to 5	103	36.8	215.8	5.8
5 to 10	22	7.9	158.6	4.3
10 to 20	23	8.2	279.5	7.5
20 to 50	8	2.9	266.0	7.2
50 to 100	10	3.6	644.9	17.4
over 100	9	3.1	2,100.7	56.6
Totals	280	100.0	3,710.7	100.0

Larochemillay, dominated by noble landowners, the vast majority of land at Limanton was held by bourgeois proprietors. Only one noble, the duc de Talleyrand, owned land at Limanton, and, with just over 450 hectares, his holdings were by no means the largest in the commune.[11] The bourgeois nature of large property owners at Limanton should not be overemphasized. The largest landowner in the commune, Antoine

Boussaraque, a retired army officer, had in fact purchased his property from a local noble, the marquis Bruneau de Vitry, in 1841. Moreover, in both localities large landowners, whether noble or bourgeois, tended to sublet their farms to local *fermiers*. These were thoroughly bourgeois individuals, by any definition of the term.

Map 11. Limanton and Larochemillay

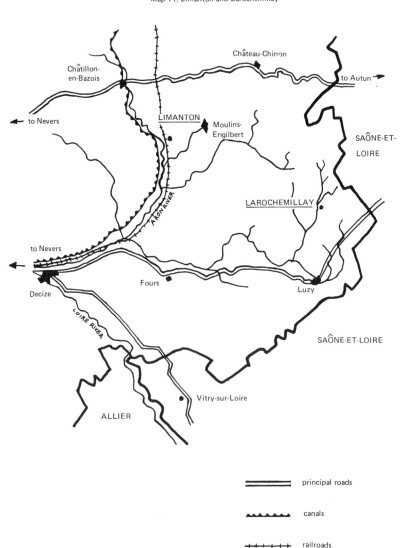

principal roads

canals

railroads

The greater concentration of landed property at Limanton is also reflected in the nature of holdings possessed by peasant proprietors. In both communes, the overwhelming majority of peasants owned less than five hectares of land, and half of these owned less than a single hectare. Such individuals were as much rural day-laborers as proprietors, with incomes derived from seasonal work on others' land as much as from their own meager plots. However, such an existence was far more characteristic of Limanton's peasant proprietors than those of Larochemillay, where a considerable number of peasants owned between ten and fifteen hectares of land and were thus able to live entirely on the output of their own farms. At Limanton in 1845, only six persons could claim this status.

Geographically, Limanton seems to have been blessed in every way that Larochemillay was not. Situated in a region of the Nivernais known as the Bazois, Limanton enjoyed the advantages of rich liassic soils formed by alluvial deposits on a limestone substratum. Even before the beginnings of the agricultural revolution, the fertile soils of the Bazois allowed farmers to reap yields of seven or eight for one, the highest in the *département*.[12] The Bazois was drained by the Aron River, which ran directly through Limanton. Along the Aron's banks lay some of the richest pastures and meadowlands of the Nivernais. Indeed the fledgling cattle-fattening industry of the eighteenth century began in the Bazois. Claude Mathieu d'Oye, the first to import charolais cattle into the Nivernais, established himself at Anlezy in the western Bazois. The rich meadows and pastures of Limanton attracted other *emboucheurs* from the Charolles, such as M. Massin and M. Lorton. In fact two of Mathieu's sons leased farms at Limanton in the late eighteenth century.[13] By the early decades of the next century, the Bazois was exporting over a hundred head of cattle a week during the spring and summer, accounting for virtually all cattle exports from the *département*.[14]

The benefits that nature bestowed on Limanton were enhanced by the hand of man in the nineteenth century. The Nivernais Canal, following the Aron, directly bisected the commune. Although many residents bitterly opposed the construction of the canal because it destroyed some of the best pastureland in the commune, by the 1840s the growing access to markets that it afforded had silenced these initial complaints. By the 1870s the commune would benefit further from the construction of a rail line paralleling the canal which linked Decize and Clamecy and thence ran to Paris. Limanton was thus able to gain access to northern markets, a crucial factor that propelled agriculture in the commune to the early adoption of new farm methods and increased cattle production.

Up to the 1840s, however, farms owned or leased by *emboucheurs* in the Bazois remained only isolated islands of progress in a sea of backward agriculture. Two-course rotations dominated farming techniques and artificial meadows were virtually unknown. As in the rest of the Nivernais, most *domaines* were worked by *métayers* whose principal efforts were concentrated on cereal production. While the rich lands they sowed produced abundant yields, sharecroppers may well have seen this as something of a mixed blessing. The heavy clay soils of the region were cultivated only with the greatest difficulty. Unlike the Morvan, where plow teams of two or four oxen were necessary, the tenacious clays of the Bazois required teams of six, eight and sometimes ten oxen. The region's limestone substratum prevented effective drainage of the land, which in excessively wet years remained too moisture-laden to plow, well into the spring, thereby threatening the success of the harvest. Peasants aptly dubbed such fields *mouilleres*. When dry, the soils would harden into a near-impenetrable consistency, exhausting both men and beasts. With as much as forty to fifty percent of the arable left in fallow each year, the operation of farms in the Bazois required considerable labor input.[15]

Effective drainage systems and the introduction of clovers would alleviate many of these problems, yet few such improvements were carried out on a large scale until the 1840s. Improvements undertaken prior to that time were generally limited to the farms leased or owned by *emboucheurs* intent on extending pasture and herbages. Most *emboucheurs* supplemented their cattle-fattening operations by becoming *gros-fermiers*, leasing several *métayer*-worked *domaines* from noble and bourgeois owners. Yet any improvements they introduced tended to be limited to the farms they directly supervised. Production on their own farms continued to stagnate under traditional two-course rotations of cereal and fallow, generally deficient in forage crops. So scarce was forage in the region that local farmers were not always sure that calves would survive the winter months in stable. "Provided we can save them from the winter," went a local proverb, "the sprouts of the spring will bring them to health." The limited influence of *emboucheurs* on agriculture in the Bazois is attested to by the fact that the cattle they fattened were usually imported from the Charolles rather than purchased locally. The indigenous morvandelle breed did not meet their needs, yet local farmers were unable to introduce the charolais for lack of sufficient fodder crops.[16]

With the penetration of the Bazois by the Nivernais Canal and the creation of a network of primary and secondary roads in the late 1830s, improvements in agriculture began to spread rapidly through the region. Between 1836 and 1854 the extent of fallow was reduced by a third while pasture increased by over sixty percent and the area given to artificial meadows more than tripled.[17] Cattle production was intensified as increased fodder enabled farmers to enlarge the size of their herds, now increasingly composed of the charolais breed. By mid-century the Bazois had become the foremost cattle-producing region in the Nièvre. Local agronomists waxed eloquent over conditions in a region that Arthur Young had declared to be merely in its infancy as far as agriculture was concerned. "The Bazois," wrote one agronomist in 1849, "with its fertilizing streams, its fruitful land, its fresh pastures grazed by magnificent white-coated cattle, constitutes the most picturesque, the most diversified, the most pleasant, and without exception, the most productive region of the Nivernais."[18]

The extent to which agriculture in the Bazois was able to reap the benefits of agrarian change can be seen when the distribution of crops over the century at Limanton is compared to that of Larochemillay. The figures in Tables 29 and 30 are based on communal reports gathered for the various government surveys of agriculture in the Nièvre.[19] It should be noted that these reports apparently were not compiled with the greatest care. The figures for 1836 are almost certainly mere estimations,

Table 29. Utilization of farmland Larochemillay and Limanton

		Limanton			
	1836	1848*	1856	1877	1885
Cereals	510 ha	477 ha	533 ha	617 ha	953 ha
Root crops	20	15	88	47	30
Artificial meadows	25	–	368	390	358
Natural meadows	500	–	722	1,607	2,225
	1,055		1,711	2,661	3,566
Wheat yields**	15.4	–	15	15	20

		Larochemillay			
	1836	1848*	1856	1877	1885
Cereals	534	1,098	885	1,577	2,712
Root crops	100	200	400	300	500
Artificial meadows	15	–	10	53	100
Natural meadows	500	–	530	957	960
	1,149	–	1,825	2,987	4,272
Wheat yields**	8	12	12	12	12

*1848 survey gave no figures on meadows
**in hectolitres per hectare

Table 30. Size of communal herds Larochemillay and Limanton

| | Limanton | | |
	1836	1856	1885
Oxen	420	1,001	1,025
Cows	250	398	550
Calves	250	184	980
Total	920	1,178	2,555

| | Larochemillay | | |
	1836	1856	1885
Oxen	480	570	580
Cows	400	450	460
Calves	500	280	150
Total	1,380	1,300	1,190

understandable given the fact that the cadastral surveys had not been completed for either commune until 1845. Moreover, it appears that local officials in both communes consistently underreported the extent of the total area under production by excluding from their enumerations the farms of small proprietors. The figures therefore pertain almost entirely to the large *domaines* of each commune.[20] These, however, appear to have been fairly accurately surveyed, at least for the years after 1845. It should also be recalled that *domaine* farming accounted for the vast majority of total farmland in each commune.

In both Limanton and Larochemillay the total area under production expanded considerably, especially at Larochemillay, where the adoption of a three-course rotation in the 1870s increased the amount of land sown in cereal crops. Yet whereas total arable land increased fivefold at Larochemillay, at Limanton the major increase in farmland came as the result of a dramatic expansion of pasture, which in turn enabled farmers in the commune to expand the size of their herds. At Larochemillay, on the other hand, no increase in pastureland was recorded until the late 1870s, and even then the increase was by no means comparable to that at Limanton. Another significant difference between the two communes was the selection of cover crops to replace fallow. At Limanton fallows were planted almost entirely in clover, while the thinner, sandier soils at Larochemillay were more conducive to the introduction of labor-intensive root crops, principally the potato.

The differences in the nature of farming at Limanton and Larochemillay can best be seen by comparing crop distributions on individual *domaines* in the two communes. Data for this has been drawn from a

15.   Domaine de la Varenne, commune of Limanton, circa 1880. The hamlet of Arcilly is
       on the ridgeline to the rear.

survey carried out in 1856 on agriculture.[21] The reports were part of an
annual agricultural survey established by the government after 1852 and
intended to provide year-by-year information on the progress of French
agriculture. While summary reports for each commune of the Nièvre
exist for most years up to 1900, the 1856 lists are unique in being the only
ones to provide information on individual farms. Compiled on the same
day as the census for 1856, the lists detail the amount of land planted in
cereals, garden crops, pasture, artificial meadows, and root crops.
Omitted was the extent of land left fallow. Because the replacement of
fallow with cover crops was the touchstone of progress in farming, it is
crucial that the amount of land left uncultivated each year be determined.

The only way that this can be ascertained is by determining the exact
size of each *domaine* in the commune. Once this is known, the extent of
fallow can be easily calculated by subtracting the total area planted in
crops and pasture from the total size of the farm. There are several
sources from which the sizes of *domaines* can be established. The most
reliable are leases or sales contracts in which *domaine* size is specified.
Unfortunately, only a handful of such contracts drawn up in the years
immediately prior to and after the 1856 survey provide this information.
The only other available source on landholdings is the cadastral surveys.

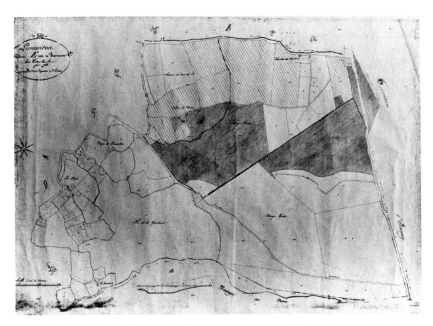

16.   The domaine de Chaume de Mousseau, commune of Limanton according to the
1845 cadastre. The shaded fields are meadow and pasture, the cross-hatched area is
arable land. The widespread use of pasture in Limanton even at this early date is
clearly evident.

However, because the cadastre lists all fields owned by each proprietor,
it is difficult to determine which fields were part of a particular farm. At
Larochemillay, for example, the cadastral entry for the marquis
Laferte-Meun reported a total of 502.10 hectares distributed in several
hundred parcels, with no indication whatsoever of which parcels
belonged to the marquis's ten *domaines* and assorted *locateries*.

The only cases in which the cadastre could be of any use in
determining the size of a particular *domaine* were those in which it was
known for certain that a proprietor owned a single *domaine* in the
commune. When this was the case, the sizes of their *domaines* in 1856
could be established by adding all acquisitions and subtracting all
alienations of land between 1845 and 1856. For example, the cadastre for
Larochemillay shows that some sixty-one hectares passed to one
Claude Cognet in 1855. As the only leases ever recorded as having been
made by Cognet pertain to the *domaine* Champphillippe, it is more than
likely that these sixty-one hectares represent not only the sole property
owned by him in the commune but the size of Champphillippe as well.
This is in fact confirmed by a testament made in 1855 in which Cognet's

father bestowed upon him the *domaine* as part of his inheritance. In all, the sizes of ten *domaines* at Larochemillay and of fourteen at Limanton could be determined with a reasonable degree of accuracy. Together these represent about a quarter of all *domaines* and approximately twenty percent of the total farmland in both communes.

Tables 31 and 32 show the distribution of crops on these *domaines*. The difference in land utilization in the two communes is striking.

Table 31. Utilization of farmland fourteen Limanton domaines** (1856)

Domaines:	Total ha.	Crops	Artificial meadows	Natural meadows	Fallow	Percent fallow
1. Arcilly (1)†	44.36	16.89	7.20	17.53	2.74	6.2%
2. Chaume Mousseau*	52.83	17.93	13.41	17.00	4.07	7.7%
3. Colombier*	48.65	26.56	6.47	10.16	5.46	11.0%
4. Arcilly (2)†	26.65	13.18	7.46	1.46	4.09	15.3%
5. Bouillots (1)†	37.38	12.39	7.60	10.06	7.33	19.6%
6. Moquereau†	57.96	12.30	7.50	26.70	11.46	19.8%
7. Bouillots (2)†	62.56	23.39	7.61	16.40	15.16	24.2%
8. Grand Anizy†	52.41	19.58	5.80	22.67	13.36	25.5%
9. Villars†	92.49	53.27	5.55	27.01	20.25	25.6%
10. Mont†	58.79	14.82	2.05	25.71	16.29	27.6%
11. Motte†	43.83	15.90	7.35	6.81	13.77	31.4%
12. Petit Champardolles*	43.57	7.16	4.15	7.75	11.12	32.2%
13. Gros Champardolles*	61.18	12.72	1.06	27.02	20.39	33.3%
14. Vauvelles†	47.75	9.70	5.76	13.06	14.23	33.3%
Mean	51.53	17.63	6.36	16.38	9.57	18.6%

†size of *domaine* determined from cadastre
*size of *domaine* determined from lease or sales contract
**woodland excluded

Table 32. Utilization of farmland ten Larochemillay domaines** (1856)

Domaines:	Total ha.	Crops	Artificial meadows	Natural meadows	Fallow	Percent fallow
1. Lavault†	59.39	29.76	–	18.00	11.63	19.6%
2. Berthelots†	70.63	30.08	–	24.00	25.16	35.7%
3. Gadelles†	35.52	13.66	–	10.00	12.86	36.2%
4. Montautaume*	54.13	19.74	–	12.00	22.39	41.4%
5. Haut Rivière*	55.58	17.46	–	15.00	23.12	41.6%
6. Grand Bois†	44.50	14.50	–	10.00	20.00	44.9%
7. Mois*	66.76	18.74	–	15.00	33.02	49.6%
8. Champphilippe*	56.25	16.25	–	12.00	28.00	49.8%
9. Quart*	70.66	21.50	–	12.00	37.16	52.6%
10. Pierrefitte*	73.07	18.48	–	15.00	39.60	54.2%
Mean	58.64	20.02	–	14.30	25.29	43.1%

†size of *domaine* determined from cadastre
*size of *domaine* determined from lease or sales contract
**woodland excluded

Whereas an average *domaine* at Limanton would have something like ten percent of its area covered in artificial meadows, these were apparently unknown at Larochemillay. Meadow and pasture were far less prevalent at Larochemillay than at Limanton, where some *domaines* had as much as half their total area under pasture. Yet the clearest indication of the progress made at Limanton as compared to Larochemillay is the extent of fallow employed in crop rotations. At Larochemillay, on seven *domaines,* between forty and fifty percent of total farmland was left uncultivated each year. On only one *domaine* had fallows been reduced to twenty percent of the total surface area. At Limanton, on the other hand, only four *domaines* had a third of their farmland under fallow; seven had between fifteen and twenty-five percent of the land in fallow, and on three, fallow had been reduced to about ten percent or less of the total acreage.

This reduction of fallows at Limanton, together with the expansion of pastureland, brought about a sharp decline in the number of adult workers needed to farm the various *domaines* of the commune. This reduction in the *domaine* work force can be measured by comparing the average number of adult male workers residing on all *domaines* in the commune for each census between 1836 and 1876.[22] The figures in Table 33 were obtained by adding all males over fifteen years of age, whether kin or servants, listed in the census as residing on a *domaine* and dividing this sum by the total number of *domaines* in the commune. This provides a rough estimation of the size of the *domaine* work force at both Limanton and Larochemillay over the course of the century.

Table 33. Mean size of *domaine* labor force (adult male kin and male servants)

Year	Limanton	Larochemillay
1836	3.7	–
1841	3.9	3.4
1846	3.3	3.3
1851	3.3	3.4
1856	3.0	3.3
1861	3.0	3.3
1866	3.1	3.1
1872	3.2	2.9
1876	3.1	3.3

In 1836 and 1841, the average number of adult males per *domaine* was, in fact, greater at Limanton than at Larochemillay. This difference was likely due to the fact that *domaines* at Limanton were generally larger than those at Larochemillay. According to a survey of farms conducted in 1892,[23] seventeen *domaines* at Larochemillay measured between forty and fifty hectares and nineteen between fifty and one hundred hectares. At Limanton only eight *domaines* were listed as between forty and fifty hectares in size; thirty were between fifty and one hundred hectares, and two were larger than one hundred hectares. The greater size of most *domaines* at Limanton therefore meant that a larger work force was needed to farm them.

After 1841, however, the average *domaine* work force at Limanton dropped sharply from 3.9 to 3.3 adult males in 1846, and to just over 3.0 for the years 1856 to 1876. This declne in the *domaine* work force coincides precisely with the years when new farming techniques were introduced into the commune. According to these figures, the average number of adult male workers per *domaine* fell by the equivalent of about one male worker. At Larochemillay, on the other hand, there is little evidence of major changes in the size of the *domaine* work force until the 1860s. In 1872 the average number of workers per *domaine* fell to under three, and then rose again to 3.3 in 1876. It is entirely possible that this temporary decline was brought about by the war with Prussia and had more to do with military conscription than with changes in farm methods.

Could the decline in the *domaine* work force at Limanton have been caused by factors other than the introduction of new farming methods? One possible cause could have been that the *domaines* themselves were becoming smaller. George Grantham has suggested that the period between 1850 and 1880 was marked by a progressive decline in the size of large farms throughout France as landowners, unable to secure a sufficient labor force due to growing rural emigration, were forced to sell off sizable portions of their properties to small peasant farmers.[24] Was a similar process at work in the Bazois? The answer to such a question must be a qualified yes, with the emphasis on "qualified."

Few *domaines* at Limanton appear to have been divided outright, at least up to the early 1870s. Until that period the number of *domaine* tenants listed in each census remained at between forty and forty-two. The variations in the number of tenants between census dates was due to the fact that landlords occasionally took over direct management of their farms and operated them with paid wage laborers rather than tenants. Only in 1876 did the number of tenants increase to forty-six, an increase that was, in fact, the result of the breakup of some *domaines*.

The only direct evidence on property holdings is the cadastre, the nature of which makes it impossible to determine the size of all *domaines* in the commune. It can, however, reveal a great deal about the fortunes of those twenty-five proprietors who owned *domaines* in the commune. In the years between 1845 and 1875, these individuals engaged in a good deal of land speculation. In any five-year period, as much as one hundred hectares or more would be acquired or sold by this group. What concerns us here is the overall balance of acquisitions and alienation made by this group and whether, on the whole, more land passed out of their control than entered into it.

The overall balance sheet for these proprietors is presented in Table 34, showing the total amount of land alienated and acquired by them for each five-year period between 1845 and 1875. The years up to 1865 were clearly beneficial for wealthy landowners at Limanton. Overall they increased their share of the commune's total farmland by 170 hectares. During the next decade, however, despite large acquisitions, this group's total share of land fell by 135 hectares. By the end of the period, however, their control of Limanton's landed resources remained unchallenged. In 1875 the amount of land they owned together was substantially the same as it had been in 1845.

Table 34. Proprietors owning 50 ha. or more (*Limanton*)

Years	Alienations	Acquisitions	Balance
1845-1850	6.24 ha	182.14 ha	+ 175.90 ha
1851-1855	119.66	58.19	− 61.47
1856-1860	27.62	68.14	+ 40.52
1861-1865	1.19	17.52	+ 16.33
1866-1870	190.80	131.39	− 59.41
1871-1875	107.85	31.38	− 76.47
Totals	453.63	488.76	+ 22.94

Such at least was their history as a whole, but what of the fortunes of individual proprietors? Of these twenty-five landowners, the holdings of five remained exactly the same in 1875 as they had been in 1845. In other words, during these three decades they made no acquisitions and alienated no land whatsoever. Ten proprietors experienced a net gain during this period. Three of these increased their holdings by ten hectares or less, three by between eleven and sixteen hectares, and four by more than fifty hectares. Of those ten landowners who suffered a net loss, the properties of four declined by less than ten hectares and another's by fourteen. The holdings of the remaining five persons declined considerably. Two showed a net loss of about forty hectares, two of more than fifty hectares and one a grand total of one hundred and six hectares. For at least three landowners, these losses appear to have occurred with the breakup of their *domaines,* which were sold off in parcels, most of which were acquired by bourgeois living in nearby

Moulins-Engilbert. In one case, division occurred as a result of an inheritance settlement. In 1874 Marie Montcharmont's one hundred and forty-three hectares were passed on to her four heirs. Her eldest son retained intact the *domaine* at Bellevaux while the rest of her property was divided between her daughters.

Given the evidence on property holdings from the cadastre, it must be concluded that most *domaines* at Limanton were not subject to massive dismemberment. In all, the properties of fifteen of the twenty-five *domaine* owners at Limanton either remained intact or showed a net increase in size. Of the ten owners who experienced a net decline in their properties, five suffered only minor losses. Of the five who experienced major losses, in only three cases were *domaines* actually divided, and in all three instances this division occurred at least two decades after the decline in the size of the *domaine* work force set in.

The shift away from the need for a large year-round work force at Limanton provoked a major reorganization of household structure among tenant farmers. The substitution of artificial meadows for fallows and the expansion of pasture sharply reduced the dependency of tenants on the adult labor of family members that had previously been secured through the incorporation of kin into the *communauté*. As this dependency declined, so too did the formation of joint families. Household structure was, in effect, "streamlined" by eliminating family units that were no longer needed, thereby reducing household complexity to either stem family types or, in most cases, nuclear families.

The changes in household structure among tenant farmers at Limanton are readily apparent in the census lists for the commune. Table 35 shows the distribution of household types among tenants at Limanton between 1820 and 1876. In 1820 and 1836, over half of all tenant households were extended, with one-third organized into joint families. During the 1840s the proportion of joint households and of extended families in general declined dramatically. By 1851 only three tenant households contained three or more family units; during the next twenty-five years never more than a single household was recorded as having a joint family structure. Indeed, by 1876 the vast majority of tenant households were nuclear in structure with only fifteen percent living in extended families, nearly all of them stem.

As the figures in Table 36 show, joint families continued to exist at Larochemillay well into the second half of the century. Up to 1846 over half of all tenant households there were joint. After mid-century, a small decline in the proportion of such households is evident. Except for 1872, when the number of joint households fell to twenty-six percent of the

Table 35. Tenant household structure (Limanton)

Year	Single person	Nuclear	Stem	Joint	Number
1820	2.5%	40.0%	22.5%	35.0%	40
1836	2.7	40.5	24.3	32.4	37
1841	2.4	61.0	9.8	26.8	41
1846	4.9	63.4	17.1	14.6	41
1851	2.5	65.0	25.0	7.5	40
1856	2.4	76.2	19.0	2.4	42
1861	–	71.4	26.2	2.4	42
1866	2.4	61.0	31.7	4.9	41
1872	–	70.7	26.8	2.4	41
1876	–	87.0	10.9	2.2	46

Table 36. Tenant household structure (Larochemillay)

Year	Nuclear	Stem	Joint	Number
1820	16.7%	15.6%	67.8%	36
1836	–	–	–	–
1841	18.4	31.6	50.0	38
1846	27.9	16.3	55.8	43
1851	27.5	32.5	40.0	40
1856	32.6	30.4	37.0	46
1861	37.5	20.0	42.5	40
1866	35.6	33.3	31.1	45
1872	43.9	29.3	26.8	41
1876	43.2	13.6	43.2	44

total, the proportion of large complex households among tenants remained fairly stable at between thirty and forty percent. The variations in the percentage of joint, stem and nuclear households between each census were due to the fact that the composition of tenant households shifted constantly between each family type. At one stage in the evolution of the household, the family would be composed of only parents and their unmarried children. As the children grew older, first one and then another would marry and bring his or her spouse into the household. Eventually the parents would die, leaving two or three married siblings residing together and the family would become a fraternal joint household, or a *frereche*. This last phase would usually be the shortest. The siblings' children would put additional pressure on the family's resources as they reached maturity until, at some point, the families would split up. Each would then become an independent nuclear household and the cycle would begin once again.

The developmental cycle of tenant households can best be seen by examining the distribution of household types when controlling for the age of the head of household, as in Table 37. Here tenant households at

Table 37. Tenant household structure by age of head of household (*Larochemillay*)

1872

Household type	Ages of Head				Mean Age	N
	−44	45-54	55-64	65+		
Nuclear	10	4	2	2	47.9	18
Stem	1	5	5	1	54.5	12
Joint			4	5	68.2	9
Fraternal Joint	–	2	–	–	47.0	2
Totals	11	11	11	8		41

1876

Household type:	Ages of Head				Mean Age	N
	−44	45-54	55-64	65+		
Nuclear	9	6	4		45.6	19
Stem			4	2	62.3	6
Joint			7	10	67.1	17
Fraternal Joint	–	2	–	–	53.0	2
Totals	9	8	15	12		44

Larochemillay are compared for the years 1872 and 1876. In both years nearly all households headed by persons under the age of forty-four were nuclear. As the age of the household head increased, so too did the complexity of the household, as more and more children were married. Joint families therefore tended to be headed by persons in their sixties, with many in their seventies. As one would expect, fraternal joint families were headed by persons in their late forties and early fifties. They also tended to be rather few in number, reflecting the inherent instability of such households.

In 1872 only about a quarter of all households were joint, the lowest proportion for the entire series. Five years later, however, this percentage rose to what may be considered a "normal" forty-three percent. By looking at the distribution of household types according to the age of the head, it can be seen that this "decline" in joint households that year was simply the result of a greater proportion of younger families among Larochemillay tenants. That year, over half the heads were under the age of fifty-four. In 1876 over sixty percent were over the age of fifty-five, so that there was a greater proportion of families in the latter stages of the household cycle that year. The decline of the joint family in 1872 was therefore more apparent than real.

The virtual disappearance of the joint family at Limanton is remarkable for the rapidity with which it occurred. In two decades—less than a generation—the number of tenants incorporating the families of two or more kin fell from one-third of all tenant families to a single household. This is not to say that the extended family itself disappeared from Limanton; it is rather that the *structure* of household organization was altered. Parents began to incorporate only a single child and his or her spouse into their *communautés* rather than several children or other kin. The *communauté* continued to serve the same purpose that it always had, to secure an adequate labor force to farm the *domaine*. Contracts of association continued to be drawn up by tenants after 1850, yet almost never involved more than two parties, usually parents and one of their sons. All stipulations of the contract remained the same as they had been in the early decades of the century, with each party agreeing to mix their property, labor, and income into a common fund that would be divided equally at the end of the agreement.

There are a number of examples indicating the ease with which tenants at Limanton adapted the formula of the traditional *communauté* to the changing nature of household organization dictated by the needs of the new husbandry.[25] In 1842 the widow of Philippe Michot and her two sons-in-law dissolved the *société* that had existed between them by verbal agreement for five years. Each received a one-third share in the profits from the *domaine* that they had leased. By the same act, Michot's widow and one of her sons-in-law formed a new *société,* while the other ceded his claim to the farm stock and equipment to his former coparceners in return for two hundred and fifty francs. By this simple arrangement, the Michot *communauté* was transformed from a joint to a stem family.

Initially a few families utilized the *société* in more traditional ways while at the same time adapting their households to the new conditions posed by changing farm methods. In 1845 Jean Courdavault and his brother-in-law, François Cassier, tenants at La Seigne, formed a *société* for the exploitation of that *domaine.* While each mixed an equal share in the common fund, it was agreed that only Courdavault and his wife would actually farm the *domaine* and would receive a three-fourths share in the profits. However, only a few such agreements were made by tenants at Limanton and there is no evidence of any similar contracts after the 1850s.

The legal arrangements of the *société* were thus easily adapted to the new requirements posed by changes in farming at Limanton. The legal conditions of the *société* remained exactly the same as always; what changed was the structure of the households covered by such agreements. By mid-century the *sociétés* at Limanton resembled the stem families that had long characterized the household structure of landowning peasant families. Tenant stem families did differ from the latter in one important way, however. Whereas among propertied peasants, ownership of the land tended to be retained by parents until their deaths, property and income among tenants were shared by all members. In this sense, at least, tenant families continued to resemble the traditional *communautés* of the Nivernais.

The extended families of Limanton tenants came to resemble those of landed peasants in yet another way. It will be recalled that tenant *communautés* at Larochemillay incorporated the families of female as well as male kin. While a distinct preference for male kin operated among these families, this tendency was tempered by the need for a large work force to farm their *domaines,* so that daughters and their husbands were brought into the association as well. Such cognatic kin ties within tenant households differed markedly from the strict agnatic ties and patrilocality characterizing landowners in the same commune.

Similar cognatic ties were evident in tenant households at Limanton during the early decades of the century. Between 1800 and 1835 some seventy-one couples were incorporated into *communautés* by marriage contracts and acts of association. Of these, forty, or about fifty-six percent, were male relatives of the head of household (brothers, sons, nephews, and so on), and thirty-one, or about forty-four percent, were female relatives (daughters, sisters, nieces). Census lists for Limanton reveal similar tendencies. The selection of relatives to share residence can be determined by tracing individual families between each census year. For example, in 1836 the *domaine* Petit Anizy was occupied by François Guillot, his two brothers Pierre and François, and his two sisters, both named Jeanne. All were unmarried at that time. The list for 1841 shows that all three brothers had married and continued to coreside at Petit Anizy. Their sisters were not listed and had presumably married men outside the commune. Between the years 1846 and 1861, only François and his family were listed as residing at Petit Anizy. By 1866 Guillot's eldest child, Pauline, had married and she and her husband lived with Guillot and his wife. We may thus conclude that, during the early stage of this family's life, selection of coresident kin had followed the principle of male preference, while during the latter stage the choice had fallen on a female relative, Guillot's daughter.

This procedure was followed for each tenant household at both Limanton and Larochemillay, and the results are shown in Table 38. At Larochemillay the incorporation of both male and female kin continued throughout the century, with female kin entering into *communautés* at approximately the same rate each decade. The families of daughters and

167

Table 38. Nature of kinship ties of new family units to heads of tenant households

Limanton

	Kin tie through				
Years	Males	%	Females	%	N
1836-1846	13	46.4	15	53.6	28
1847-1856	10	55.6	8	43.4	18
1857-1866	20	69.0	9	31.0	29
1867-1876	9	90.0	1	10.0	10

Larochemillay

	Kin ties through				
Years	Males	%	Females	%	N
1846-1856	24	55.8	19	44.2	43
1857-1866	15	53.6	13	46.4	28
1867-1876	16	57.1	12	42.9	28

other female relatives were an important source of labor, so cognatic kin ties within tenant households were formed at a fairly steady rate. At Limanton, however, as the need for additional labor declined, fewer and fewer couples were incorporated into tenant households. Also apparent is a distant change in the nature of kin association. Between 1836 and 1856 the families of daughters and sisters were incorporated at about the same rate as those of male kin. Over the next two decades, however, the proportion of female relatives and their families sharing residence with the heads of tenant households declined noticeably. It would appear that, as the structure of tenant households shifted from joint to stem families under the impact of agrarian change, the principle of male preference came to dominate the choice of coparceners.

This increasing trend towards patrilocal residence practices among Limanton tenants should not be taken as an indication that parental attitudes about who would share in the labor and benefits of the *domaine* were changing. It is probable that a general tendency to favor sons over daughters had always existed regarding inheritance settlements and in residence practices. Prior to the Revolution, landowning peasants concentrated property on their sons and excluded their daughters as much as possible from succession to land. Even in tenant households, most families incorporated into the *communauté* were those of male rather than female kin, a preference that was most marked during the early stages of household development. The association of female kin was due more to the necessity for securing a sufficient work force than to any weakening of the principle of male preference. With the advent of labor-reducing farm techniques, large numbers of adult workers were no longer needed. As this need declined, so too did reliance on female kin. Not only were fewer and fewer extended families formed but, when they were, parents selected sons rather than daughters as coparceners.

The same kind of changes in tenant household organization evident at Limanton were occurring throughout the Nivernais wherever farm production was rationalized. Only in areas such as Larochemillay where reliance on primitive farm methods persisted did the large *communauté* survive. There is no evidence that the decline of the joint household was a result of cultural change, of an intrusion of modern values and the discarding of traditional ones. Indeed, the inhabitants of villages such as Limanton would surely have been surprised to learn that social scientists and politicians were alarmed that the demise of the large *communauté* reflected a growing demoralization of the peasantry. For tenants, the *communauté* never really disappeared. Associations continued to be formed around the same rights and obligations as had always been the case. What had altered was merely the structure of the household, not its purpose or function.

CHAPTER NINE

From Subsistence Peasant to Capitalist Farmer

The introduction of new farm methods signaled the end of the large *communautés* in the Nivernais. Yet changes in household structure were not the only effect of the agricultural revolution on tenant families. Even more significant were its effects on tenure, the relationship of tenants to the market, and the overall standard of living of tenant families. At this point, it may be useful to recall the distinction made by Robert Redfield between "peasants," for whom agriculture is primarily subsistence farming, and "farmers," who treat agriculture as a business. In a certain sense, farming for sharecroppers up to the nineteenth century could be considered a business insofar as surpluses derived from their share of production were marketed. However, by the very nature of *métayage,* only a very limited part of total farm produce was left to direct producers and was usually consumed entirely by the family. The landlord's share, as well as the marketing of all cattle and other farm animals, was directly controlled by the landlord himself. Thus, the direct involvement in the market by *métayers* remained fairly limited. Though not entirely subsistence peasants, sharecroppers, prior to the 1840s, could by no stretch of the term fit into Redfield's category of "farmers."

With the agricultural revolution, this aspect of tenants' relationship to production was entirely transformed. This change was brought about when *métayage* came to be replaced by a form of tenure known as *fermage*. Under *fermage* the tenant leased a farm for a fixed rent and was solely responsible for all marketing of production. The market thereby became the direct concern of the tenant himself. In fact the transformation of tenure in the Nièvre was one of the most important consequences of the agricultural revolution, not only because of its

170

effect on tenants themselves, who clearly benefited from it, but because of its role in accelerating the process of agrarian change.

The Debate on Tenure

In the late 1840s the *Société départemental d'agriculture de la Nièvre,* organized in 1840 as a vehicle to disseminate information on new agricultural techniques, began to address itself to the issue of the relationship between tenure and agricultural progress. The question at hand was whether new farm methods could be successfully introduced within the existing framework of *métayage* tenure. The question sparked a vigorous debate over the merits and vices of *métayage.* Opponents of sharecropping argued that *métayage* afforded little opportunity for either landlords or tenants to reap the potential benefits of the new husbandry and that sharecropping was itself the principal obstacle to improvement. Supporters of sharecropping agreed that, as generally practiced in the region, *métayage* was indeed harmful to agriculture. They felt, however, that it could be easily adapted to the demands of the new husbandry because landowners, by retaining control over their property, would be assured that their commands and instructions would be properly carried out. The debate was not merely academic. The members of the *Société* were themselves wealthy landowners for whom the progress of agriculture was of vital importance. Their arguments reflected the concerns of landowners throughout the Nivernais who were struggling to increase production and experimenting with different forms of tenure relations as much as with innovations in farming.

Among a host of agronomists and government officials there was little doubt that *métayage* posed a formidable barrier to agricultural improvement. "The miserable condition of *métayers,*" wrote the marquis de Chambray in 1834, "was not only an obstacle to improvement but even a cause of deterioration."[1] Chambray's conclusions were shared by most local administrators, who pounded the same points home in report after report on the conditions of agriculture in the Nièvre. The committee organized in the canton of Moulins-Engilber in 1848 to report on working conditions in their district declared that "the mode of exploitation known as *métayage* is the cause of decadence in agriculture." The committee for the canton of Luzy agreed:

> One cannot say that agriculture is merely stagnating; it is in decline. . . .
> The conditions of sharecroppers are such that any modifications in the system of farming, and thus any improvements, are all but impossible. . . .

The proprietor invests the least amount of capital as possible, the *métayer* the least amount of labor as possible. Production is miserable.[2]

The subprefect of Château-Chinon reported in 1853 that *métayage* "is a cause of deterioration in agriculture. The sharecropper, who is always poor, lives from day to day, without any thought of the future, without any idea of improvement. Provided his family can eat, he is content."

The poverty of sharecroppers not only inhibited their ability to invest in improvements but bred such deep hostility toward their landlords that any cooperation in farming between the two was almost impossible. To the myriad anxieties inherent in farming itself were added the vexations of a form of tenure that can only be described as draconian. To receive a mere half share or less of the fruit of a year of hard and heavy labor may have been entirely within the bounds of the law, but to many tenants it appeared downright immoral. Complaints that resulted in dismissal from a farm that had been worked for years, sometimes even generations, could not help but create resentment. When such a fate befell Etienne Bertin, his indignation gushed forth in bitter exasperation.

> The blow was truly a bitter one. On this farm . . . I had spent twenty-five years of my life, the best years of my full maturity. To all who knew me, was I not Tiennon of La Creuserie? To everybody my person seemed inseparable from the farm. . . . Yes, I was strongly linked, linked by all the fibers of my nature, to this land from which a gentleman was driving me without any other reason than that he was the master.[3]

Animosity of this kind could manifest itself in a thousand different ways—in petty thefts, evasions and outright destruction of property, all committed against the landlord and generating mutual resentment and mistrust. "Everywhere," wrote one member of the *Société d'agriculture*, "sharecroppers are the enemies of proprietors. Chicanery is substituted for good faith, wastage for loyal division of shares, and defiance for equitable accord. Thus, all proprietors complain of the state of their *domaines*, of the meager profits that they derive from them, and of the progressive diminution of their harvests. Such is the fruit of *métayage*."[4]

Landlords had to be continually on guard against their tenants, no better proof of which is a manual written in the eighteenth century by a wealthy Morvan proprietor, Isaïe Bonfils.[5] His stated aim was to provide counsel on how best to protect oneself against the *friponneries* of tenants. Rule number one: "Never believe the promises of a peasant. He studies for hours at ways to trick his master." A careful landlord will list each and every tool of his *domaine* before turning it over to a tenant lest the *métayer* later claim to have brought it with him. He will also make frequent visits to his farm, at least every month, to assure himself of the health of the farm stock, for a clever tenant will claim that a cow had died from disease or was killed by a wolf when in fact it had been consumed or sold. "It is especially important to be careful before and after parish feastdays or when there is a marriage. If you grant them one pig on such an occasion, they'll slaughter two." If the farm is equipped with a horse, then a landlord must be sure that his tenant employs it only on tasks directly related to the *domaine,* since *métayers* are notorious for loaning out animals to their neighbors.

According to Bonfils, sowing provides tenants with a number of opportunities for theft. Therefore be sure to oversee this operation. If a tenant appears to be relieving himself behind a bush, he's more than likely scooping out a pile of grain to be recovered later. The *mauvais métayer* may take hours to sow a field, but he's only attempting to try his master's patience in order to carry out his schemes. A bashful landowner who fails to search the petticoats and bodices of his tenants' wives and daughters during the picking of fruit trees will later discover that they have retrieved three-fourths of the fruit for themselves. Finally, if a landlord has been fortunate enough in having found a relatively honest fellow to farm his land, refuse absolutely to allow him to depart before the expiration of the lease. Threaten him with the baillif if necessary: "The peasant has much fear of the law."

Bonfils's attitudes regarding the proper management of one's *domaine* were probably justified for conditions of the eighteenth century. By the nineteenth century, however, landlords were no longer interested in merely preserving their revenues against tenant theft but were actively seeking ways to increase production. Virtually all recognized that *métayage* prevented most tenants from accumulating enough capital for reinvestment. In 1835 the costs of improving a farm of one hundred hectares were estimated at 40,000 francs alone.[6] Capital investment on this scale was far beyond the means of *métayers*. During the debate over tenure in the *Société d'agriculture,* J. B. Avril, a critic of *métayage,* produced figures to show that the sharecroppers on the *Sociéte's* own model farms actually earned less than a family of day-laborers.[7] Any investment in improving production would, therefore, have to be made by the landowners themselves. In many cases, this is precisely what happened. This sudden interest by landlords in the condition of their farms was considered so remarkable that the practice was given a new tenurial designation. *Métayage ameliorée* thus came to be distinguished from the traditional *métayage ordinaire,* where tenants were effectively left to their own resources. This reform of sharecropping, so it was argued, would not only ensure that the owner's commands would be obeyed but would allow the tenant to share in the benefits of increased profits.

Proponents of *métayage ameliorée* were quick to point out that these benefits were not entirely material. When the Marquis d'Espeuilles adopted this system, an observer noted a distinct change in the attitudes of his tenants. "The influence of *métayage ameliorée* on the condition of sharecroppers is remarkable. A spirit of order and proper work habits is developing among them. They possess clean and decent households, they live better and, as a result, can work harder."[8] Once *métayers* saw the benefits that were possible when they were guided by their enlightened masters, their stubborn resistance would disappear. As one writer put it, "The proprietor will be the head, the *métayer* the arms, but arms which are loyal and obedient to all commands."

Unfortunately, such moral improvements were not always forthcoming. According to the theory behind *métayage ameliorée,* tenants should have eagerly welcomed the new interest that landlords were showing in their farms since both owner and tenant stood to gain equally from any improvements. Indeed, the principle of equality was seen as the very foundation of sharecropping. The owner supplied the land, seed, and stock; the tenant the labor. Both divided profits equally. But this was not how most tenants saw it. While improvements did require a substantial financial outlay, they also necessitated considerable increases in labor. In fact, labor was one of the largest single factors involved in transforming production. In 1854 one member of the *Société d'agriculture,* after visiting a *domaine* whose owner had succeeded in doubling wheat yields in ten years, concluded that "this success has been obtained by much ingenuity and perseverance, but not by considerable financial sacrifice."[9] True, improvements required the purchase of more and better cattle, the construction of new stables and barns and the acquisition of improved plows; but creating drainage and irrigation ditches to improve soil meant many long hours of back-breaking labor. Liming the soils required weeks of turning the marl into the earth as well as numerous cartings to lime quarries. Stone and lumber for new farm buildings had to be hauled to the farm as well. All these tasks were shouldered by the tenant and his family and represented a considerable physical investment.

If the introduction of the new husbandry was to be successful, the tenant himself had to be assured that he would benefit directly from his increased efforts. Theoretically, at least, these would surely be realized by tenants. While he received only a half share of total farm production, if profits rose so too would the size of his share. It was only just, therefore, that tenants should contribute something towards increasing production. In reality, however, the situation was not that simple. As Avril pointed out, *both the landowner and the tenant had to be assured that increased profits made possible from improvements would be at least double the sum of their initial investments*.

> In effect, if we consider first the landowner, it is evident that he will resist any project of improvement that would not be double the interest on his capital since he receives only half the product. As to the sharecropper, any improvement must pay him at least double the value of his labor since he will divide the product with the proprietor.[10]

In other words, the proprietor who invested 10,000 francs in improving his farm had to realize an eventual gain of 20,000 francs. The same would be true for his tenant. However, the amount of time usually required before investments could be covered by increased profits was ten to fifteen years, depending on the market price of farm commodities. Barring any unforeseen disasters, the proprietor would be sure to realize a net profit. The same was not always true for tenants, simply because their leases ran for only three years and they had no guarantee that the leases would be renewed. If a tenant should cooperate with his landlord in undertaking such a project and then find himself turned out of the farm after three years, his own investment in labor would have been for nothing. Another factor often overlooked by critics of *métayage* was the effect on tenant income when arable land was transformed into pasture. It took two to three years before new pastureland was able to produce sufficient grasses for grazing. During that time such fields contributed nothing to the tenant's income and, in fact, actually cut directly into his subsistence. His only gains in such a project would be realized several years later, assuming that he continued to occupy the *domaine*.

Tenants' uncertainty as to whether or not their leases would be renewed had some basis in fact. At Larochemillay census returns show that between thirty and forty percent of all tenant families changed their residence between each five-year interval of the census. Thirty-five percent of tenant families were listed as having lived or the same *domaine* for only a single census year, and twenty-eight percent for only two consecutive census years. In other words, sixty-three percent of all tenant families in the commune remained at one *domaine* for less than ten years. Frequent changes of residence were the usual experience of most tenant families, and it is unlikely that many viewed the time, effort, and money involved in improving farm production of a particular *domaine* as in any way benefiting them.

In fact, the years between 1840 and 1860 were marked by increasing frustration on the part of landlords who attempted to induce *métayers* to cooperate in the implementation of improvements. Every initiative appears to have provoked grumbling, delays, and outright resistance on the part of tenants. "Proprietors," claimed one writer, "are positively prevented from introducing improvements every day by the neglect, bad will or even outright refusal with which their *métayers* oppose them. . . . All attempts usually collapse before the invincible spirit of routine."[11] The 1848 commissions investigating local working conditions came to similar conclusions.

> Any attempt at improvement begins with investments in money and in labor. . . . But it is difficult to clearly regulate the share of each party and the fear of being cheated, joined to the spirit of routine, most often prevents even the most advantageous improvements. The sharecropper contributes only an amount of labor strictly necessary for the work he has executed for centuries, changing neither his tools or methods of farming.[12]

The note French rural economist Etienne Jouzíer echoed the same view decades later. "The independent spirit of the sharecropper, his own self-interest, will not fail to take its revenge. Any innovation coming from 'le maître' will end in failure, any improvement will be delayed indefinitely."[13]

Proprietors attempted to resolve this problem by inserting clauses into their leases assigning their *métayers* specific tasks to be performed and enforcing them by strict surveillance. Direct participation by landowners in the implementation of farm improvements was viewed by most agronomists as the only real means of increasing production under *métayage*. Avril, himself a critic of sharecropping, admitted that substantial benefits could be produced under such tenure so long as constant supervision by proprietors was maintained. He was also quick to point out, however, that the interests of the *métayer* also had to be táken into consideration. "Orders ought never to be such that they cannot be modified by the *métayer's* own opinion, and his interests ought also to weigh in the balance. If one wishes to utilize the labor of *métayers* it is, above all, necessary to appreciate that part of the profits which he should receive in all fairness."

Yet constant surveillance by landowners could also be a drawback, particularly in a region such as the Nivernais where most wealthy proprietors resided in Paris rather than on their estates. Because of this many government officials advocated the substitution of *fermage* for *métayage*. Under *fermage* the proprietors would furnish land, tools, and animals plus a year's seed in return for a fixed annual rent. The entire management of the farm would be assumed by the tenant, including the repair of all buildings and equipment and any costs for improvement. Avril argued that under *fermage* there would exist sufficient incentive for tenants to increase productivity since, by paying a fixed rent, any increase in farm profits would be to their advantage. "It cannot be doubted that a *fermier,* who alone profits from the care and work devoted to improve farming, would receive more advantage than the sharecropper whose situation will almost always lead him to oppose improvements."

Avril cautioned that such a transition in tenure relationships would not be made without difficulties. Few tenants at that time possessed sufficient capital to invest in costly improvements. Even after improvements had been made, a *fermier* would have to have enough money to cover at least the first two years of his lease; enough for the first year's rent plus enough to cover the second year should any crop losses occur or the price of farm products fall.[14] Since few tenants had this kind of capital, lack of competition between potential lessors would have the effect of keeping down rents.

Recognizing these problems, Avril advocated that landowners finance the costs of improvements themselves under the system of *métayage ameliorée,* thereby creating the foundation for progress in agriculture and also for the accumulation of capital by tenants that would enable them to take up *fermage* leases. "After sharecroppers, through better farming, order and economy, have achieved a financially comfortable position, they will hasten to take over farms on money leases. By the same token, proprietors, finding experienced and finacially solvent men, will no longer fear to entrust their properties and will be able to free themselves from a daily surveillance which rarely gives them advantageous returns."

Avril also emphasized that, if *fermage* was to succeed, leases would have to be lengthened to nine or even twelve years. Crop rotations then being employed in the Nivernais required at least three or four seasons, involving the successive planting of wheat, spring grains, artificial meadows, and root crops. Long leases were therefore necessary if a tenant was to be able to take full advantage of the new husbandry on each section of his farm.

To many, Avril's suggestions seemed impossible. As one critic exclaimed, "The reform of tenure is well nigh impossible in a country such as ours where proprietors consider a lease of twelve years as akin to outright alienation." In fact, it appears that the majority of landowners in the Nièvre did adopt *fermage*. According to census figures, by 1851 53.5 percent of all tenants in the Nièvre were *fermiers*. In 1866, when the government undertook its monumental survey of agriculture in France, *métayage* was reported as having virtually disappeared from the cantons of Nevers, Saint-Pierre-le-Moutier, Saint-Benin-d'Azy, Decize, and Pougues. By 1872 the percentage of *fermiers* in the Nièvre had increased to 69 percent of all tenants and in two decades it rose to 84 percent.[15]

Métayage did not disappear entirely, however. In the southeastern regions of the *département* and particularly in the Morvan, it remained the predominant form of tenure. This geographic distribution of tenure forms can be readily seen in the following maps, based on cantonal returns from the 1852 and 1872 agricultural surveys.[16] By mid-century the cantons in the center, north and south showed the percentage of tenant-held farms worked by *fermiers* to range from 85 percent to 97 percent. In the cantons bordering on the Bourbonnais and in those of the Morvan, *métayers* comprised between 60 and 70 percent of all tenants. During the next two decades, *fermage* continued to spread throughout the Nièvre and began to penetrate even the Morvan. In the cantons of Château-Chinon, in the central Morvan, the percentage of tenants listed as *métayers* fell from 43.4 to 12.5 percent. In Lormes, in the northern Morvan, this proportion dropped from 47.4 to 11.1 percent. *Fermage* increased in the southern Morvan as well, though not as rapidly. In the canton of Luzy, where over 70 percent of all tenants were *métayers* in 1852, by 1872 only 42 percent were. This decline in *métayage* was noted with satisfaction by the subprefect who called it "a revolution" in tenure relations.[17]

It is noteworthy that the transition to *fermage* occurred on the greatest scale in precisely those regions of the Nivernais where agricultural production increased most rapidly after the 1840s. *Métayage* continued in the Morvan, not because landowners there chose to embark on improvements within the framework of sharecropping but because the new husbandry failed to develop within the region until relatively late in the century. This was due largely to the physical isolation of the Morvan, which continued to lack adequate means of communication and transport facilities. High transport costs made it difficult to export agricultural products out of the region while at the

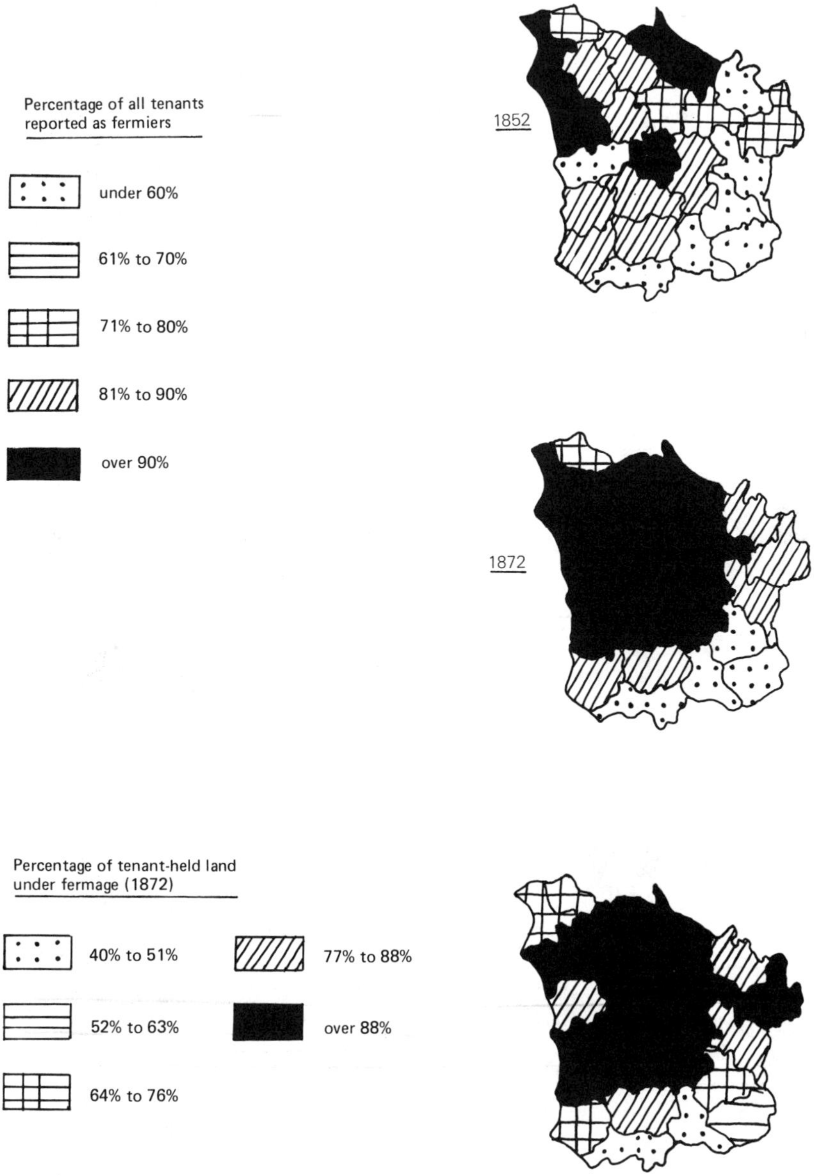
Percentage of all tenants reported as fermiers
under 60%
61% to 70%
71% to 80%
81% to 90%
over 90%
1852
1872
Percentage of tenant-held land under fermage (1872)
40% to 51%
52% to 63%
64% to 76%
77% to 88%
over 88%

Map 12. Distribution of Tenure in the Nièvre

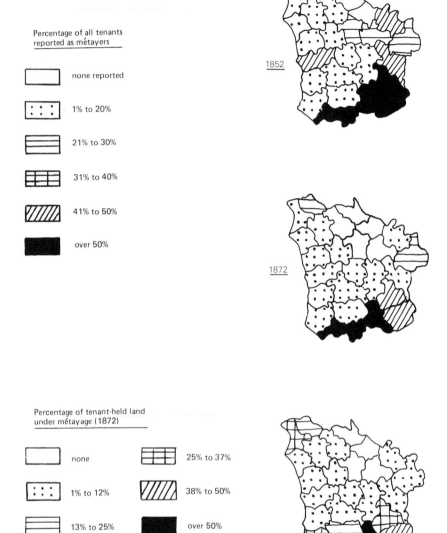

Percentage of all tenants
reported as métayers

- none reported
- 1% to 20%
- 21% to 30%
- 31% to 40%
- 41% to 50%
- over 50%

1852

1872

Percentage of tenant-held land
under métayage (1872)

- none
- 1% to 12%
- 13% to 25%
- 25% to 37%
- 38% to 50%
- over 50%

Map 12. Distribution of Tenure in the Nièvre (continued)

180

same time inhibiting the importation of lime needed to improve soil fertility. M*étayage continued to exist within an agricultural econo*my that was essentially backward.

This geographic distribution of *fermage* and *métayage* is reflected in the development of tenure relations at Limanton and Larochemillay. The transition to *fermage* at Limanton is evident in both census lists and lease contracts. Table 39 shows the percentage of tenants listed as either

Table 39. Tenure relations at Limanton according to census lists

Years	% Fermier	% Métayer	N	Years	% Fermier	% Métayer	N
1820	20.0	80.0	40	1856	66.7	33.3	42
1836	18.9	81.1	37	1861	66.7	33.3	42
1841	36.6	63.4	41	1866	63.4	36.6	41
1846	46.3	53.7	41	1872	82.9	17.1	41
1851	47.5	52.5	40	1876	91.3	8.7	46

fermiers or *métayers* for each census year. In 1820 and 1836 only a fifth of all tenants were *fermiers*. During the 1840s this percentage began to rise so that in 1856, 1861 and 1866 two-thirds of all tenants in the commune were listed as *fermiers,* and by 1876 only four tenants were *métayers.* Unfortunately, census lists for Larochemillay do not permit a comparison to be made between the two communes. In most years, census-takers listed tenants as either *cultivateurs* or *laboureurs,* terms which mask the specific form of tenure under which their farms were held. Only in 1846 and 1876 was a clear distinction made. In 1846 only 4.6 percent of the tenants in the commune were listed as *fermiers,* and by 1876 this percentage had risen to only 17.9.

A comparison of leases made between 1800 and 1864 for *domaines* in each commune reveals that *métayage continued to dominate tenure relations at Larochemillay even as landowners at Limanton* were adopting *fermage* agreements. In all, one hundred and two leases were drawn up at Limanton and one hundred and thirteen at Larochemillay.[18] The percentage of *fermage* and *métayage* contracts for each twenty-year period after 1800 is shown in Table 40. While the vast majority of leases at Larochemillay were sharecropping agreements, at Limanton the percentage of *fermage* contracts rose from 35 between 1800 and 1820 to almost 50 between 1821 and 1840, and to nearly 70 during the next decades.

Even more significant was the growing length of leases at Limanton. During the first twenty years of the century, half of all leases were for periods of one or three years, with no lease longer than six years. Between 1821 and 1840 over 68 percent of all leases were for more than

Table 40. Tenure relations according to leases

Limanton

	Form of tenure		Length of lease in years					
Years	% fermage	% métayage	1	3	6	9	12	N
1800–1820	35.0	65.0	6	4	10			20
1821–1840	48.6	51.4	3	7	14	10		35
1841–1864	68.1	31.9	4	8	16	15	4	47

Larochemillay

	Form of Tenure		Length of Lease in Years:					
Years	% fermage	% métayage	1	3	6	9	12	N
1800–1820	22.4	77.6	4	6	37	2		49
1821–1840	9.7	90.3	5	9	15	2		31
1841–1864	15.2	84.8	3	21	8	1		33

six years and over a fourth were for nine years (the first nine-year lease was made in 1835). Between 1841 and 1864 only four leases were for a single year while over 40 percent were for nine years or more. At Larochemillay, on the other hand, the length of leases not only failed to increase but actually tended to decrease. Between 1800 and 1821 three-fourths of all leases were for six years; only one-fifth were for either one or three years. During the next two decades, only 48 percent were for six years, while 45 percent were for one or three years. By the last period, almost three-fourths of all contracts at Larochemillay were for three years or less.

This development of tenure relations at Limanton and Larochemillay had far-reaching effects on the lives and fortunes of tenants in both communes. The transition to *fermage* at Limanton not only allowed tenants to exercise greater control over the marketing of farm products but resulted in a significant increase in tenant wealth as well. The persistence of *métayage* at Larochemillay did not, however, mean that the condition of tenants remained unchanged. In fact, there is every indication that the living standards of *métayers* actually declined somewhat after 1850 as a result of increased exactions demanded of them by landlords faced with rising prices and stagnant agricultural production. The divergence of tenant fortunes was not merely the result of rising incomes experienced by Limanton tenants but was accelerated by a parallel decline in the incomes of their counterparts at Larochmillay. As tenants at Limanton were increasing their control over the operation of their farms and were in effect becoming independent capitalist farmers, tenants at Larochemillay remained subject to the will and dictates of their landlords and remained little more than hired hands.

The Divergence of Tenant Fortunes

Certainly one of the most important changes brought about by the transition from *métayage* to *fermage* was its effect on the relationship between tenants and the market. Under *métayage* direct control over the sale of farm produce was tightly restricted. There were several reasons for this. In the first place, that portion of farm production accruing to the *métayer* was largely consumed by his own family, leaving little in the way of marketable surpluses. Second, the marketing of the lessor's share was in most cases controlled by the landowner himself or by his agent. Most leases stipulated that harvested crops were to be stored in the landowner's granary. With large stocks of grain thus accumulated from several *domaines*, wealthy landowners were in a position to withhold grain from the market until prices began to rise in the late winter and early spring, thereby ensuring them a greater profit.[19]

Similar control by the landlords was exercised over the sale of cattle and other farm animals. It was clearly in their interest to do so, since, by allowing their *métayers* to carry out such transactions, they ran a risk of being cheated by an unscrupulous tenant who could easily pocket part of the proceeds without his master's knowledge. This control over cattle sales is made explicit in Emile Guillaumin's *Life of a Simple Man*. Throughout Bertin's memoirs, sales and purchases of cattle were invariably managed by Bertin's landlord or his agent. At local fairs, Bertin's role was usually that of a herdsman awaiting his landlord's decision on when to seel and at what price.[20] Such control enabled landlords to determine the price at which cattle would be sold and thereby virtually dictate to his tenant the income that he would derive from his own labor. This domination of landlords and their agents at local markets is evident from a description of a cattle fair given by Emile Guillaumin.

> The fairs are the principal field of action for the *fermiers-généraux* (agents of landowners) . . . . To better display their domination they are always escorted by several of their *métayers* whose thin and sad countenances belie the seeming well-being of their ruddy faces. When they sell, prices are discussed in low voices with the merchants, all of whom they know, dealing in blocks for a herd of animals from several *domaines*, and indicating to each of the *métayers* the price of his own merchandise . . . . To effect purchases of animals outside of the presence of their sharecroppers does not embarrass them in the least.[21]

Landlord control over the marketing of farm produce had direct consequences on tenant livelihood. It must be remembered that the economies of a *domaine* were, from the point of view of the tenant, household economies. Indeed it is often impossible to make distinctions between the two. Decisions by landlords affecting what was to be grown, how many animals were to be purchased and the price at which they were to be sold may have been carried out with a view of obtaining the highest possible revenues from their estates, yet for the *métayer* such decisions affected the very quality of their lives. These two views were not always the same and at times conflicted. In one passage from his memoirs, Etienne Bertin recalled a violent scene that took place between his parents and their landlord over just such a question.

> My father wanted to sell one of the sows and some little ones because food was scarce that year. But the master declared that he wished to keep the mother and let the little ones grow bigger.
> "We can buy bran," he said.
> That word was like fire to powder, for they were convinced that, when settling up at the previous Martinmas, more had been reckoned for bran than had been bought. They also considered as absolutely ridiculous the price of the fat oxen which had been sold when my father was not present. At different times my mother had sworn that Fauconnet should repent before he died.[22]

Bertin's mother took the opportunity to demand that any further purchases of bran should not be charged to them. A bitter argument ensued that ended with the dismissal of Bertin's father and a threat of prosecution for slander. Yet even without such open conflicts, landlord control over the operation of the *domaine* could be a trying experience even for the most patient of sharecroppers. As Bertin was later to remark of one of his landlords, "What was so unbearable for us was the nearness of the master, his constant presence."

Tenants who held their farms under *fermage* contracts, however, carried out all sales and purchases themselves. The *fermier* was the sole master of the *domaine*, subject only to the provisions that his landlord wished to insert into the lease.[23] Legally, he held the farm in a kind of usufruct, his only obligations being to return the farm at the termination of his lease in the same condition in which it had existed when he had taken it up. This held true for farm stock as well. At the end of each lease, the *fermier* was required to return a stock of animals of a value equivalent to that stated in the original contract. During the life of the lease, he could sell and purchase animals as he pleased and keep the profits from such transactions. Victor de Cheverry's description of a *fermier* household in the 1860s gives the impression that this ability to conduct all market transactions was considered important enough to be the sole preserve of the head of household. "The *maître de communauté*, subject to the same labor as the other members of the association, also carries out all purchases and sales. It is he who goes to the fairs and markets, and it is he who manages all external business . . . All the accounts of the *communauté* rest with him and it is left to him, by right of honor, to drive the cattle."[24]

Yet increased independence of *fermiers* was not the only difference distinguishing them from *métayers*. After 1850 tenant wealth at Limanton began to far outstrip that of Larochemillay tenants. After mid-century, as Limanton landlords were adopting progressively longer leases at fixed rents, their tenants were able to reap increasing profits from agriculture as prices rose and production expanded. At Larochemillay landlords employed just the opposite strategy. *Métayage* was preserved and the length of leases grew increasingly shorter. In fact landlords in both communes were working toward the same goal, to increase their own revenues, but because conditions at Limanton and Larochemillay were so vastly different the methods by which their common goal was achieved came to differ as well.

Tenant relations at Larochemillay developed within an agrarian economy that remained undeveloped well into the second half of the century. Increases in productivity could be achieved only by expanding fodder crops through the introduction of artificial meadows. This would have enabled farmers to enlarge their herds, which in turn would increase soil fertility by providing greater stocks of animal fertilizers. The lime-deficient soils of the Morvan could not, however, support clovers or alfalfa without considerable marling of the soil. The poor condition of local roads made transport costs extremely high and the importation of marl thus prohibitive. Because the bulk of landlord income was derived from his share in farm production, revenues could be increased only as a result of a rise in the market value of agricultural goods. Yet higher revenues obtained in this manner merely reflected the general inflation of prices for all commodities after mid-century and therefore did not represent a growth in real income.

Landlords operating within the framework of *métayage* did possess one means of increasing their incomes. Besides their share in farm produce, they also levied a money rent known as the *bellemain*. This was intended to cover the tenant's share of state taxes as well as rent for the use of farm buildings. During the 1850s landlords at Larochemillay progressively increased this charge as a means of raising their incomes. For example, a *métayage* contract drawn up in 1843 for the *domaine* at

Mesle stated that the tenant was to pay two hundred and fifty francs in *bellemain*. The same contract declared that the lessor's share of farm production was valued at five hundred francs. Another sharecropping agreement for Mesle, made ten years later, declared that the lessor's share was valued at five hundred and twenty-nine francs, indicating that no significant increase in productivity had occurred in over a decade. However, the tenant was held to pay three hundred francs in *bellemain*. In other words, while the value of production rose less than six percent in ten years, the price of the *bellemain* increased by twenty percent. In another case the marquis Bertrand de Rivière fixed the *bellemain* for his *domaine* at Rivière at two hundred and fifty francs in 1850. The same contract stated that his share would be comprised of one hundred double decaliters of rye, twenty of wheat and twenty-five of oats, valued at four hundred and eleven francs. Ten years later another *bail à métairie* for Rivière gave the same quantities of cereals for the lesson's share. The *bellemain*, however, had been increased to three hundred and fifty francs.

Such increases in the *bellemain* could not be justified on the basis of a rise in state land taxes. In 1852 the average rate of taxation for a hectare of arable land in the Nièvre was reported to be 1.20 francs. Twenty-two years later the rate was 1.19 francs. During the same period, the rate of taxation for a hectare of meadowland actually declined from 3.92 francs to 3.59 francs.[25] Landlords at Larochemillay were able to demand such rent increases largely because of growing competition among tenants to secure a farm. Antoine Desforges, who resided for several years in the nearby commune of Flety, wrote that "the rents are clearly exaggerated, but the fault lies with the tenants who make war upon one another rather than coming to some sort of agreement. I have often counseled them to organize themselves. Some recognize the necessity but do not dare. Others, more royalist than the king, consider me to be revolutionary when I speak to them about it."[26] Guillaumin found the situation in the Bourbonnais to be much the same. Landlords there employed one-year leases that they renewed at their will. "The masters can change the conditions whenever they please by increasing the *impôt colonique* (the Bourbonnais term for the *bellemain*). . . . Sharecroppers usually accept it since moving to another farm is always a cause of dread and means considerable expense. They prefer to accept such unjust conditions and remain where they are."[27]

The *bellemain* was a heavy charge for sharecroppers and its progressive increase cut deeply into family incomes. An additional fifty or one hundred francs in rent could easily wipe out any meager profit a tenant might realize at the end of a hard year of labor. The precarious nature of sharecropper incomes can be understood when revenues and expenses are analyzed for a typical *domaine* at Larochemillay during the 1860s. The figures in Table 41 represent an approximate assessment of farm income and costs for a fifty hectare *domaine* for one year.[28] The principal sources of earnings were sales of grain which totaled about 1,740 francs. Vegetables and courtyard products added another 510 francs. Cattle sales were another major source of revenue. Each spring the oldest pair of oxen from the farm's plow team would be sold to local butchers or *emboucheurs* from the lowlands. These would be replaced by heifers which were broken into the yoke by light work such as carting or harrowing so that, by fall, they would be ready to shoulder the heavier burden of plowing. With the sale of sheep and pigs, revenues for farm animals could total about 1,600 francs. Thus, a farm of this size would probably bring in a gross income of some 3,860 francs.

From these earnings the lessor would deduct his half as well as the *bellemain* and various other lesser charges known as *menus suffrages*. These included a few chickens, a dozen eggs, and perhaps a kilogram of butter. This left the sharecropper with approximately 1,550 francs from which he had to deduct wages for farm servants and additional labor hired during the harvest season. From what remained the tenant had to feed his own family. Various government inquiries into living standards of rural families during this time place the cost of feeding a family of five at about 300 to 350 francs a year. Assuming that the *domaine* was worked by a *communauté* of three families, their subsistence needs would represent a total cost of approximately 1,000 francs. After all these deductions are made, a tenant's total profit for the year amounted to a mere 60 francs. This "profit" could easily be eaten away by various purchases of salt, pepper, candles, oil, and the like, none of which could be produced on the farm. If the *bellemain* were increased by 50 francs or more, the sharecropper would be faced with the choice of either reducing his standard of living or moving to another farm in the unlikely hope that conditions might be better elsewhere. The livelihood of most *métayer* families was evidently one of never-ending poverty, of a perpetual existence on that precarious dividing line between subsistence and privation. The death of cattle from disease, a late winter, or insufficient rain might mean a drop in his landlord's revenue, but for the *métayer* it could spell ruin. As Guillaumin put it, "Their conditions are such that they can only vegetate in misery."

In direct contrast to the situation at Larochemillay, landlords at Limanton adopted a policy of increasing production as much as possible and doing so by providing tangible economic incentives for their tenants. To be sure, the expansion of the agrarian economy at Limanton was made possible by the commune's geographic location, yet landlords assured themselves that farm revenues would be increased by the active

Table 41. Farm revenues and expenses Larochemillay

Distribution of crops		Farm animals	
10 ha. rye	3 ha. potatoes	6 oxen	4 calves
2 ha. wheat	10 ha. pasture	4 cows	40 sheep
.5 ha. oats	23 ha. fallow	4 heifers	10 pigs
1.5 ha. buckwheat			

Revenues

Wheat: 12 hectoliters   per ha. × 2 ha. = 24   hectoliters
                               less seed   5   "
                                             ───
                                              19   " @ 20 f./hectoliter   380.00 f.

Rye: 12   "   per ha. × 10 ha. = 120 hectoliters
                               less seed   25   "
                                             ───
                                              95   " @ 13 f./hectoliter   1,235.00 f.

Oats: 12   "   per ha. × .5 ha. = 6   hectoliters
                               less seed   2.5   "
                                             ───
                                              3.5   " @ 6.50 f./hectoliter   22.75 f.

Buckwheat: 12   "   per ha. × 1.5 ha. = 18   "
                               less seed   2.5   "
                                             ────
                                             15.5   " @ 6.50 f./hectoliter   100.75 f.

Potatoes: 100   "   per ha. × 3 ha. = 300   "
                               less seed   60
                                             ───
                                             240   " @ 1.50 f./hectoliter   360.00 f.

Peas and beans	80.00 f.
Courtyard products	70.00 f.
2 oxen weighing 400 kg. each @ 1.20 f./kg.	960.00 f.
1 cow weighing 300 kg. @ 1.00 f./kg.	300.00 f.
1 calf weighing 60 kg. @ 1.20 f./kg.	72.00 f.
20 sheep @ 10 f. each	200.00 f.
2 pigs @ 40 f. each	80.00 f.
	3,860.50 f.
Landlord's share in farm production	1,930.25 f.
Bellemain	300.00 f.
menu suffrages	20.00 f.
Labor hired during harvest season	400.00 f.
1 male servant	100.00 f.
1 female servant	50.00 f.
Subsistence needs of family*	1,000.00 f.
Total Expenses:	3,800.25 f.
Total Tenant Profit:	60.25 f.

*Assuming three families of six adults and nine children

and willing participation of their tenants. Because tenants were themselves able to benefit from economic development, improvements in agriculture were introduced in their direct interest and not against it. By employing long-term leases at fixed rents, tenants made every effort to increase farm production and thereby their own profits. This was especially true for tenants who concentrated on cattle raising. Between 1851 and 1879 the net revenue derived from a hectare of meadow in the *département* as a whole increased by forty-nine percent. However, the rate of *fermage* for a hectare of first-class meadowland rose during the same period by only thirty-seven percent.[29]

Just how much a tenant at Limanton could profit from these arrangements is evident in the following calculation of earnings and expenses for a fifty-hectare farm at Limanton (table 42).[30] Unlike the *domaine* at Larochemillay, where almost half the farmland was left in fallow, only a fifth of the Limanton *domaine* was left uncultivated each year, which increased considerably the number of hectares planted in crops. The use of artificial meadows further allowed Limanton tenants to maintain twice as many head of cattle as could the tenants at Larochemillay. These factors, together with greater yields, meant that a similar-size farm at Limanton could produce annual revenues that exceeded those at Larochemillay by 3,000 francs.

Labor costs for Limanton tenants tended to exceed those at Larochemillay, in part because a larger area of farmland was placed into production, and also because wages in the Bazois tended to be higher than those in the Morvan. Moreover, the Limanton tenant, as a *fermier*, was obliged to pay all state land taxes as well as insurance costs, which together added over 500 francs to his expenses. Nevertheless, despite greater production costs, the Limanton tenant stood to make an annual profit of 1,600 francs.

When compared to the revenues earned by a landlord of a fifty-hectare *domaine* at Larochemillay, the 2,500 francs rent obtained by the Limanton *domaine* does not, at first glance, appear to have justified the latter's strategy. Indeed a tenant's profits at Limanton could potentially equal the yearly rent obtained by his landlord, a rather remarkable fact when one considers the traditional view of French landlords as rackrenters unwilling to allow the least amount of potential profit escape their grasp. Yet it should also be noted that the rents derived from *fermage* contracts were pure profits entailing no expenses whatsoever on the part of the lessor. Insurance, taxes, the repair of buildings and equipment, and the purchase of new animals—all were entirely the responsibility of the *fermier*. At Larochemillay these charges could easily reduce a landlord's revenues by 500 francs or more. In addition, the landlord who leased his farm to a *fermier* was sheltered from both the vagaries of the market and any calamities of nature. In effect, landlords at Limanton were willing to accept lower immediate returns in exchange for anticipated increases in the value of their land. A brief look at leases for individual *domaines* in the commune shows that this policy was not without its merits. In 1842 the *domaine* at Grand Anizy was let for six years at a rent of 1,460 francs. In 1860 it was let for nine years at 1,650

Table 42. Farm revenues and expenses Limanton

Distribution of crops		Farm animals:	
10 ha. wheat	16 ha. pasture	12 oxen	5 calves
5 ha. oats	7 ha. clover	1 bull	50 sheep
2 ha. rye	10 ha. fallow	6 cows	10 pigs
		12 heifers	

Revenues

Wheat: 15 hectoliters   per ha. × 10 ha. = 150 hectoliters
                             less seed   25   "
                                          ——————
                                          125   " @ 20 f./hectoliter   2,500.00 f.

Oats: 15   "   per ha. × 5 ha. = 75 hectoliters
                             less seed   12.5   "
                                          ——————
                                          62.5   " @ 6.50 f./hectoliter   406.25 f.

Rye: 15   "   per ha. × 2 ha. = 30 hectoliters
                             less seed   10   "
                                          ——————
                                           20   " @ 13.00 f./hectoliter   260.00 f.

Peas and beans	80.00 f.
Courtyard products	70.00 f.
4 oxen weighing 500 kg. each @ 1.20 f./kg.	2,400.00 f.
2 cows weighing 400 kg. each @ 1.00 f./kg.	800.00 f.
1 calf weighing 60 kg. @ 1.20 f./kg.	72.00 f.
20 sheep @ 10 f. each	200.00 f.
2 pigs @ 40 f. each	80.00 f.
Total revenues:	6,868.20 f.

Expenses:	
Fermage	2,500.00 f.
Menus suffrages	20.00 f.
Labor hired during harvest	550.00 f.
2 male servants	500.00 f.
2 female servants	300.00 f.
Taxes	400.00 f.
Insurance	125.00 f.
Subsistence needs of family*	800.00 f.
Total expenses:	4,695.00 f.
Total tenant profit:	1,673.00 f.

*Assuming two families of four adults and six children

francs. The *domaine* at Colombier, leased for 4,000 francs a year in 1840, brought its owner 5,000 francs in 1863. The annual rent for Bouillots in 1847 was 1,800 francs. By 1862 it had risen to 2,000 francs.

Tenants as well as landlords at Limanton benefited from the expansion of agriculture. One aspect of growing tenant wealth is reflected in the size of marriage dowries provided their children. Dowries were considered to be a kind of advance on a child's inheritance and their value can thus be taken as an indication of their parents' level of wealth. While only a handful of marriage contracts were drawn up by this group between 1800 and 1864, the trend towards larger and larger dowries, after mid-century is evident. In the ten contracts made up to 1845, the average value of daughters' dowries was 294 francs. Only one girl received more than 500 francs. After 1850, however, the marriage portions given to tenants' daughters rose dramatically. Of the seven contracts drawn up between 1850 and 1864, five girls received dowries of 1,800 francs or more, two of whom received more than 3,000 francs. The average for all the dowries was 1,411 francs, almost five times the average for the previous four and one-half decades.

Occasionally, the contracts reveal the growing wealth of individual families. When Anne Doreau married Jean Mathe in 1828, she received as her dowry a trousseau valued at 200 francs and 400 francs in cash. When their daughter Louise married in 1864, they were able to provide her with a trousseau valued at 500 francs plus an additional 3,000 francs in cash that was declared to be independent of her eventual inheritance rights. The parents of Agathe Roy, *métayers* at Limanton, were able to give their daughter, at the time of her marriage in 1836, a trousseau and cash with a total value of 350 francs. When Agathe's own daughter married in 1863, she was provided with a trousseau valued at 600 francs and a donation of 1,200 francs.

The clearest evidence of a rise in tenant incomes at Limanton is seen in the growing number of land purchases made by them after 1850. According to the cadastre, only three tenants owned any land in the decade following its compilation in 1846. In 1861, 1866, and 1872, the number of landowning tenants rose to nine, or about a fifth of all tenants. In most cases the amount of land held by these persons was between one and two hectares, yet many acquired fairly substantial holdings in the course of a decade or so of purchases. François Guillot, tenant at Grand Anizy, acquired some seven hectares between 1855 and 1869. His neighbor Jean Regnier purchased a similar amount of land between 1868 and 1876. Claude Vadrot, a *fermier* at Arcilly, made six separate purchases of land between 1863 and 1875 totaling five and one-half hectares. Denis Merlin, *fermier* at Villars, bought over eight hectares between 1859 and 1879. Perhaps the greatest success was that of Louis Bondoux. In eight different purchases made between 1859 and 1876, he acquired a total of twenty-one hectares.

The extent of land acquisition by Limanton tenants is evident in the figures given in Table 43. Here tenant land acquisitions are broken down into five-year periods according to whether the land was acquired through an inheritance or by purchase. It should be noted that the figures here represent only land acquired in the commune of Limanton. Several contracts drawn up by notaries for tenants during this period indicate that purchases of land were also made in adjoining communes and would not show up in the cadastre. The figures in this table do not, therefore, represent the total extent of tenant land acquisitions.

Table 43. Tenant landowners at Limanton

Years	Acquisition by			Alienation through			Balance
	Inheritance	Purchase	Total	Succession	Sales	Total	
1845–1850		5.75 ha	5.75 ha		.29 ha	.29 ha	+ 5.46 ha
1851–1855		2.86	2.86		3.69	3.69	− .83
1856–1860	2.33 ha	8.84	11.17		1.27	1.27	+ 9.90
1861–1865	4.47	16.93	21.40		1.17	1.17	+20.23
1866–1870	.83	10.86	11.69	1.90 ha	1.10	3.00	+ 8.69
1871–1875	.01	1.86	1.87	13.35	3.51	16.86	−14.99
Totals	7.64	47.10	54.74	15.25	11.03	26.28	+33.92
(%)	(14%)	(86%)		(58%)	(42%)		

In the decade between 1845 and 1855, Limanton tenants as a group purchased a total of 8.7 hectares. During the next ten years they acquired a total of 32.5 hectares, most of it through purchases. In the next five years, a further 11 hectares were acquired, nearly all by purchases. Interestingly, the period after 1870 was marked by a sudden drop in acquisitions. This abrupt halt in land purchases was probably the result of the disruptions caused by the Franco-Prussian War and the subsequent occupation of the Nièvre by Prussian troops. A sudden fall in meat prices in the 1870s certainly added to the problem by cutting into farm profits. During these same years, the total amount of land held by Limanton tenants fell by 15 hectares. While part of this decline was due to sales, most of the land passed on to heirs who were not themselves tenants or who did not reside in the commune.

Land acquisition by Limanton tenants becomes even more striking when compared to acquisitions made at Larochemillay tenants during the same period. The level of land acquisition in that commune came nowhere near that recorded at Limanton (Table 44). Furthermore, half the land acquired by tenants at Larochemillay between 1845 and 1875 was through inheritances, compared to only fourteen percent for tenants at Limanton. If we compare the distribution of tenant holdings at each census date for Limanton and Larochemillay, as in Table 45, the differences between the two communes become even more striking. Up to 1851, while the percentage of tenant proprietors in both communes was approximately the same, the holdings of Larochemillay tenants tended to be somewhat larger than those at Limanton. After this date, however, both the number of tenants at Limanton who owned land and the size of their holdings increased. At Larochemillay during the same period, not only did the number of landowning tenants remain fairly constant, but the average size of their holdings declined by one-half. Between 1851 and 1860, four tenants sold lands totaling some eight hectares, and by the 1860s purchases of land virtually ceased to take place. If land can be taken as a measure of wealth, then the position of tenants at Larochemillay was certainly declining at precisely the same time that the fortunes of their counterparts at Limanton were expanding.

Table 44. Tenant landowners at Larochemillay

Years	Acquisition by			Alienation through			Balance
	Inheritance	Purchase	Total	Succession	Sales	Total	
1845–1850	–	–	–	–	–	–	
1851–1855	5.87 ha	2.10 ha	7.97 ha	–	6.97 ha	6.97 ha	+ 1.00 ha
1856–1860		2.71	2.71		.81	.81	+ 1.90
1861–1865	5.41	.27	5.68				+ 5.68
1866–1870	3.04	3.19	6.23	1.20	2.02	3.22	+ 3.01
1871–1875	.60	6.20	6.80				+ 6.80
Totals	14.92	14.47	29.39	1.20	8.90	10.10	+ 19.29
(%)	(50.8)	(49.2)		(11.9)	(88.1)		

Increased wealth and greater independence in the management of the farm were not the only characteristics that came to distinguish Limanton tenants from the *métayers* of Larochemillay. As the economy of the Nivernais expanded, this independence and wealth became the basis of an entirely new set of relations between tenants and production. The *domaine* became less a means of securing subsistence and more a business enterprise. The tenant himself became less a peasant producing crops with the aim of securing subsistence and payment of ground rent,

Table 45. Tenant holdings

Limanton

	Size of holdings				% of all	mean size of
Years	−1 ha	1–2.9 ha	+3.0 ha	N	tenants	holdings
1846	1	2		3	7.3%	1.4 ha
1851	1	2		3	7.5	1.3
1856	1	1		2	4.8	1.9
1861		6	3	9	21.4	2.6
1866	5	2	2	9	22.0	2.1
1872	3	3	2	8	19.5	2.0
1876	5	2	1	8	17.4	1.1

Larochemillay

	Size of holdings				% of all	mean size of
Years	−1 ha	1–2.9 ha	+3.0 ha	N	tenants	holdings
1846	1	1	1	3	7.0%	3.1 ha
1851		2	1	3	7.5	3.1
1856	1	3		4	8.7	2.1
1861	1	3		4	10.0	1.7
1866	1	5		6	13.0	1.5
1872	1	2		3	7.5	1.6
1876	1	1		2	4.5	1.8

and more a capitalist farmer producing and marketing commodities with the aim of reinvesting profits to expand production. This is not to argue that farmers are distinguished from peasants simply because they produce for the market. Virtually all known peasant societies engage in market production to some extent. However, the marketing of cash crops for a peasant is usually prompted by the inability to meet subsistence needs solely within the existing social and economic conditions of production. The aim of the peasant is subsistence. For the farmer, however, crops are sold not only to provide goods and services for him and his family, but also to permit the expansion of his enterprise. The aim of the farmer, therefore, is reinvestment.[31]

To be sure, such a distinction is often hazy when applied to specific cases. It is, nonetheless, a useful analytical model. It is important to recognize, moreover, that such distinctions are determined by the relationship of the direct producer to the means of production. Peasants aim at subsistence not because of cultural limitations on the expansion of output through the reinvestment of capital, but because the nature of productive relations prohibits this expansion beyond mere subsistence. Such limitations were manifest at Larochemillay. By the same token, *fermiers* at Limanton were themselves able to expand production because of the development of a specific set of social relations permitting them to do so.

The extent of reinvestment carried out by *fermiers* is evident in the budgets of the Pervy *communauté* examined in 1860 by Victor de Cheverry.[32] As in all of the family studies carried out by LePlay and his followers, considerable attention was given to the precise sources of family income and the uses to which these were put. The purpose was to reveal the level of material prosperity of each representative family type. The Pervys, who leased a farm of over one hundred hectares, were clearly well off. The total value of the family's income that year (in kind and in money) amounted to just over 21,160 francs. What concerns us here is the extent to which this income was reinvested into their farm. After deductions for the *fermage,* taxes, and household consumption, the *communauté* was left with some 15,160 francs. Of this, 2,820 francs, or 18.6 percent of the total, was set aside as ready cash as well as the *pecules* of each individual family. The remaining 12,338 francs were reinvested in the farm. Unfortunately, because de Cheverry made a distinction between income allotted to household needs and income utilized for business investment, no breakdown of the uses to which this sum was employed was provided.

Evidence from Limanton would suggest that a considerable part of this capital was invested in the purchase of cattle. Of course, detailed budgets do not exist for Limanton tenants. There is every indication, however, that reinvestment on a scale similar to that of the Pervys' was carried out at Limanton, especially in the development of cattle raising and cattle fattening. In 1853, for example, Claude Laboux took up a lease for the *domaine* at Villars which, at that time, included a stock of animals with a declared value of 5,000 francs. At the time of the agricultural survey three years later, Laboux was recorded as possessing a stock of some seventy-four head with a market value of 13,125 francs. Clearly, Laboux had invested considerable money in the acquisition of additional animals, as indicated by the existence of ten *vaches d'embouche* included among his herd. Similarly, when Francois Guillot, a tenant at Arcilly, renewed his lease in 1852, the contract stated that the *domaine* stock was valued at 5,921 francs. In 1856 Guillot possessed a stock with a market value of 42,160 francs, including one hundred and twenty-four *boeufs d'embouche.* There is evidence of other *fermiers* at Limanton engaging in similar practices of acquiring animals for fattening, and on a scale that required considerable financial outlay.

The Return to Preferential Succession

Limanton *fermiers* after 1850 were far removed from the cycle of subsistence farming that had characterized their parents' condition only a generation before. Economic development and the transition to *fermage* not only swelled tenant fortunes but transformed their relationship to production and the market. Yet in one important aspect productive relations surrounding *domaine* farming remained unaltered. While the term "capitalist farmer" has been used here to describe Limanton tenants during this period, in a strict sense its use is not accurate. Capitalism defines a set of productive relations in which those who control and direct the means of production and those who labor constitute two separate classes.

This was clearly not the situation for Limanton tenants, for whom both the management of the enterprise and the provision of labor were combined in the domestic unit. *Domaine* farming remained essentially household production. Management, production, and consumption were organized along kin lines with only limited reliance on wage labor in the form of domestic servants. While by no means subsistence peasants, *fermiers* at Limanton were not fully capitalists either. Because of this, traditional practices of regulating property relations within the *communauté* continued to be carried out. That is, property relations within the productive unit were governed by kinship ties rather than capitalist relations. There is no better proof of this than the manner in which inheritances were settled.

At this point, it may be useful to review the law governing contracts of association as put forth in the Napoleonic Code. Individuals who entered into a *société* shared equally all property brought into the association as well as all profits derived from the employment of that property. Thus, each coparcener had a claim to any property acquired through the investment of profits obtained as a direct result of funds confounded in the *société*. This last provision was utilized by Limanton tenants in such a way as to exclude all but a single heir from succession to real estate. Prior to the agricultural revolution, this aspect of the law had largely been a dead letter. After deductions had been made for rent, hired labor, and taxes, little was left of the tenant's share of farm production that could be invested in the purchase of property. Virtually all proceeds from the farm were directly consumed by the tenant and the members of his household. Once tenant incomes expanded beyond immediate subsistence needs to the point where farm profits could be invested in the purchase of land, then any property so acquired was subject to the provision. Any land that was purchased with profits derived from the funds held in common by members of the *société* was not, therefore, directly subject to the laws governing inheritance. Property acquired in this manner had to be divided first between the coparceners and only then could the law requiring equal division of each coparcener's property take effect. This was precisely the strategy employed by Limanton tenants to concentrate real estate on a single heir.

After 1850 the *communautés* of Limanton tenants were reduced to an association of a single married child, usually a son, and the parents. When either or both parents died, two separate acts were necessary to settle their estates. First, all profits and debts arising from the *société* were divided equally between the remaining members of the association. After these transactions were put in order, the inheritance claims of all the heirs could be dealt with. Just how this worked so that a single heir was favored can be made clear in the following example.

In 1853 the *société* of Jean Guerin and his two sons was dissolved. Guerin's youngest son then ceded his rights in the former association to his father and older brother, who then formed a new *société*. In 1863 Querin died leaving five heirs, one of whom, his eldest son Jean, was also his coparcener. The funds from their *société* were evaluated at 4,345 francs, which included both the profits from the exploitation of the *domaine* they had farmed and 161 francs' annual revenue from several hectares of land acquired during the life of the new *société*. This fund was divided equally between Guerin's eldest son and his widow, each of whom received 2,172.50 francs. The value of Guerin's personal estate, after debts, came to 5,463 francs. Half of this went to his widow and the rest was divided among his five children, including Jean, his eldest. Thus, not only did his son Jean receive an extra 2,172 francs beyond his inheritance, but, with his mother, he retained ownership of the land purchased by the *société*.

Most tenant successions at Limanton were handled in the same way. In all, some twenty-seven tenants had acquired land in the commune between 1845 and 1875. Of these, seven sold off their land during their lifetime; the dispositions of a further seven extended into the period not covered by the cadastre. Of the remaining thirteen persons, ten passed all their land on to a single heir. Of the three who did not, two succeeded in excluding most of their heirs from the lands they had acquired. Claude Vadrot, for example, who had formed a *société* with his eldest son and the husband of one of his daughters in 1861, purchased a total of 5.71 hectares between 1863 and 1875. In 1889 the cadastre records that this land was divided equally between his son and daughter. A third son received nothing. Similarly, Denis Merlin, whom census lists after 1861 show as having resided at Villars with a son-in-law and one of his unmarried sons, divided his 5.5 hectares between these two in 1884. His six other children did not receive any part of this land. In only one case did a tenant divide his land among all his heirs. In 1881 Jean Billebaut's two hectares were partitioned among his four surviving children. It may have been that Billebaut never entered into a *communauté* with any of his children and so was prevented from concentrating the land on a single heir. Interestingly, however, two of his heirs subsequently sold their parcels to Billebaut's youngest son, three years after the holding had been divided.

Although well on the way to becoming capitalist farmers in the full sense of the term, farm production at Limanton nonetheless continued to be based essentially on the domestic unit. Tenants thus retained practices associated with traditional household organization and sought to concentrate family-owned land by passing it on to a single heir. This development is fascinating when one considers the history of the *communauté* from the beginning of the modern era. Up to the seventeenth century, it had been a property-owning association concerned with allocating rights to real estate among its members. By the end of the seventeenth century it had developed into a labor-sharing association in which land ownership was no longer a concern. With increased living standards and the ability to acquire land in the nineteenth century, the *communauté* became once again a family-based landowning corporation. In a very real sense, the *communauté* in the Nivernais had come full circle.

CHAPTER TEN

La Vie en Commun

The object of this book has been to examine the ways in which family patterns in the Nivernais were affected by the transformations in rural society from the close of the medieval period to the nineteenth century. In pursuing this investigation, a great deal of emphasis has been placed on what may be termed the quantifiable aspects of family life, on household structure, on the nature of kin ties and property relations within the *communauté*. Considerable attention has been given to legal, social, and economic factors affecting peasant production, since the peasant farm is seen as the foundation of household organization. To a great extent, this thrust has been conditioned by the nature of the source materials available on rural families in the Nivernais. Yet wills, marriage contracts, acts of association, and other such documents tend to reveal only the most formal aspects of family life. Couched in the dry, legal jargon of the notary, they rarely provide insight into the personal and emotional aspects of *la vie en commun*. By its sheer size, the *communaté* differed from most French peasant households. Yet was it unique in another sense as well? How did the organization of such domestic groups affect the lives of those who lived and worked under such arrangements? Did the life experience of the *parsonnier* differ from persons who rarely coresided with any relatives beyond their immediate family? In short, what did it mean to live in a *communauté*?

Conservatives in nineteenth century France had ready answers to such questions. They viewed the *communauté* as a collective institution which imbued its members with respect for parental authority, a sense of family cohesiveness and an attachment to time-honored beliefs and traditions. It performed a vital social function by tempering a recklessness inherent in human nature. Family solidarity provided individuals with a sense of place and purpose, without which life in the countryside was meaningless and unbearable.

By the same token, the demise of the *communauté* meant the loss of an institution that checked rapacious ambition and self-interest. When de Cheverry revisted the Pervy family in 1885, he witnessed to his bitter disappointment the dissolution of the association. For him, the breakup of the Pervys was only another example of the widespread decline of traditional values that had characterized rural life for centuries. The loss of such values not only weakened the financial position of the former coparceners, but destroyed the sense of cohesiveness that had given meaning to life.

> The husband, retired with his share, becomes a day laborer; the wife leaves Paris to become a wet nurse; the children are abandoned. The husband, discouraged, ceases to work and love of the family gives way to love of the cabaret.[1]

The disintegration of family life led to flight from the countryside. Rural exodus was thus seen as a direct consequence of the destruction of family patterns by modern values. As early as 1851, one member of the *Societé de agriculture de la Nièvre* claimed that the demise of the *communauté* was severing the roots of young peasants, "pushing young people from the paternal hearths to seek uncertain careers elsewhere."[2] Joseph Imbart de la Tour, one of the Nièvre's most prominent notables, cited "the decline of paternal authority, egoism and ambition, of morality and the disappearance of the spirit of the family"[3] as the leading causes of rural immigration. Rural depopulation was not merely an unfortunate aspect of modern times, but was a serious problem for landowners who were forced to pay increasingly higher wages to rural workers. The responses to the government's agricultural survey of 1866 are littered with complaints about the difficulty of attracting hired help at even the highest wages.[4]

Certainly one of the principal motivations behind the growing interest in the *communauté* during the nineteenth century was the belief that its preservation could in some way stem the tide of rural emigration. With little hope that peasants, who were so thoroughly battered by the onslaught of modern values, would ever reconstitute on their own the traditional *communautés,* de Cheverry argued that this goal could only be achieved with the active assistance of wealthy landowners. "The mission of the proprietor," wrote de Cheverry, "ought not to be limited to the surveillance of the farm. He has to inspire confidence, to assume the functions of that protective mother, the old *communauté.*" The result of such practices would be "greater attachment to the soil . . . a pacification of spirits. Such is the goal for which the Union of Social Peace strives."[5] The reconstitution of the traditional *communauté* would further benefit society since the socialization of members within the *communauté* had a direct consequence on landlord-tenant relations. As conservatives viewed it, the patriarchal *communauté* served to socialize members not only to respect parental authority, but one's social superiors as well. As de Cheverry put it:

> The authority of the *maître* and the obedience given him are not learned by words, but by the example of tradition. . . . As the awareness of the young child grows, the deference that everyone gives to the *maître* becomes apparent to him, and the more he grows, the more he accepts the authority of him whom all obey. . . . When the child becomes a man, he is obedient and respectful without even perceiving it.[6]

Thus, the obedience and deference acquired under the influence of the family patriarch would extend to all representatives of authority. The values of the *communauté* and the preservation of social harmony were intimately linked to one another. Individuals raised in a paternalistic environment would provide a willing and obedient work force that would foster the progress of agriculture and economic development in general. Ironically, there is no evidence indicating that conservatives were at all aware that the decline of the large *communauté* was itself the result of the very economic progress they so eagerly desired.

Clearly, such a view was colored by ideological bias. What appears to some as respect for authority, may, to others, seem more like mental inertia or lack of initiative. Antoine Desforges, who spent a few years in a small Morvan commune near Larochemillay, felt that the *communauté* had many positive aspects. Individuals were sheltered from the hardships and hazards of old age, sickness, and the loneliness of widowhood. Yet the *communauté* also had its drawbacks. "It habituates passive obedience and destroys the energy of the spirit of initiative. Crowded together in houses that are too small, members of *communautés* are subject to immorality and promiscuity." All in all, Desforges applauded the demise of the *communauté,* "notwithstanding the displeasure of amateurs of the picturesque."[7]

What then were the characteristics of life in the *communauté?* To be sure, the first impression one gets is that of an overcrowded and cramped living space. Desforges claimed while some of the houses in the Morvan that had been built recently were comfortable enough, most were older buildings so unsanitary that they should have been closed by public health authorities. The tenant houses described by Dupin in 1846 were generally without adequate ventilation, a sole window providing light and fresh air. If a fire was burning, the smoke filled the entire building, forcing the residents to open the doors even in the coldest weather. The house in which Pervy *communauté* lived was of a type built in the sixteenth century.[8] A large central room served as the *salle de communauté*. Here the women prepared the family's meals, the members ate (the men first, followed by the women), business transactions were carried out, and the evening *veilles* observed. To each side were two bedrooms, each occupied by a couple who slept only with their smallest children. Either because the individual bedrooms were too small or because of a desire for greater privacy, older children and adolescents slept together with the elderly in the main hall: twelve persons in all, brothers, sisters, cousins, aunts, uncles, nephews and nieces. All crammed into five beds, "the head of one touching the feet of another."[9]

Cramped living space seemed always to grow even smaller as new babies arrived with each passing year. Of course, living in a large *communauté* could alleviate somewhat the burdens of pregnancy and childbearing, since a woman could count on the support of several female kin close at hand. All too often however, babies arrived in quick succession, turning the farmhouse into a nursery in a matter of weeks. Jeanne Marie Ducourdarde, maîtress of her *communauté* at Limanton and already the mother of three children, one not yet a year old, gave birth to her fourth child in March, 1827. Ten days later, her step-daughter Marie, gave birth to her second child. Between March 1809 and March 1811, six new babies were born into the Martin *communauté* at Limanton, three during a two-week period of May, 1810! Marriage practices contributed to the close arrival of new babies. It was common for two and even three children to marry at once, bringing their new spouses into the household. François Guillot, his sister Jeanne, and his younger brother François were all married on April 25, 1837, and together formed a *communauté* at Petit Anizy in Limanton. In February, 1839, the elder François' wife gave birth to a baby boy, followed by another baby born to the younger François and his wife four weeks later.

Within the *communauté* there existed a strict division of labor, made necessary by the numerous farm tasks to be performed. As in most peasant families, men occupied themselves with the heavier work of plowing and cultivation, women with the various tasks of food preparation. Also consigned to women were the care of the garden plot, sheep,

17.   Fairly typical day-laborer's house in the Morvan, circa 1880. Like those of sharecroppers, the building was poorly ventilated, living space was cramped and the floors earthen.

and pigs. Women cultivated flax, ministered to the sick and, in the summer, helped their menfolk bring in the harvest. In the large *communauté*, however, division of labor extended beyond sex lines. In the Pervy *communauté*, one man would perform the work of a blacksmith, another would double as a carpenter, another as a herdsman or wheelwright. As youngsters grew up, they would be apprenticed to a particular occupation, thereby assuring a replacement for the future. Among the women, one would be assigned to cultivate the garden, another would watch over the sheep while another maintained the courtyard. So burdened were these women with their various tasks that one was chosen to care for the children of all—a kind of domestic day-care center for working mothers. One woman, usually the wife of the head of household,[10] would act as the *maîtress de communauté*, directing the tasks of the women and serving as a counterpart to the *maître*.

Such occupational specialization, made necessary by the size of the domestic unit, could create problems. "There is always the cowman, the gardener, the sower," recalled Etienne Bertin. "The cowman never works in the garden, the gardener scarcely knows anything of plowing, nor how to care for the beasts. When they come to separate, each finds himself at a loss."[11] Bertin himself had never had an opportunity to sow the fields, a task that had been reserved for the *maître* or his eldest son.

18. Courtyard of a large Nivernais domaine. The three-story farm house is just left of
     center, the stables and barn flanking the courtyard on the right, sheep and pig pens
     on the left. Note the manure pile, typically as close to the farm house entryway as
     the barn door.

As a result, when he took over his own farm for the first time, his fields
were so poorly sown that his harvest was seriously affected and he had
to endure the jeers of his neighbors.

While de Cheverry repeatedly emphasized that such a division of
work tasks fostered a collectivist spirit of cooperation among members,
the history of the Pervys reveals that, in fact, major conflicts occured.
The greatest bone of contention appears to have been the manner in
which household accounts were kept by the *maître*. Control of these was
not only his sole preserve but were kept secret from other members. The
maître's nephew repeatedly demanded to know how much had been
made on the sale of grain and at what price a pair of oxen had been sold.
"The youth of today," he told his irritated uncle, "are very curious."
But this was not the only clash between members. In 1876 the youngest
son of the *maîtress* died soon after his return from the army. His death
was followed in a short time by that of her daughter-in-law's son. These
calamities, compounded by the dissension over the household budget,
brought the two women into open conflict.

As for the two mothers, they were inconsolable. The human heart holds
strange mysteries. At times, grief brought them together, at other times it

19.   Morvan peasant and his three sons, 1873.

split them apart. The mother-in-law and daughter-in-law could no longer support each other, the misery of one seeming an outrage to the sadness of the other. After some months of this, it was evident that the life in common had become impossible. The two men resolved to separate.[12]

Given the nature of living and working conditions within *communautés*, it is easy to visualize how conflicts over events and developments affecting the lives of each member could lead to clashes of personalities. The Pervys were fairly well off, their property at the time of their dissolution having been evaluated at 80,000 francs. The poverty of most sharecropping *communautés* was certainly not conducive to an atmosphere of tranquility. Indeed Emil Guillaumin, who had himself been raised in such a household, gives the impression that *la vie en commun* was anything but harmonious. "There existed perpetual dissensions between one person and another. The group divided itself into subgroups of enemies, never speaking to the other except to exchange insults. Noxious poison of miserable rivalries! No hope of evasion!"[13] No hope because the conditions of agriculture and tenure demanded that the members remain together. "Misery maintained cohesion."

Necessity bound families together; proximity made for conflicts. In rare instances notary records provide glimpses of this. In 1793 a *tribunal de famille* was convoked in Preporche to hear a complaint brought by Marie Cousson, widow of Claude Cousson, against her son-in-law François Bouillot.[14] Cousson actually had several complaints. She demanded that the *communauté* that had existed between the two couples be divided in six equal parts, two for the Bouillots and the remaining shares for herself and her other children. She also complained that Bouillot had sold a pair of oxen belonging to the *communauté* and had used the proceeds to buy land for himself. This, too, she demanded should be divided between them. Her son-in-law countered with the claim that, since one of her children was still a minor, he had no right to an equal share in the partition. He further denied that the money obtained from the oxen had been used to purchase land. This, he claimed, had been bought with his own *propres* and was rightfully his. As for the oxen, this money had been returned to the *communauté*. His mother-in-law, he said, knew this to be true but was simply attempting to steal what she had no right to. He also had a bone to pick with her over some 370 *livres* which he had lent to the *communauté* but which had never been returned to him. "Where is it?" he wanted to know.

The arbitrators chosen by both sides did their best to sort out the dispute, but in the end generally sided with Marie Cousson. The land was ordered divided and Bouillot held to show proof of his claim to the 370 *livres*. Whether these judgements were carried out is difficult to determine since these tribunals had little means of enforcing their decisions. What is certain is that there was little love lost between the in-laws.

Of all the sources on the conditions of life within *communautés*, perhaps the most valuable, and certainly the most revealing, are the memoirs of Etienne Bertin. In 1823 Bertin was born into a *communauté* formed by an association between his father and uncle. His earliest experiences were of incessant conflict between the two. His uncle had suffered from the effects of frostbite since his participation in Napoleon's Russian campaign. His inability—or unwillingness—to work was a source of continued argument. Finally, Bertin's father had enough and the *communauté* was dissolved. Yet the antagonisms that had built up over the years turned the partition into a bitter dispute, particularly between Bertin's mother and her in-laws.

> At the time of the removal there were painful discussions as to the sharing of the tools, furniture, linen and household utensils. My grandmother was to accompany us, and that complicated things still more. My aunt, who disagreed with her most, wrangled with her about what she ought to take, and snatched sheets and towels out of her hands. My father had a calmer temperament and sought to avoid these disputes, but my mother, quick and impetuous, was constantly in a rage with my uncle or aunt, and sometimes with both. It used to terrify me to hear them shouting and shaking their fists with menacing gestures as though they would strike each other.[15]

Years later, when Bertin was a young man, a quarrel with his parents ended in his decision to leave the household. His parents, by scraping together every sou they could spare, had been able to purchase substitutes for his two brothers when they reached draft age. Yet their ever-deteriorating financial position, caused in large part by their landlord's double-dealing, meant that they would be unable to prevent Bertin's conscription should his lottery number come up. Although Bertin was spared from the army, his resentment at what he saw as favoritism on the part of his helpless parents determined his choice: he would leave.

This experience seemed to have deeply affected Bertin. Years afterwards, when he had married and established his own household, he was careful to avoid favoring any of his children in the least way, even to the point of buying them the same clothes at the same time. Despite these efforts at good parenting, he was unable to prevent a growing hostility between his daughter and daughter-in-law after she moved in with them. "When there are three families in one house, things never go on long without some friction." The friction, in this case, arose over the tasks of preparing the family's meals, each woman considering the other to be lazy or inept. Hostility between the two eventually ended in a bitter argument over which family was to have use of the carriage for a day. Bertin did his best to arbitrate the matter, but, "from that day, the two sisters-in-law never spoke except to mock or to vilify each other."[16]

The clash of personalities finally led to the breakup of the household, with Bertin's daughter and son-in-law leaving to take up another farm. Bertin's wife, anxious over her daughter's ill health and pregnancy, paid frequent visits to her, bringing her cheese, fruit, and milk. So bitter was the feeling between the two sisters-in-law, however, that even this parental solicitude was a source of further resentment. "We shall have enough to do," the daughter-in-law complained, "if all that comes in at the door is to go out of the window; we shan't be able to supply ourselves." In order to preserve what was left of his household, Bertin and his wife agreed to stop furnishing their daughter with gifts—at least openly. "But Rosalie's sharp eyes were everywhere, and it was very difficult for Victoire to make the smallest thing disappear without her knowledge. There were more and more violent scenes when she discovered that some gift had been made, unknown to her."[17]

It is noteworthy that most of the family feuds recalled by Bertin took place between in-laws. Arguments between blood relatives could be heated, often bitter, but the parties had at least grown up together and a common life experience may have served to temper bruised egos. Families are, in a sense, small societies, their members held together by their own ways of dealing with one another. An in-law, however, was an outsider, a stranger accepted only in part and unfamiliar with the customs of his or her new relatives. So common were conflicts between in-laws that the theme found its way into the culture of the Nivernais. Local folk songs attest to it.

> J'ai un mechants belle-mère,
> Grand-Dieu, qui ne veut pas me voir,
> Ah! tous les jours elle dit à mon mari:
> ——Quand donc la fera-tu mourir?[18]

A favorite game played by children in the Morvan in the nineteenth century was "*La Belle-mère*."[19] One girl would play the evil mother-in-law, another her hapless, overworked and underfed daughter-in-law, while a third would play the girl's faithful maternal aunt who had come to ask the belle-mere how her niece was getting along. The other children would chant, "She gives her nothin' but mouldy old bread!" After further evidence of mistreatment by the belle-mère (a few blows here were considered appropriate), the aunt would rescue her niece and take her home where she would be well fed and clothed, the rest of the children ganging up on the belle-mère to mete out her just punishment. This finale appears to resemble today's game of "Slaughter the Pig" and one assumes that the person chosen to be La Belle-mere was either the least liked or the smallest child in the village.

Families could try to soften the harrowing experience of moving into a new family by a practice known as *mariage per echange*. Frequently in the Nivernais, brothers would choose as their wives two sisters who could be expected to get along with one another and thus assure the future tranquility of the household. So common was the practice that it found its way into the customary laws of the province.[20] This was what Bertin's older brothers did, although one was a not entirely willing groom, having already set his eyes upon another girl.

> But my mother made him understand that, as he would always have to live with his brother, it would be more to his interest that they should have sisters for wives, that this would be some guarantee of harmony in the household. As she had considerable ascendancy over him she succeeded in persuading him.[21]

The results were far more successful than Bertin's mother expected. After his father died, hostility between his mother and one of her daughters-in-law threatened to break up the household. "But in spite of occasional disagreements, my brothers got on fairly well. They reckoned they could get on still better together than separately, as long as their children were not grown up." The family did split, but it was their mother who was asked to leave, much to her surprise. She spent the rest of her years alone, venting her rage at the filial treachery of her sons.

There is, in all of this, little evidence of the picturesque patriarchal family bound together by the two-sided coin of paternal authority and filial devotion. If anything bound families together, it was economic necessity, pure and simple. People stuck together because they needed to, but as a result were also stuck with each other as well. With the agricultural revolution came the opportunity for independence. Young families that had been forced to live with their in-laws, to endure parental domination, the frictions between relatives and the restrictions of the large *communauté,* seized the first chance for freedom. In his response to a survey on living conditions in the Nivernais in 1894, M. de Lespinasse noted the change.

> The tendency today in the countryside is to have a home of one's own. . . .A young family prefers to live even penniless if this will give them independence. As soon as they marry, they set up their own household. . . .Large farmers now have only servants to help with the work of the farm.[22]

By then, large *communautés* came to be formed less frequently even in the Morvan. Children "quit the paternal hearth in order to free themselves from their parents' authority and to earn some money that they will spend in increasing their own well-being."[23] The decline of the *communauté* in the Nivernais may have been lamented by folklorists as the final, dying gasp of the Old Regime and with dread by landowners fearing the loss of a passively obedient work force; for those who actually experienced the realities of *la vie en commun,* its passing was more than likely greeted with one long sigh of relief.

Glossary

affranchissement—franchises granted to individual serfs or to an entire community specifiying rights and delineating obligations to their lord.

apanage—property given to younger sons and daughters as a means of support.

arrêt—royal decree.

bellemain—the cash portion owed by sharecroppers in addition to the half-product of the farm.

bordelage—a form of feudal tenure peculiar to the Nivernais; hence *bordelier.*

cahiers de doleance—formal lists of grievances drawn up in 1789 by each parish and the *estates* of each province and city in France.

censive—manorial rent-paying lands; usually at a fixed amount of cash; hence, *censitaires.*

charivari—usually a noisy mock serenade to a newlywed couple, *charivari* could be invoked against anyone seen as transgressing community-held standards of behavior.

corvée—labor dues paid to the manorial lord and/or the crown.

dénombrement—enumeration of properties and rights of a fief.

élévage—cattle raising; hence, *éléveur.*

embouche—cattle fattening; hence, *emboucheur.*

fermage—lease agreement; hence, *fermier.*

feu—hearth; household.

formariage—fine on marriage to individuals not dependent on the same lord.

frereche—joint household comprised of brothers.

gabelle—salt tax; the Franch crown held a monopoly on the sale of salt and apportioned the amount to be purchased by the inhabitants of those provinces subject to the tax.

grenier à sel—warehouse and administrative office for the *gabelle.*

intendant—royal govenor in pre-Revolutionary France.

journalier—day-laborer; generally denoting individual owning no land.

laboureur—plowman; in the Nivernais, denotes sharecropper.

mainmorte—mortmain; the lord's right to a share of the estate of a serf after his death.

manouvrier—can denote a landless peasant or a peasant owning or leasing a small farm or *manouvrie*.

mercuriales—official price list of farm products sold in major towns of each *département*.

métayage—sharecropping; hence, *métayer*.

meubles—movable property.

parsonnier—sometimes *personnier*; coparcener, or person sharing jointly in ownership of property.

partage—formal division of property.

préfet—administrative head of each *départment*. Introduced by Napoleon, the prefet's powers were akin to those of the former *intendants*.

propes—property held by individuals outside the marital community or the *communauté*.

seigneur—manorial lord.

taille—royal tax levied on commoners in pre-Revolutionary France.

taille à volonté—arbitrary tallage on dependents of a manor.

terrier—record of boundary lines of landholdings of a manor.

vingtième—theoretically, an income tax of one-twentieth of value of all property; introduced in the early eighteenth century, it soon became simply an addition to the *taille*.

Administrative Division

Pre-Revolutionary France was a compilation of a complex system of administrative units imposed one upon the other throughout the history of the Old Regime. One or more provinces, when not directly subject to the crown's administrative authority, were administered by the *généralité* headed by the *intendant*. Each *généralité* was in turn divided into *éléctions* composed of individual parishes. The provinces of the Nivernais and the Bourbonnais directly to the south were joined into the *généralité de Moulins*. An entirely separate bureaucratic apparatus administered the *gabelle*, each province divided into districts known as *greniers à sel*. Because they were distinct systems, *éléctions* and *greniers à sel* rarely coincided.

This bewildering array of administrations was abolished by the Revolution in 1789, which divided France into *départements* eventually headed by the prefect. The province of the Nivernais became, for the most part, the *département* of the Nièvre, the Bourbonnais the *département* of the Allier. Each *département* was subdivided into *arrondissements,* each divided into cantons made up of the individual communes.

Land Measures

The system of land measurements of the Old Regime was even more confusing than its administrative system. A veritable plethora of units for measuring land existed, virtually every province using its own system. Even within a province, there existed myriad systems for measuring land. Thus, in the Nivernais one could measure land in *boisselées, razellées, coupées, arpents, journaux,* and so on. Usually, a single document would employ all of these together. Compounding this problem was the fact that a *boiselée* at the town of Decize differed in size from a *boiselée* at Nevers. Fortunately, the Revolution introduced the metric system as a uniform system for all of France, although local inhabitants continued to employ the measures of the Old Regime well into the nineteenth century. The standard unit of land measurement was henceforth the *hectare,* about 2.5 acres. For the purposes of clarity, property holdings referred to in the book have been recalculated into hectares.

Appendix

Association between Comte, Teupeuier, Perrin and others,
(January 21, 1816)

Before Louis DelaGrange, public notary herein undersigned, residing in the town and commune of Moulins-Engilbert, comes Louis Teupeuier and by his authority Jeanne, his wife, Philippe Perrin, Pierre Mathe and by his authority Pierrette, his wife, all brothers and brother-in-law, plowmen and coparceners residing at the *domaine* of La Varenne, commune of Limanton, who have on this day admitted into their *communauté:* Pierre and Jeanne Teupeuier, children now of legal age of said Louis Teupeuier and Jeanne Perrin; Denis Mathé and by his authority Etiennette Cheurlin, his wife, son of said Pierre Mathé and Pierrette Perrin; these latter four residing with their fathers and mothers, uncles and aunts at the said *domaine* of La Varenne and here present and consenting and who, in order to acquire rights into the *communauté,* commingle all the fruits of their labor. The *communauté* will be composed of nine heads, that is two for Louis Teupeuier and his wife, two for Pierre Mathe and his wife, one for Philippe Perrin, two for Pierre and Jeanne Teupeuier and the last two for Denis Mathé and Cheurlin and his wife. In the event the *communauté* dissolves, that which will be held in common will be divided in nine equal portions, including grains and profits from the sale of animals, with the exception of the linen and clothes belonging to each party which will not be susceptible to division and which will not be part of the *communauté*. The beds of each member of the *communauté* will not be part of the said *communauté*, belonging to each member, as well as the chests which contains their linen and clothes. Such has been consented, stipulated and accepted by all those present.

Marriage Contract, January 3, 1782

Before the notary of the Duchy of the Nivernais herein undersigned residing in the town of Moulins-Engilbert, comes Lazare Martin, proprietor, and by his authority Françoise Dudragne, his wife, and by their authority Philibert Martin, their son, residing with them in the village of Noëuille, parish of Villapourçin, parties of the first part; and Dominique Laudet, also proprietor, and by his authority, Françoise Lambert, his wife, and by their authority Etienette Laudet, their daughter, residing with them in the village of Champrobert, parish of Saint-Jean-Goux, parties of the second part. The said Philibert Martin and Etienette Laudet proceeding under the authority of their said fathers and mothers, with their advice and consent, have made between them a treaty of marriage which here follows:

Know that the said Philibert Martin and Etienette Laudet have promised to marry and will reside in the company and in the *communauté* of said Lazare Martin and Françoise Dudragne; the said betrothed will make only one head in all movables of any nature existing and to come and in any acquisitions of real estate. In order to acquire rights in the *communauté* for one head only, the said betrothed will be held to confer the sum of 300 *livres,* which sum has been presented and paid to said Lazare Martin and Françoise Dudragne by the said Dominique Laudet and Françoise Lambert. . . . Furthermore, after the celebration of the said marriage, the said betrothed will hold in *communauté* all movable property existing and to come and in any acquisitions of real estate.

In consideration of which marriage, the said Dominique Laudet and Françoise Lambert have constituted as dowry to the said Etienette Laudet, their daughter, the sum of 800 *livres* and in addition a trousseau valued at 50 *livres,* composed of a bed consisting of two mattresses, the one filled with feathers and the other without feathers; an embroidered comforter and six drapes of cloth; of two chairs, two plates, a wooden coffer with lock holding about 12 *boisseaux* according to the measures of Moulins-Engilbert; of clothes for her daily use and nightgown, the said trousseau to be given the day following her marriage. By which sum of 800 *livres* and said trousseau, said Dominique Laudet and Françoise Lambert have apanaged the said Etienette Laudet, their daughter. By means of said dowry and apanage, the said Etienette Laudet has herein renounced to any succession of her said father and mother in favor of Françoise Laudet, her sole brother.

And on the part of the groom, his said father and mother have constituted him as his dowry all paternal and maternal rights to fall in their succession. In addition to which the said Lazare Martin and Françoise Dudragne declare that they have apanaged Michel Martin, their youngest son, with the sum of 800 *livres,* and Françoise Martin, their daughter, an equal sum of 800 *livres*; by means of which said Michel and Françoise Martin will be held to renounce any succession of their said mother and father. Said Martin and Dudragne reserve the right to dower and apanage with a like sum their other children.

It is further agreed that in the case that the said Lazare Martin and Françoise Dudragne should marry another of their sons whom they have not apanaged and that said sons not yet apanaged should desire to remain in their company and *communauté,* the girl that he will marry will be held to confer in their said *communauté* a sum of 300 *livres,* and by commingling such a sum, the said son and girl will acquire rights in the said *communauté* for one head; and in order to acquire a right in the said marital *communauté* of the said son, the son of 300 *livres,* and their son will pay the said marital *communauté* 300 *livres.* And the balance of 500 *livres* will pass to his heirs in direct line as their *propres.* . . .

In the event that the said *communauté* is dissolved by death or otherwise, the said bride will have the choice of living at the expense of the said *communauté* with no reduction of her rights; or by renouncing this right, she will take all her personal goods which she has brought into the *communauté,* together with all property passing to her by inheritance free and quit of any debt. . . .

The above has been stipulated, consented to, and accepted by the said parties, who are obliged to execute the provisions according to the law. Passed at said Moulin-Engilbert in the afternoon of the 13th of January, 1782, in the presence of the undersigned notaries. All parties having declared they cannot read or write, we as notaries have signed for them.

Notes

Notes to Chapter One

1. Andre Marie Jean-Jacque Dupin, *Le Morvan: Topographie, agriculture, moeurs des habitants; état ancien, état actuel* (Paris, 1853), p. 94.

2. Ibid., p. 100.

3. An excellent summary of this may be found in Lutz K. Berkner, "Rural Family Organization in Europe: A Problem in Comparative History," *Peasant Studies Newsletter* 1, no. 4 (1972), pp. 145-156. See also Walter Goldschmidt and Evalyn Kunkel, "The Structure of the Peasant Family," *American Anthropologist* 73 (1971), pp. 1058-76, and David Sabean, "Aspects of Kinship Behavior and Property in Western Europe Before 1800," in *Family and Inheritance: Rural Society in Western Europe (1200-1800)*, ed. Jack Goody et al. (London, 1976), pp. 96-111.

4. Marion J. Levy, Jr., "Aspects of the Analysis of Family Structure," in *Aspects of the Analysis of Family Structure*, ed. Ansley Coale et al. (Princeton, 1965), pp. 1-63.

5. Jack Goody, "Strategies of Heirship," *Comparative Studies in Society and History* 15 (1973), pp. 3-20.

6. Rudolf Braun, *Industrialisierung und Volksleben* (Zurich, 1960); Joan Thirsk, "Industry in the Countryside," in *Essays in the Economic and Social History of Tudor and Stuart England*, ed. F. J. Fisher (Cambridge, 1961), pp. 70-88.

7. Lutz K. Berkner, "Inheritance, Land Tenure, and Family Structure in Lower Saxony," in *Family and Inheritance*, pp. 71-95.

8. Braun, *Industrialisierung;* Thirsk, "Industry in the Countryside."

9. These differences are discussed in T. N. Madan, "The Joint Family: A Terminological Clarification," in *Family and Marriage*, ed. John Mogey (Leiden, 1963), pp. 7-16.

10. Ibid., pp. 12-13.

11. Lutz K. Berkner, "The Stem Family and the Developmental Cycle of the Peasant Household: An Eighteenth-Century Austrian Example," *American Historical Review* 77, no. 2 (1972), pp. 400-401; William Douglas, "Rural

Exodus in Two Spanish Basque Villages: A Cultural Explanation," *American Anthropologist* 72 (1971), p. 1108; Conrad Arensberg, *The Irish Countryman* (New York, 1937), p. 81; Sigrid Khera, "Social Stratification and Land Inheritance Among Austrian Peasants," *American Anthropologist* 75 (1973), p. 816; John W. Cole, "Social Process in the Italian Alps," *American Anthropologist* 75 (1973), p. 773.

12. Joel Halpern, *A Serbian Village* (New York, 1967), p. 135; Christiane Klapisch and Michel Demonet, " 'A uno pane e uno vino,' La famille rurale toscane au debut de XVe siècle," *Annales, E.S.C.* 27 (1972), p. 881; David Mandelbaum, *Society in India* (Berkeley, 1970), p. 35; Olga Lang, *Chinese Family and Society* (New Haven, 1946), p. 17.

13. Meyer Fortes, Introduction to *The Developmental Cycle in Domestic Groups*, ed. Jack Goody (Cambridge, 1958). See also Berkner, "The Stem Family," and E. A. Hammel, "The Zadruga as Process," in *Household and Family in Past Time*, ed. Peter Laslett (Cambridge, 1972), pp. 335-374.

14. Goldschmidt and Kunkel, "The Structure of the Peasant Family," p. 1062.

15. Mandelbaum, *Society in India*, p. 125; Lang, *Chinese Family and Society*, p. 141; Halpern, *A Serbian Village*, p. 168; Klapisch and Demonet, "A uno pane e uno vino'," p. 881n; M. G. Kulkarni, "Family Patterns in Gokak Taluka," *Sociological Bulletin* 9 (1960), p. 60; S. C. Dube, *Indian Village* (Stanford, 1967), p. 115; Andrejs Plakans, "Seigneurial Authority and Peasant Family Life: The Baltic Area in the Eighteenth Century," *Journal of Interdisciplinary History* 5 (1975), pp. 652-653.

16. Eric Wolf, *Peasants* (Englewood Cliffs, N. J., 1966), p. 69.

17. E. A. Hammel, "The Zadruga as Process," and "Household Structure in Fourteenth-Century Macedonia," to appear in *Mediterranean Family Organization*, ed. J. K. Campbell (Oxford).

18. R. Boutrouche, *Crise d'une société; seigneurs et paysans du Bordelaise pendant la Guerre des Cent Ans* (Paris, 1947), pp. 119-122; Emmanuel Le Roy Lauderie, *The Peasants of Languedoc*, trans. John Day (Chicago, 1974), pp. 29-36; Klapisch and Demonet, " 'A uno pane e uno vino' ", p. 885.

19. Goldschmidt and Kunkel, "The Structure of the Peasant Family," pp. 1062-1063.

20. Plakans, "Seigneurial Authority and Peasant Family Life," p. 634-5.

21. J-C Peyronnet, "Famille elargie ou famille nucleaire? En Limousin au debut du XIXe siècle," *Révue d'histoire modern et contemporaine* 22 (1975), pp. 569-582, and Frank McArdle, "Another Look at 'Peasant Families East and West'," *Peasant Studies Newsletter* 3, no. 3 (1974), pp. 11-14.

22. Joel Halpern and David Anderson, "The *Zadruga*, a Century of Change," *Anthropologica* vol. 12, no. 1 (1970), p. 92.

23. C. Geertz, "Ritual and Social Change: A Javanese Example," *American Anthropologist* 59 (1957), pp. 33-34.

24. Wolf, *Peasants*, pp. 68-70.

25. Peter Laslett, Introduction to *Household and Family*, p. 65.

26. Robert Wheaton, "Family and Kinship in Western Europe: The Problem of the Joint Family Household," *Journal of Interdisciplinary History* 4 (1975), p. 623.

27. Wheaton, "Family and Kinship," p. 617; Dube, *Indian Village,* pp. 138-140; Mandelbaum, *Society in India, op. cit.,* pp. 48-50; M. S. Gore, "The Traditional Indian Family," in *Comparative Family Systems,* ed. M. F. Nimkoff (Boston, 1965), p. 214; William Morrison, "Family Types in Badlapur: An Analysis of a Changing Institution in a Maharushtrian Village," *Sociological Bulletin* 7 (1959), pp. 45-67.

28. William J. Goode, World Revolution and Family Patterns (New York, 1963).

29. Ibid., p. 23. While Goode's arguments may be somewhat extreme, similar arguments have been advanced by industrial sociologists. See, for example, Clark Kerr, et al., *Industrialism and Industrial Man: The Problems of Labor and Management in Economic Growth* (Cambridge, Mass., 1962), and Charles A. Myers, *Labor Problems in the Industrialization of India* (Cambridge, Mass., 1960).

30. Alain Corbin, *Archaisme et modernité en Limousin en XIXe siècle, 1845-1880* (Paris, 1975), pp. 286 and 460.

31. Joseph Fievée, "Note confidentielle sur le département de la Nièvre, in Guy Thuillier, *Aspects de l'économie nivernais au XIXe siècle* (Paris, 1966), p. 497.

32. Paul Cornu, "Grèves de flotteurs sur l'Yonne aux XVIIIe et XIXe siècles," *Cahiers du Centre* (Jan. 1911), pp.   .

33. Frederic LePlay, *L'Organisation de la famille* (Paris, 1871), p. 82.

34. Alfred Kroeber, *Anthropology* (New York, 1948), p. 284; George M. Foster, "What is Folk Culture?" *American Anthropologist* 55 (1953), pp. 159-173; Robert Redfield, *Peasant Society and Culture* (Chicago, 1956).

Notes to Chapter Two

1. J. Gaudemet, *Les communautés familiales* (Paris, 1963), p. 20; Paul Destray, "Etudes sur les vieilles associations nivernaises," *Comité des travaux. Travaux historiques et scientifiques. Bulletin philologique et historique* (1920), pp. 377-394.

2. M. Dupin, *Le Morvan: Topographie, agriculture, moeurs des habitants, état ancien, état actuel* (Paris, 1853), p. 94.

3. Paul Bastid, *De la fonction sociale des communautés taisible en l'ancienne droit* (Tours, 1916), p. 20.

4. E. Glasson, "Communautés taisibles et communautés coutumières depuis la redaction des coutumes," *Nouvelle révue historique de droit français et étranger* 23 ser. 3, (1899), pp. 527-539.

5. Bastid, *Communautés taisibles* 22, pp. 47-48.

6. *Coutume de Nivernais,* chap. 22, art. 2.

7. M. Dupin, ed., *La coutume de Nivernais accompagnée d'extraits du*

commentaire de cette coutume par Guy Coquille (Paris, 1864), p. 304.

8. Paul Destray, "Contributions à l'histoire de l'association en Nivernais; La région de Clamecy," *Mèmoires de la société academique du Nivernais* 24 (1922), pp. 7-12.

9. Walter Goldschmidt and Evalyn Kunkel, "The Structure of the Peasant Family," *American Anthropologist* 73 (1971), pp. 1058-76.

10. *Coutume de Nivernais* chap. 33, art. 17.

11. Ibid., chap. 6; see also Réné de Lespinasse, "Notice sur les redevances roturiers du Nivernois appelées bordelages," *Bibliothèque de l'École des Chartes* 4, ser. 6 (1868), pp. 140-55, and Antoine Boucomont, *Des mainmortes personnelles et réele en Nivernais* (Paris, 1897).

12. Guy Coquille, *Histoire du pays et duché de Nivernais* (1612).

13. Victor de Cheverry, "Fermiers à communauté taisible du Nivernais," Les ouvriers des deux mondes, 5 (1885), p. 38.

14. L. Turpin, "Les anciennes communautés de laboureurs et la coutume du bordelage," *Bulletin de la société nivernais des lettres, arts et sciences* 5, ser. 3 (1909), p. 203.

15. Dupin, *Coutume de Nivernais*, p. 202.

16. Réné de Lespinasse, ed., *Registre-terrier de l'évêché de Nevers redigé en 1287* (Nevers, 1869).

17. Dupin, *Coutume de Nivernais*, p. 229.

18. Paul Mohler, *Le Servage et les communautés serviles en Nivernais* (Paris, 1900), pp. 135-137.

19. Andred Bossuat, "Le Servage en Nivernais au XVe siècle d'aprés les registres du Parlement," *Bibliothèque de l'École des Chartes* 117 (1959), pp. 111-112.

20. J-F Baudiau, *Le Morvand, ou essai géographique, topographique et historique sur cette contrée* (Nevers, 1865), pp. 169-170. On the wars of this period, see Henri de Flamare, *Le Nivernais pendant la Guerre de Cent Ans* (Nevers, 1928).

21. M. L. Mirot, "Note pour servir à l'histoire du Nivernais et du Donziais de 1360 à 1404 d'après les comptes de la Recette Générale et des Châtellenies," *Société académique du Nivernais* 39 (1937).

22. Bossuat, "Le Servage," pp. 91, 101-102.

23. Ibid., pp. 103-104.

24. The inhabitants of the county of Château-Chinon justified their resistance by claiming that the king had freed them from serfdom. In fact, Charles VI, when he confiscated the county in 1389, had confirmed all franchises granted by its previous lord during the fourteenth century. These had been made to particular families and not, as was claimed by serfs in the fifteenth century, to all the subjects of the county. See Réné de Lespinasse, *Le Nivernais et les comtes de Nevers* (Paris, 1911), 1: 264.

25. Bossuat, "Le Servage," pp. 96-99.

26. Mohler, *Le Servage*, p. 105.

27. A. D. Nièvre, 1 F 270, *Fonds Bruneau de Vitry.*
28. Dupin, *Cotume de Nivernais,* pp. 483-488.
29. These and the following case were derived from A. D. Nièvre, Série E, *Registre des minutes notariales de Decize,* excerpts of which were published in Paul Destray, "Contribution à l'histoire de l'association en Nivernais: Qui peut vivre en communauté?" *Bulletin de la société nivernais des lettres, arts et sciences* 27, no. 1 (1926), pp. 149-157.
30. Ibid., pp. 168-170.
31. *Cotume du Nivernais,* chap. 8, art. 10, 11, 12, and 16.
32. A. D. Nièvre. 1 F 59-60, *Fonds de Bruneau de Vitry.*
33. A. D. Nièvre, 2 F 243, 246, 247, 260, 272-296, 431-471, *Fonds du Bourg de Bozas.*
34. Boucomont, *Des mainmortes,* p. 107.
35. Bibliothèque municipale de Nevers, Ms. *Lieve déclaration des cens, rentes et bordelages due au terrier de Saint-Baudière* (1780).
36. Bibliothèque municipale de Nevers, Ms. 33, *Lieve au terrier de Decize, Champvert, Gannay, Charrin et dépendances* (1775); A. N. Q¹ 825¹, *Aveux et dénombrement de la fief de la Forêt* (1775), *de La Verechère* (1771), *de La Villette* (1779); A. D. Nièvre, 1 F 292, *Dénombrement de la fief de Champrobert* (1779).
37. A. D. Nièvre, 1 F 60 and 63, *Fonds Bruneau de Vitry.* For Prye and Azy, see above, footnote 33.
38. Turpin, "Les anciennes communautés," pp. 212, 228-229.
39. Lespinasse, *Le Nivernais et les comtes de Nevers,* 3: 597.
40. The 1490 customs have been published in A. Boucomont, "l'Ancienne coutume du Nivernais," *Révue historique de droit français* (1897), pp. 770-820.
41. A. de Villenaut, "Registres-terriers des seizième et dix-septième siècles," *Bulletin de la société nivernais des lettres, arts et sciences* ser. 3, V (1892), p. 83.
42. *Ancienne coutume du Nivernais,* chap. 5, art. 6.
43. *Coutume du Nivernais,* chap. 6, art. 11.
44. Dupin, *Coutume du Nivernais,* p. 197.
45. Bibliothèque municipale de Nevers, Ms. 2 N 304, *Sentence rendue au bailliage de Nevers au subject des bordelages* (1753).
46. Ibid.
47. A. N., L 1000, *Terrier de l'abbaye de Bellevaux* (1782).
48. A. N., Q¹ 825¹, *Aveux et dénombrement de la fief de La Verechère* (1771).
49. A. D. Nièvre, 1 F 292, *Dénombrement de la fief de Champrobert* (1779).
50. *Coutume du Nivernais,* chap. 34, art. 14.
51. A. D. Nièvre, Series L, *Cahiers de doleances, parish of Neuffontaines.*
52. A. D. Nièvre, 1 F 168, *Fonds Bruneau de Vitry.*
53. A. D. Nièvre, 2 C 831-836, *Administration des domaines. Contrôle des actes des notaires et sous-signée privée. Bureau de Larochemillay.*

Notes to Chapter Three

1. Karl Marx, *Capital* (New York, 1909), pp. 784-848. The classic study of this is R. H. Tawney's *The Agrarian Problem in the Sixteenth Century* (London, 1912). See also Robert Brenner, "Agrarian Class Structure and Economic Development in Pre-Industrial Europe," *Past and Present,* no. 70 (1976), pp. 30-75.

2. Antonie de Boislisle, ed., *Correspondances des contrôleurs des finances avec les intendants des provinces* (Paris, 1874), no. 599.

3. Sources on taxation were: "Traité due révenue et dépense de France de l'année 1607," *Révue rétrospective ou bibliothèque historique* ser. 1, 4 (1834), pp. 84-130; Nicolas Remond, "Sommaire traicté de révenue et dépense des finances de France," *Varietées historiques et litteraires* 6 (1856), pp. 156-184; Lazare Ducrot, *Le Nouveau traité des aides, tailles et gabelles* (Paris, 1643).

4. Marcel Marion, *Les Impots directs sous l'Ancien Regime* (Paris, 1910). The intendants for the generality of Moulins complained repeatedly about alleged fraud in claims for tax exemptions. D'Argouges, intendant in 1684, reported to the contrôleur generale that in the Nivernais "there are so many people who claim exemption and these are so poorly based that I need your help in reducing their claims and making them carry their share of taxes." Boislisle, *Correspondances,* no. 136.

5. Population estimates for 1625 were derived from Ducrot, *Le Nouvreau traité*; for 1664, François Desmaisons, *Nouveau traité des aids, tailles et gabelles* (Paris, 1643); Guy Cabourdin, "Gabelles et démographie en France au XVIIe siècle," *Annales de démographie historiques* (1969), pp. 293-314; for 1696, "Extrait du Mémoire de la Généralité de Moulins en 1698," in *État de la France. Extraits des mémoires dressées par les intendants de Royaume par l'order du Roi Louis XIV* (London, 1737), 5: 94.

6. Boris Porshnev, *Les Soulévements populaires en France au XVIIe siècle* (Paris, 1963), pp. 662-676.

7. Cabourdin, "Gabelles et démographie."

8. A. Vassayière, ed., *Proces-verbal de la généralité de Moulins, dressée en 1686 par l'intendant Florent d'Argouges* (Moulins, 1911).

9. "Extrait du Mémoire," p. 94.

10. Ducrot, *Le Nouveau traité.*

11. Emmanuel Le Roy Ladurie and Jeanne Recurat, "L'État des vents des sel vers 1625," *Annales. Économies, sociétés, civilisations* XXIV, No. 4 (1969), pp. 999-1010.

12. "Extrait du Mémoire," p. 94.

13. Sebastien le Prestre Vauban, "Description géographique de l'élection de Vézélay," in *Mémoires des intendants sur l'état des généralités dressées pour l'instruction du duc de Bourgogne,* ed. Antonie Boislisle (Paris, 1881), p. 740.

14. Ibid.

15. The following are only some of the more important works among a

considerable body of literature on this subject. Paul Raveau, *L'Agriculture et les classes paysannes: La transformation de la prorièté en Haut Poitou au XVIIe siècle* (Paris, 1926); Gaston Roupnel, *La Ville et la campagne au XVIIe siècle. Étude sur la population du pays dijonnais* (Paris, 1955); Louis Merle, *La Métairie et l'évolution de la Gatine poitevine* (Paris, 1958); Pierre Goubert, *Beauvais et le Beauvaisis de 1600 à 1730* (Paris, 1960); Jean Jacquart, *La Crise rural en Ile-de-France, 1550-1670* (Paris, 1974).

16. A. D. Nièvre, 2F 317, *Fonds du Bourg de Bozas.*

17. *Coutume de Nivernais,* chap. 6, art. 23.

18. The *cahiers* for the parish of Mhere complained that "the onerous condition of such properties inhibits their commercial circulation," while that of Mont-et-Marré demanded the conversion of *bordelage* tenures to *cens* because "it is well known that *bordelages* are almost impossible to sell when this becomes necessary." A. D. Nièvre, Series L, *Cahiers des doleances.*

19. A. D. Nièvre, 1 F 127, 129 and 397, *Fords Bruneau de Vitry.*

20. A. D. Nièvre, 1 F 296, *Fonds Bruneau de Vitry.*

21. A. D. Nièvre, 1 F 100 and 103, *Fonds Bruneau de Vitry.*

22. A. D. Nièvre, 2 F 279, *Fonds du Bourg de Bozas.*

23. A. D. Nièvre, 1 F 403, *Fond Bruneau de Vitry.*

24. A. D. Nièvre, 1 F 104, 213, 215, 218, 263-264, 297, 299-300, 323, 349-350, 364, 376, 402, 403, *Fonds Bruneau de Vitry.*

25. Guy Coquille, *Questions et réponses sur les coutumes de la France* (Paris, 1612), No. 276.

26. A. D. Nièvre, 2 F 243, 246, 247, 260, 272-296, 431-435, 457, 471, 476-479, 483, 595, *Fonds du Bourg du Bozas.*

27. A. D. Nièvre, 1 F 67, *Fonds Bruneau de Vitry.*

28. Nancy Fitch, "The Demographic and Economic Effects of Seventeenth Century Wars: The Case of the Bourbonnais, France" (Paper given at the Social Science History Association Annual Meeting, October, 1977), p. 16.

29. Porshnev, *Soulèvements,* pp. 662-663. Also, Andre Lequai, "Les Émotions et séditions populaires dans la généralité de Moulins aux XVIIe et XVIIIe siècles," *Révue d'histoire économique et sociale* 42 (1965), pp. 45-65.

30. Porshnev, *Soulèvements,* p. 60.

31. Roland Mousnier, ed., *Lettres et mémoires adressées au chancelier Sequier (1633-1649)* (Paris, 1964).

32. A. D. Nièvre, Series B 39, *Presidial de Saint-Pierre-le-Moutier.*

33. Boislisle, *Correspondances,* nos. 450 and 519.

34. "Extraite du Mémoire," pp. 93-94.

35. Jean Boichard, *La Vie rural entre Loire et Allier* (Paris, 1971), p. 29.

36. Jacquelaine Hecht, "La Vie de Francois Quesnay," in *Francois Quesnay et la Physiocratie* (Paris, 1958) 1: 245-246.

37. Arthur Young, *Travels in France During The Years 1787, 1788 and 1789* (New York, 1969), pp. 173-176.

38. A. D. Nièvre, 1 F 67 and 85, *Fonds Bruneau de Vitry.*

39. *Coutume de Nivernais,* chap. 6, art. 23.

40. Romain Baron, "La Bourgeois de Varzy au XVIIe siècle," *Annales de Bourgogne* 36 (1964), pp. 161-208.
41. A. D. Nièvre, 2 F 483, *Fonds du Bourg de Bozas.*
42. Vauban, "Description géographique," pp. 740-741.

Notes to Chapter Four

1. A. D. Nièvre, Sèries M, *Listes nominatives, 1820.*
2. A. D. Nièvre, Sèries M, *Tableau du nombre et de la division des côtes compriés aux rôles de la contribution fonçières de l'annee 1835.*
3. Jean Baudiot, *Annuaire statistique, administratif et commercial de dé-partement de la Nièvre* (Nevers, 1829), p. 82.
4. Sebastien le Prestre Vauban, "Description géographique de l'éléction de Vézelay en 1696," in Antoine de Boislisle, *Mémoires des Intendants sur l'état des généralités dressées pour l'instruction du Duc de Bourgogne* (Paris, 1881), p. 740.
5. J. Leváinville, *Le Morvan. Étude de géographie humaine* (Paris, 1910), p. 244.
6. In 1860 the commune of Poil was created from the western third of the commune of Larochemillay. Statistics and references made to Larochemillay throughout this paper are based on the present boundaries of the commune.
7. A. D. Nièvre, Cadastre 140, Larochemillay.
8. Arthur Young, *Travels in France During the Years 1787, 1788 and 1789* (New York, 1965), pp. 305-307.
9. Dupin, *Le Morvan: Topographie, agriculture, moeurs des habitants; état ancien, état actuel* (Paris, 1853), p. 11.
10. *Annales de Poussery* (1947), p. 394.
11. Antoine Desforges, *La Vie dans un coin du Morvan* (Nevers, 1911), p. 12.
12. France. Ministre de l'agriculture et du commerce, *Statistique de la France* (Paris, 1840).
13. Emile Guillaumin, *The Life of a Simple Man,* trans. Margaret Holden (London 1919), p. 52.
14. A. D. Nièvre, 1 F 292, *Dénombrement de la fief de Champrobert;* 2 C 835 *Contrôle des actes des notaires et sous signatures privés,* Bureau de Laro-chemillay; Réné de Nomazy, *Le Chartrier de Riviere, fief de la baronnie de la Larochemillay en Morvan* (Nice, 1955).
15. A. D. Nièvre, 2 C 831-836, *Contrôle des actes des notaires et des sous-signatures privés,* Bureau de Larochemillay, and 3 Q 16 *Régistres des actes des notaires et sous-signatures privés,* Bureau de Luzy.
17. A. D. Nièvre, 4 E 253 Larochemillay and 4 E 275 Saint-Jean-Goux.
18. Customary laws governing succession were supplanted by the laws of 17 Nivôse, Year II. *Bordelage* was completely abolished by the law of July 17, 1793.
19. A. D. Nièvre, Séries L, *Cahier de Château-Chinon.*
20. A. Vayssière, ed., *Proces-verbal de la Généralité de Moulins dresseés en*

1686 par Florent d'Argouges (Moulins, 1686); Claude Marion Saugrain, *Dénombrement du royaume* (Paris, 1709); A. D. Nièvre, *Cartes pour servir au département de la taille,* 1 C 230 *Éléction de Château-Chinon,* 1 C 293 *Eléction de Nevers.*

21. Emil Bin, *Le Morvan: Moeurs, coutumes, language, histoirettes, légendes, croyances populaires, topographie, histoire, monuments* (Château-Chinon, 1902).

22. See below, chapter six.

23. Antoine Desforges, "Curieuse délibérations des paroisses des environs de Châtillon-en-Bazois en 1790," *Mémoires de la société académique du Nivernais* 43 (1941), p. 40.

24. A. D. Nièvre, 1 C 312, Villapourçon, 1786.

25. Guillaumin, *Life of a Simple Man,* pp. 74-75.

26. Ibid., p. 172.

27. Seventy-one percent of the 1,179 societies classified by George Murdock in his *Ethnographic Atlas* are either patrilocal or virilocal. Some of the factors cited by anthropologists for such male preference are high population densities in areas of intensive cultivation and frequency of warfare. Under these conditions, families supposedly strive to concentrate male strength within the domestic group. See William Divale and Marvin Harris, "Population Warfare and Male Supremacy," *Transactions of the New York Academy of Sciences* (New York, 1975).

28. *Coutume de Nivernais,* chap. 34, art. 14. In the northern region of the province, this rule was not observed.

29. Jean-Lucien Gay, *Les Effects pécuniaires du mariage en Nivernais du XIVe au XVIIIe siècle* (Paris, 1953), p. 189.

30. Residence patterns for the households of sharecroppers were as follows:

Kin tie through		
males	Parents and married son(s)	18
	Married brothers	3
	Married brothers and married son(s)	10
Kin tie through females	Parents and married daughter(s)	14
Kin tie through both	Parents and married son(s) and married daughter(s)	14
males and females	Married brothers and sisters	2
	Married brothers and sisters and their married children	8
	Married brother(s) and kin of their son(s)- or daughter(s)-in-law	4

31. Guillaumin, *Life of a Simple Man,* p. 117.

32. Victor de Cheverry, "Fermiers à communauté taisible du Nivernais," *Les ouvriers des deux mondes* 5 (1885), pp. 6-7. Also, Desforges, *Un Coin du Morvan,* p. 25.

33. The extent of class endogamy at Larochemillay can be seen in the

following table showing the percentage of grooms marrying within the same class.

Occupation of Bride's Father:

Occupation of Groom:	*Laboureur*	*proprietaire*	*journalier*	No.
Laboureur	59.8%	28.1%	12.2%	82
Proprietaire	22.2	68.3	7.9	63
Journalier	26.8	21.1	46.7	71

34. Guillaumin, *Life of a Simple Man*, p. 90.

35. Desforges, *Un Coin du Morvan*, p. 23. Also, de Cheverry, "Fermiers à communauté," p. 23.

36. De Cheverry, "Fermiers à communauté," p. 19.

37. Ibid., p. 19-20.

38. Jean Drouillet, *Folklore du Nivernais et du Morvan* (La-Charité-sur-Loire, 1959), p. 166.

39. A. D. Nièvre, 4 E 253 and 275.

40. Drouillet, *Folklore*, p. 166.

41. J-F Baudiau, *Le Morvan, ou éssai géographique, topographique et historique sur cette contrée* (Nevers, 1865), p. 40.

42. Dupin, *Le Morvan*, p. 28.

43. Vauban, "Déscription géographique," p. 741.

44. N. Monod, "Les Maisons-types dans la région de Montsauche (Morvan)," in *Enquête sur les conditions de l'habitation en France: Les maisons-types* (Paris, 1894), p. 374.

45. J. Simon, *Statistique de la commune de Fretoy* (Château-Chinon, 1883), pp. 9-10.

46. A. D. Nièvre, Series L, *Cahier de doleance de Château-Chinon.*

Notes to Chapter Five

1. Quoted in Philippe Sagnac *Le Législation civile de la Révolution française (1789-1804). Essai d'histoire sociale* (Paris, 1898), p. 220n.

2. J. de Maumigny, *Étude sur Guy Coquille, publiciste et juriconsulte* (Paris, 1910), and Joseph Caillot, *La Coutume de Nivernais etudiée dans ses differences avec le droit common coutumier* (Paris, 1887).

3. Sagnac, *La Législation civile*, pp. 217-226.

4. Ibid., pp. 218-224.

5. M. Mavidal and C. Laurent, eds., *Archives Parlementaires de 1787 à 1860* (Paris, 1901), 59: 681-83.

6. A. N. D. III 382, *Lettres addressée à la Committee Législatif.*

7. Laws of 9 Fructidor Year III, 3 Vendémaire, Year IV and 18 Pluviose, Year V.

8. Law of 4 Germinal, Year VIII.

9. *Code Napoléon*, art. 913.

10. Paul Bastid, *De la fonction sociale des communautés taisibles en l'ancien droit* (Tours, 1916), p. 153.

11. *Code Napoleón*, art. 784. However, such renunciations could be made only after the parents had died.

12. *Recueil des lois composant le Code Civil, avec les Discours des Orateurs du Gouvernement, les Rapports de la commission de Tribunat, et les Opinions omisés pendant le cours de la discussion, tant au Tribunat qu'au corps législatif* (Paris, 1804), 7: 260 and 277-278.

13. *Code Napoleón*, arts. 13, 34, and 37.

14. Ibid., arts. 38 and 39.

15. Victor de Cheverry, "Fermiers à communauté taisible du Nivernais," *Les Ouvriers des deux mondes* 5 (1885), pp. 41-2.

16. De Cheverry, "Fin des communautés taisibles du Nivernais," *Union du Nivernais et du Bourbonnais, Réunion régionale de 11 avril 1886* (1886), p. 49.

17. *Annales de Poussery* (1840).

18. Dupin, "Lettre à M. Etienne, de l'Academie française, à la suite d'une excursion dans la Nièvre, et d'une visite à la commuauté des Jault 22 septembre 1840," in Dupin, *Le Morvan: Topographie, agriculture, moeurs des habitants; état ancien, état actuel* (Paris, 1853), p. 94.

19. Albert Maron, "La Communauté des Jault: Une association agricole de l'ancien France, des origins de la féodalite jusqu'a l'année 1847," *La Réforme Sociale* 10, ser. 2 (1890), pp. 259-276; Charles Prieuret, "Une Association agricole en Nivernais: Histoire de la Grosse Communauté des. Jaults, 1580-1847," *Bulletin de la société nivernaise des lettres, sciences et arts* 2 (1927), pp. 333-383.

20. De Cheverry, "Fermiers," p. 49.

21. Maron, "La Communauté des Jaults," p. 276.

22. See, for example, Robert A. Nisbet, *The Social Bond: An Introduction to the Study of Society* (New York, 1970) and "State and Family," in *Social Change*, ed. Nisbet (New York, 1972), pp. 190-210.

23. A. D. Nièvre, Series L, *Tribunaux*.

24. A. D. Nièvre, *Tableaux alphabètiques des partages* for the following: 2 C 2040-2041 and 3 Q 5, Bureau de Château-Chinon; 2 C 2250 and 3 Q 16, Bureau de Luzy; 2 C 2301-2302 and 3 Q 18, Bureau de Moulins-Engilbert.

25. A. D. Nièvre, 2 C 831-836, Bureau de La Roche Millay. *Contrôle des actes des notaires et sous-signatures privés;* 3 Q 16, Bureau de Luzy, *Registres des actes des notaires et sous-signatures privés*.

26. A. D. Nièvre, Cadastre 140, Larochemillay.

27. A. D. Nièvre, Series M, *Tableau du nombre et de la division des côtes comprisés aux rôles de la contribution foncière de l'année 1835*.

28. *Coutume de Nivernais*, chap. 24, arts. 1 and 2.

29. The increase in the number of *côtes* for the *arrondissements* of the departement of the Nièvre was as follows:

	1835	1852	% increase
Château-Chinon	12,687	18,563	46.3
Nevers	16,053	20,263	26.2

Cosne	23,287	29,383	26.2
Clamecy	31,834	37,943	19.2

30. Jean Boichard, *La Vie rurale entre Loire et Allier* (Paris, 1971), pp. 32-33.

31. Paul Meunier, *La Nièvre sous la Convention* (Nevers, 1895), p. 335.

32. Gabriel Vanneureau, *Le District de Moulins-Engilbert pendant la Révolution* (Nevers, 1962-1966), 1: 73-86 and 162-168.

33. M. le Marquis de Saint-Phalle and M. Pinet de Maupas, *Enquête sur le situation et les besoins de l'agriculture. Réponses faites au questionnaire général* (Nevers, 1867), p. 5.

34. A. D. Nièvre, *Cartes pour servir au département de la taille*, 1 C 230, Éléction de Château-Chinon; 1 C 293, Éléction de Nevers. Series M, *Statistique agricoles, Enquête agricole de 1892.*

35. Archives municipale de Larochemillay, *Listes nominative de 1846, 1856, 1866, and 1876.*

Notes to Chapter Six

1. Guy Coquille, *Les Coutumes du pays et duché de Nivernois avec les annotations et commentaires* (Paris, 1625); see also, Jean Drouillet, *Folklore du Nivernais et du Morvan* (La-Charité-sur-Loire, 1959), pp. 51-60.

2. Dupin, *Le Morvan*, pp. 1-2.

3. Emil Blin, *Le Morvan, moeurs, coutumes, language, historiettes, légendes populaires, topographie, histoire, monuments* (Château-Chinon, 1912).

4. A. Hovelaique and G. Hervé, *Recherches éthnographiques sur le Morvan* (Paris, 1894). In fact, the inhabitants of the Morvan were physically distinct from their neighbors in surrounding regions, as recruitment reports testify. Between 1806 and 1814, over twenty percent of all recruits from the Morvan were rejected as being too short, compared to fifteen percent from the rest of the *département.* (Jean Baudiot, *Annuaire statistique, administratif et commercial du département de la Nièvre* [Nevers, 1829]). Such physical differences, due to the poorer diets of the region, persisted throughout the century. See H. Labit, *Topographie médicale du département de la Nièvre* (Paris, 1892).

5. A. Levainville, *Le Morvan. Étude de géographie humaine* (Paris, 1909), pp. 133-134.

6. P. Gillet, *Annuaire de département de la Nièvre* (Nevers, 1809).

7. A. D. Nièvre, Séries M, *Statistique agricoles et des récoltes. Résponses au questions proposées au sous-prefets* (1815).

8. Marlière, *Rapport statistique sur l'arrondissement de Clamecy* (Clamecy, 1856).

9. L. Mirot, "Notes pour servir à l'histoire du Nivernais et du Donziais de 1360 à 1409 après les comptes de la Recette générale et des Châtellenies," *Bulletin de la société académique du Nivernais* 39 (1937),

10. The jurisdictional limits of the two customs are discussed in: Leon Mirot and André Bossuat, *Les Limites et la réunion du Nivernais et du Donziais;* P.

Meunier, "Bailliage provincial-Duché pairie de Nivernais," *Bulletin de la société nivernaise des lettres, sciences et arts,* ser. 3, V (1937).

11. *Costumes d'Auxerre,* art. 202.

12. A. D. Nièvre, Séries M. *Listes nominatives de 1820.*

13. A. D. Nièvre, Séries M. *Statistiques agricoles de 1852.*

14. A. D. Nièvre, Séries M. Statistiques agricoles de 1872. There are numerous instances of communal reports returned to mayors to be redone because they were erroneously filled out the first time.

15. Figures derived from *Statistique générale. Résultats généraux de l'enquête de 1882* (Nancy, 1884).

16. The average rate of the *impôt fonçier* between 1851-1853 and 1879-1881 remained at 1.64 francs. Ministère des finances, *Nouvelle évaluation du revenue fonçier des propriétés non-batiés de la France* (Paris, 1884).

17. Figures derived from Le Duc de Boullainvilliers, *L'État de la France* note (London, 1709).

18. Vauban, "Rapport sur l'éléction de Vézelay."

Notes to Chapter Seven

1. M. Taverna, "Une ville affamée: Nevers pendant la Révolution," *Mémoires de la société académique du nivernais* 21 (1921), p. 81.

2. Guy Thuillier, *Aspects de l'économie nivernais au XIXe siècle,* (Paris, 1966), pp. 16-17.

3. François Quesnay, "Fermiers," in *Oeuvres économique et philosophiques de F. Quesnay,* ed. Auguste Oncken (New York, 1888), pp. 159-192.

4. "In the Upper Morvan a third of the land is cultivated. That is, one-sixth in rye, one-sixth in spring grains. When each sixth part has been cropped for two harvests they are left in fallow and another third is sown, with each third left uncultivated for eight years, serving only as pasture." A. D. Nièvre, M 1162, *Situation d'agricole et des recoltes, 1810-1935. Réponses aux questions propesées au sous-préfet de Château-Chinon* (1815). On the Nivernais proper, see Roger Dion, *Le Val de Loire,* (Tours, 1934), pp. 533-559.

5. Baron J. de Terline, *L'Agriculture dans l'Amognes à la fin du XVIIIe siècle d'après la relation contemporaire inedité de J-C Flamen d'Assigny,* (Nevers, 1927), p. 27.

6. Dion, *Le Val de Loire,* p. 33.

7. Arthur Young, *Travels in France During the Years 1787, 1788 and 1789,* (New York, 1865), pp. 279-280.

8. Emile Guillaumin, *The Life of a Simple Man,* trans. Margaret Holden (London, 1919), pp. 202-203.

9. Terline, *L'Agriculture dans l'Amognes,* p. 41.

10. Thuillier, *Économie nivernais,* p. 16n.

11. A. N., F10 285, *Lettre de 25 Nivôse An II de la Société Populaire de Brutus le Magnanime à la Convention National.*

12. J. Levainville, *Le Morvan, étude de géographie humaine* (Paris, 1908), pp. 490-491.

13. M. Le Prieur, *Histoire du district de La-Charité-sur-Loire* (Nevers, 1937), pp. 26-28.

14. Bibliothèque municipal de Nevers, 2 N 326, *Observations presentées pour Louis Ballerat, fermier, demeurant en la commune de Saint-Caise; contre le sieur François Paignon, proprietaire demeurant à Nevers* (1809).

15. A. D. Nièvres, M 1162, *Réponses aux questions proposées au sous-préfet de Nevers* (1815).

16. Young, *Travels in France*, p. 170.

17. Terline, *L'Agriculture dans l'Amognes*, p. 43.

18. Joseph Fièvèe, "Note confidentielle de Fièvèe sur le département de la Nièvre (16 fevrier 1815)," in Thuillier, *L'Économie nivernais*, p. 497.

19. A. D. Nièvre, 7 M 1161/2, *Notice sur la statistique bovine de l'arrondissement de Nevers* (1819).

20. Eric Kerridge, *The Agricultural Revolution* (London, 1967), p. 27.

21. George Grantham, "The Diffusion of the New Husbandry in Northern France, 1815-1840," *Journal of Economic History* 38, no. 2 (June 1978), pp. 311-37.

22. Figures were derived from: Ministère des travaux publiques de l'agriculture et du commerce, *Archives Statistiques* (Paris, 1 37).

23. A. D. Nièvre, M 1162, *Réponses aux questions proposées au sous-préfet de Nevers* (1815).

24. Jean-Claude Toutain, "La Consommation alimentaire en France de 1789 à 1964," *Économies et sociétés, Cahiers de l'I.S.E.A., V, No. 11 (Novembre, 1971), pp. 1946-1947.*

25. *G. Desert, "Viande et poisson dans l'alimentation des français au milieu de XIXe siècle," Annales, E.S.C. 30 (1975), pp. 519-533.*

26. According to Toutain's figures, some 769,000 tons of beef were consumed in France between 1835 adn 1844; by the decade 1895-1905 this amount had risen to 1,716,000 tons.

27. Toutain, "Consommation alimentaire," p. 1942.

28. "All the roads near us leading to Saint-Saulges and Châtillon are impassable for three months of the year. All local roads are too narrow, obstructed by stones and trees or crossed by creeks which impede travelers each winter." Terline, *L'Agriculture dans l'Amognes*, p. 41.

29. The royal route skirting the Loire was the only road completed in the *département* by the Revolution. Of the twenty leagues of road between Nevers and Luzy, eleven remain incomplete; between Clamecy and Nevers only eight of eighteen leagues were finished; between Nevers and Château-Chinon ten leagues were completed and eight remained unfinished. No bridges crossed the Allier River, cutting off communication with the Bourbonnais. Taverna, "Une ville affamée," p. 24.

30. "We declare that the roads to the town of Decize, Saint-Saulge, Nevers,

Moulins-Engilbert and Luzy are impassible and that one can't move goods or cattle to the markets of these places without considerable loss." (Parish of Langy.) "The Nivernais needs means of communication to nearby cities; lacking such roads the commerce of parishes only three or four leagues away are interrupted at least five months of the year because the roads are so bad that one cannot even drive cattle to these towns." (Parish of Cercy-la-Tour.) A local official gave the following description of road conditions at La-Charité in 1794: "The poor state of roads forces carters to cross sown fields and these cut a path so large that a major part of the harvest is destroyed." LePrieur, *La District de La-Charité-sur-Loire*, p. 28.

31. *Rapport statistique sur les routes départementales de la Nièvre* (Nevers, 1834).

32. M. le marquis de Saint-Phalle and M. Pinet de Maupas, *Enquête sur les besoins et la situation de l'agriculture. Réponses fait au questionnaire général* (Nevers, 1867), p. 65.

33. O. Delafond, *Progrés agricole et amelioration du gros bétail de la Nièvre* (Paris, 1849), p. 33.

34. P. Boisseau, *Traité d'agriculture* (Cosne, 1887), p. 9.

35. Figures on agriculture derived from the following sources: For 1805, P. Gillet, *Annuaire du département de la Nièvre pour l'an XI* (Nevers, 1805); for 1815, Ministère de l'instruction publique et des beaux-arts. Comité des travaux historiques et scientifiques. *Notices, inventaires et documents. Statistique agricole de 1815* (Paris, 1914); for 1837, Ministère de l'agriculture et du commerce, *Statistique de la France. Agriculture* (Paris, 1840); for 1852, *Statistique général. Statistique de la France,* ser. 2, 8 (Paris, 1860); for 1862, *Statistique de la France. Résultats généraux de l'enquête décennale de 1862* (Strasbourg, 1870); for 1872, A. D. Nièvre, M 1156, *Statistique agricole,* 1872; for 1882, Statistique général. *Résultats généraux de l'enquête décennale de 1882* (Nancy, 1887). For a critique of these sources, see Réné Musset, "Les Statistiques agricoles françaises: etude critique," *Annales d'histoire économique et sociale* (1933), pp. 284-291, and Bertrand Gille, *Les sources statistiques de l'histoire de France* (Paris, 1964).

36. A. D. Nièvre, 7 M 1162/2, *Rapport des sous-préfet sur la statistique bovine de l'arrondissement de Château-Chinon* (1819).

37. Figures derived from 1815 and 1862 government surveys cited above. Government surveys of agriculture report the following numbers of cattle in the Nièvre:

	1815	1830	1837	1852	1862	1882
Bulls	11,781	13,177	12,005	5,400	4,022	2,563
Oxen	29,172	45,161	40,427	41,155	44,484	42,504
Cows	31,262	47,222	51,558	61,168	63,789	76,072
Heifers	9,766	26,819	22,365	36,869	40,832	21,759
Calves	14,978	——	——	——	29,748	37,038
	96,959	132,379	126,355	144,592	182,875	180,026

38. On the cattle and fattening industry of the Nivernais, see Delafond, *Progrès agricole;* Le comte de Pazzis, *Enquête sur la situation de bétail dans le département de la Nièvre* (Paris, 1875); M. de Damas d'Anlezy, *En Nivernais, étude de la production animale dans la canton de Saint-Benin-d'Azy* (Nevers, 1907); Achille Naudin, *L'Industrie de l'elévage dans la Nièvre* (Paris, 1916); Jean Meuvret, "Les Amognes," *Annales géographie* (1926), vol. 35, pp. 236-244; Thuillier, *L'Économie nivernais,* pp. 13-32.

39. Figures derived from government surveys noted above.

40. "Rapport de M. Bouche," *Bulletin de la société centrale d'agriculture et d'industrie du département de la Nièvre* (1840-1841), pp. 191-212. Joseph Imbart de la Tour, *Réponse au questionnaire de la grande enquête agricole de 1888, notamment en ce qui concerne le Nivernais* (Nevers, 1888), The total value of agricultural production, as measured in francs, increased from 34,836,000 f in 1837 to 77,931,000 f in 1852, an increase of 123%. During the next ten years the value of production rose to 204,985,000 f, or by 163%.

41. A. D. Nièvre, 6 M 2160/5; prices are averages for markets at Nevers, Saint-Pierre-le-Moutier, Cosne, Donzy, La-Charité, Pouilly, Premery, Saint-Amand, Clamecy, Corbigny, Lormes, and Tannay.

42. Lucien Gueneau, *L'Organisation du travail à Nevers aux XVIIe et XVIIIe siècles* (Nevers, 1919). In 1829, the sub-perfect for Château-Chinon reported that large numbers of cattle were being withheld from the market by farmers due to the intense drought that year. A. D. Nièvre, M 1156, *Tableau de situation de divers produits de l'agriculture* (Château-Chinon).

43. The average weights of cattle slaughtered in the Nièvre (in Kilograms) during the first half of the century were as follows:

	1816	*1820*	*1833*	*1840*
Oxen	283	283	279	230
Cows	173	170	174	133

Sources: *Archives statistiques* and *Statistique de la France (1840).*

44. Philippe Thienneaut, *La Crise actuelle et l'agriculture* (Clamecy, 1886), p. 6.

45. See especially Thuillier, *L'Économie nivernais,* pp. 21-26.

46. Farmers sought to protect their crops from *foulots* by crossing two sheaves of straw and chanting, "Foulot, j'te maudis; n'pass par ici . . . Foulot, foulot! Retourne-toi comme t'es venu!" Jean Drouillet, "Notes d'un folkloriste. Costumes de moisson en pays nivernais," *Annales du pays nivernais* 2 (1972), p. 27.

47. M. de Chambray, *De l'agriculture et de l'industrie dans la province de Nivernais* (Paris, 1834), pp. 13-14.

48. Pierre Boisseau, *Traité d'agriculture* (Cosne, 1887).

49. Guillaumin, *Life of a Simple Man,* p. 47.

50. Terline, *L'Agriculture dans l'Amognes,* p. 16. Responses furnished by Saint-Phalle to the 1866 survey indicate that a single hectare of arable may have required as much as four days of plowing.

51. Achille Naudin, *L'Industrie de l'élévage*, p. 244. None of the leases passed at the communes of Larochemillay or Limanton carried such clauses, at least up to 1864. It is possible that clauses of the type noted by Naudin, which were drawn up in the early years of the twentieth century, were inserted only after rural emigration threatened to drain off needed manpower. Similar clauses existed in leases drawn up in the Bourbonnais just to the South.

52. As late as 1882 only 64,571 hectares of meadow were irrigated by creeks or man-made ditches, while 37,452 hectares of meadow were not irrigated at all.

53. *Enquête sur la situation et les besoins d'agriculture. Proces verbaux des séances de la commission départementales et dépositions*, (Paris, 1867) 9: 418-419.

54. Taurin-Theodore Robin, *Guide théoretique et pratique des cultivateurs* (Nevers, 1861), p. 120.

Notes to Chapter Eight

1. A. D. Nièvre, M 1156, *Statistique agricole* (1882); J. Levanville, *Le Morvan. Étude de géographie humaine* (Paris, 1910), p. 164.

2. A. D. Nièvre, M 1156, *Statistique agricole (1836, 1852, and 1882)*.

3. A. D. Nièvre, 4 M 1141/4, *Rapport et correspondances des préfets et sous-préfets, état d'ésprit de la population (Château-Chinon, 1853)*.

4. A. D. Nièvre, M 1156, *Statistique agricole, Biches (1882)*.

5. A. Marlière, *Statistique de l'arrondissement de Clamecy* (Clamecy, 1859), pp. 217, 241, and 385.

6. A. Hovelaque and G. Hervé, *Recherches éthnologuiques sur le Morvan* (Paris, 1894).

7. A. D. Nièvre, 4 M 1141/4, *Rapport*.

8. Emil Blin, *Le Morvan: Moeurs, coutumes, language, historiettes, légendes, croyances, populaires, typographie, histoire, monuments* (Château-Chinon, 1902), p. 70.

9. Cultivation of potatoes and other root crops such as sugar beets required three separate plowings to prepare the seed bed. After planting, a further plowing was necessary to cut down weeds; this was followed by a later weeding carried out by hand. Labor costs for root crops were in fact twice that of cereals. According to the 1866 Agricultural Survey, these totaled 2.20 francs per hectare for potatoes, 2.82 francs for sugar beets, and only 1.05 francs for wheat or rye. M. le marquis de Saint-Phalle and M. Pinet de Maupas, *Enquête sur la situation et les besoins de l'agriculture. Réponses faites au questionnaire général* (Nevers, 1867), pp. 32 and 41.

10. A. D. Nièvre, M, *Listes nominatives* (1820).

11. A. D. Nièvre, *Cadastre. 140, Larochemillay; 142, Limanton*.

12. A. D. Nièvre, M 1162, *Résponses aux questions proposées de sous-préfet de Château-Chinon relativement à l'agriculture de son arrondissement (1815)*.

13. Le Comte de Pazzis, *Enquête sur la situation du bétail dans le département de la Nièvre* (Paris, 1875), pp. 3-4.

14. A. D. Nièvre, 7 M 1161/2, *Rapport du sous-préfet sur la statistique bovine de l'arrondissement de Château-Chinon* (1819).

15. The 1836 agricultural survey for the canton of Châtillon-en-Bazois, roughly equivalent to the Bazois itself, reported a total of 4,412 hectares in fallow and 5,596 hectares in crops.

16. A. D. Nièvre, 7 M 1161/2, *Rapport*.

17. According to annual statistics on agriculture in the canton of Châtillon-en-Bazois, fallows which had totaled 4,412 hectares in 1836 had been reduced to 3,402 hectares by 1852 and to 2,496 hectares by 1859.

18. O. Delafond, *Progrès agricole et amélioration du gros bétail en la Nièvre* (Paris, 1849), p. 33.

19. A. D. Nièvre, M 1156, *Statistique agricole, Limanton and Larochemillay.*

20. Only seventeen of the one hundred and seventy-four resident proprietors at Larochemillay (i.e., those persons listed in both the 1856 census and the cadastre) were covered by the survey that year. In Limanton, only thirty-five of one hundred and thirty-six resident proprietors were surveyed. As the following figures show, the smaller the holding the more likely it was to be ignored.

Proprietors listed in 1856 census and owning:		Proprietors listed in 1856 survey:	Percentage not surveyed:
Larochemillay			
under 1 ha.	68	0	100.0%
1 to 5	76	10	86.8
5 to 20	30	7	76.7
	174	17	92.0
Limanton			
under 1 ha.	63	3	95.2%
1 to 5	52	18	65.4
5 to 20	21	14	33.3
	136	35	74.3

21. A. D. Nièvre, M 1156, *Statistiques agricoles, Larochemillay and Limanton.*

22. Archives municipales de Limanton and Larochemillay, *Listes nominatives, 1836 to 1876.*

23. A. D. Nièvre, M 1156, *Statistiques agricoles, Limanton and Larochemillay (1892).*

24. George Grantham, "Scale and Organization in French Farming, 1840-1880," in *European Peasants and Their Markets,* ed. William N. Parker and Eric L. Jones (Princeton, N.J., 1975), pp. 293-326.

25. A. D. Nièvre, 3 Q 18, *Registre des actes des notaires et sous-signatures privès. Bureau de Moulins-Engilbert.*

Notes to Chapter Nine

1. Le Marquis de Chambray, *De l'agriculture et de l'industrie dans la province de Nivernais* (Paris, 1834), p. 24.

2. A. N. C. 960, *Enquête sur le travail agricole et industrielle (1848). Nièvre, cantons of Luzy and Moulins-Engilbert.*

3. Emil Guillaumin, *The Life of a Simple Man,* trans. Margaret Holden (London 1919), pp. 203-204.

4. *Annales de Poussery* (1847), p. 12.

5. "Extrait des mémoires d'Isaïe Bonfils," *Mémoires de la société académique du Nivernais* 7 (1898), pp. 60-92.

6. Guy Thuillier, *Aspects de l'économie nivernais au XIXe siècle* (Paris, 1969), p. 26.

7. The Société owned five *métairies* at Poussery totaling 256 hectares and worked by a labor force of eleven males, eleven females and eight children. Total income for the tenants was stated by Avril to be 5,466 francs, less a *bellemain* of 1,365 francs, leaving 4,101 francs. Avril estimated that, to feed all members of the family, it would cost approximately 4,735 francs. As he put it, "It is pointless to push the calculations any further." *Annales de Poussery* (1847), pp. 393-394.

8. *Ibid.*, p. 52.

9. E. de Chambure, *Une domaine du Morvand* (Nevers, 1854). The farm was located in the commune of Saint-Hilaire and described by Chambure as "an oasis in the wilderness."

10. Avril's arguments were made before various meetings of the Société and were printed in the association's journal, *Annales de Poussery,* in 1847.

11. Taurin-Theodore Robin, *Guide théoretique et pratique des cultivateurs* (Nevers, 1861), p. 15.

12. A. D. Nièvre, 10 M 1164, *Enquête sur le travail industrielle et agricole* (1848).

13. E. Jouzier, *Économie rurale* (Paris, 1910), p. 399.

14. Enquête sur la situation et les besoins de l'agriculture. Procès verbaux des seances de la commission départementales et dépositions (Paris, 1866), p. 363.

15. Statistique général, *Résultats du dénombrements de 1851 and 1872* (Strasbourg, 1853, Nancy, 1874); M. le Marquis de Saint-Phalle and M. Pinet de Maupas, *Enquête sur la situation et les besoins de l'agriculture. Réponses au questionnaire général* (Nevers, 1867). There is evidence that during the initial stages of the transition to *fermage* some tenants proved unable to shoulder the burdens of investment. When the Marquis d'Espeuilles leased his *domaines* for a fixed money rent in the 1840s, his tenants were unable to invest enough capital to improve production, and the marquis was forced to return to sharecropping. In 1852 the commission on agriculture in the *arrondissement* of Nevers reported that "the progress of agriculture has not been great enough to give the profession of *fermier* the importance that it will one day have. This is due in part to the fact that most do not have sufficient capital to bring the land to its full productive potential." *Annales de Poussery* (1852), pp. 46-47, 52.

16. A. D. Nièvre, M 1156, *Statistiques agricoles* 1852 and 1872).

17. A. D. Nièvre, 4 M 1141/4, *Rapports et correspondances des préfets et sous-préfets, état d'ésprit de la population* (Château-Chinon, 1853).

18. A. D. Nièvre, 3 Q 16, *Registres des actes des notaire et sous-signatures privées. Bureau de Luzy.* 3 Q 18, *Bureau de Moulins-Engilbert.* Omitted were those leases made to agents and subcontractors who would sublet *domaines* to tenants.

19. Thuillier, *Économie nivernais,* p. 19. Such practices were a further source of friction between landowners and tenants. See, for example, Guillaumin, *Life of a Simple Man,* pp. 66-67, 152-154, 162-163, 201-203.

20. Guillaumin, *Life of a Simple Man,* pp. 25-26, 162.

21. Guillaumin, *En Bourbonnais: La Propriété et l'agriculture, les moeurs, les diverses categories de travailleurs* (Paris, n.d.), pp. 12-13.

22. Guillaumin, *Life of a Simple Man,* pp. 60-61.

23. Provisions of this type usually stipulated that the tenant was not to graze animals on medowland after March 25 and forbade him to sublet the farm without permission. In a number of leases at Limanton, in the 1850s and 1860s, tenants were held to plant a stipulated number of hectares in clover and were to apply so much marl on certain fields.

24. Victor de Cheverry, "Fermiers à communauté taisible du Nivernais," *Les Ouvriers des deux mondes* 5 (1885), p. 12.

25. Ministère des finances, *Nouvelle évaluations du révenue fonçier des propriétés non-bâties de la France* (Paris, 1884).

26. Antoine Desforges, *La Vie dans un coin du Morvan* (Paris, 1911), p. 12.

27. Guillaumin, *En Bourbonnais,* p. 26.

28. The distribution of crops and the number of farm animals for such a *domaine* are here based on the communal survey of 1856. Yields for cereals and other crops are derived from figures reported in the survey of 1852 for the canton of Luzy. Revenues were determined by the average prices for animals, cereals and other crops as given in the *départemental mercuriales* for the years 1860 to 1864.

29. Estimates place the net revenue of a hectare of pasture in the Nièvre at 79.97 francs in 1851 and 119 francs in 1879. According to government agricultural surveys, the average *fermage* for a hectare of pastureland in the canton of Châtillon-en-Bazois rose from 100 francs in 1852 to 137 francs in 1882. For a hectare of second-class pasture, the increase was even less, rising from 90 francs to 108 francs, or about twenty percent. *Nouvelle évaluations du révenue fonçier;* A. D. Nièvre, M 1156, *Statistiques agricoles* (1852 and 1882).

30. As in the Larochemillay farm, the figures here are based on the communal survey of 1856 and prices for farm products during the 1860s.

31. For a discussion of this, see Eric Wolf, "Types of Latin American Peasantry: A Preliminary Discussion," *American Anthropologist,* 57 (1955), pp. 452-471.

32. De Cheverry, "Fermiers à communauté," pp. 24-37.

Notes to Chapter Ten

1. Victor de Cheverry, "Fin des communautés taisibles du Nivernais," *Union du Nivernais et du Bourbonnais. Réunion régionale du 11 avril 1886* (1886), p. 49.

2. *Annales de Poussery* (1840-1841), p. 76.

3. Joseph Imbart de la Tour, *La Causes morales et économiques de la désertion des campagnes* (Paris, 1909), p. 4.

4. *Enquête sur la situation et les besoins de l'agriculture. Proces-verbaux des séances de la commission départementales et dépositions* (Paris, 1866), p. 360.

5. De Cheverry, "Fin des communautés," pp. 52-53.

6. Ibid., p. 49.

7. Antoine Desforges, *La Vie dans un coin du Morvan* (Paris, 1911), p. 22.

8. M. Dupin, *Le Morvan: Topographie, agriculture, moeurs des habitants. État ancien, état actuel* (Paris, 1853), pp. 3-4.

9. De Cheverry, "Fermiers à communauté taisible du Nivernais," *Les Ouvriers des deux mondes* 5 (1885), p. 5.

10. In the Pervy *communauté* the maîtress was not the husband of the maître but the widow of the former head of the household. In most *communautés* at Limanton and Larochemillay, the master and the mistress were also husband and wife.

11. Emil Guillaumin, *The Life of a Simple Man,* trans. Margaret Holden (London, 1919), pp. 102-103.

12. De Cheverry, "Fin des commuanutés," p. 47.

13. Guillaumin, *Panorama de l'évolution paysanne (1870-1935)* (Paris, 1935), pp. 12-13. Guillaumin also cited rising living costs after 1850 as a factor that intensified conflicts within the *communautés*. Younger members demanded more money for living expenses from parents who were unable to furnish it.

14. A. D. Nièvre, Series L, *Tribunal de Moulins-Engilbert.*

15. Guillaumin, *Life of a Simple Man,* p. 2.

16. Ibid., p. 189.

17. Ibid., pp. 199-201.

18. Achille Millien, *Chants et chansons. Litterature orale et traditions du Nivernais* (Paris, 1906-1910), 1: 263.

19. M. Burley, *Le Morvan, coeur de la France* (Paris, 1959), 2: 25-26.

20. *Coutume du Nivernais,* chap. 8, art. 25.

21. Guillaumin, *Life of a Simple Man,* p. 39.

22. M. de Lespinasse, "Les Maisons-types dans la region de Nevers," in *Enquête sur les conditions de l'habitation en France: Les maisons-types,* ed. Alfred Fovile (Paris, 1894), p. 351.

23. N. Monod, "Les Maisons-types dans la region du Montsauche (Morvan)," in ibid., p. 374.

Bibliography

I. Manuscripts deposited in the Archives Nationales at Paris

C 960   Enquête sur le travail agricole et industrielle (1848).

D III 382   Questions relatives aux succession et substitutions. Pétitions individuelles et collectives. Mémoires relatif aux lois concernant les successions et donations, l'egalité des partages.

D III 1-310   Correspondances et pétitions relatives à des constatations en matière de législation, à jugements civils, à des nominations de fonctionnaires de l'ordre judiciaire.

F^{10} 203^a Rapports des préfets (1807-1812).

F^{10} 212^b Comité d'agriculture. Commission d'agriculture et des actes (1789-An 3). Pétitions, mémoires, plaintes et observations des particuleurs et corps constituées.

F^{10} 285   Comité d'agriculture. Pétitions (1790-An 3).

F^{10} 331   Comité d'agriculture. Mémoires et Pétitions (An 2-3). Application des lois, amélioration des cultures.

L 998-1000   Titres concernant les abbayes de Notre-Dame-d'Apponay et de Bellevaux.

S 3303$^{5-19}$ Titres, aveux, baux et dénombrements.

Q^1 825^1 Aveux et dénombrements des fiefs de Villette-les-forges, Champrobert, Lavault, La-Corvée, Montaron, La Forêt, La Verechère.

II. Manuscripts deposited in the Archives départementales de la Nièvre

B 39   Présidial de Saint-Pierre-le Moutier.

Série C   Relèves des aveux, dénombrements, fois et hommages. Contrôles dans les bureaux de la généralité depuis leur creation et copies d'éxtraits pour les paroisses.

1 C 156   Bureau de Larochemillay.

1 C 159   Limanton, Moulins-Engilbert, Maux, Saint-Honoré, Vandenesse.

Sous-série   1 C Cartes pour servir au département de la taille.

1 C 230   Élection de Château-Chinon (1750-1764).

1 C 232   Élection de Château-Chinon (1789).

1 C 293   Élection de Nevers (1760).

1 C 298   Élection de Nevers (1789).

1 C 299-312   Rôles d'impositions des paroisses. Élection de Nevers.

Sous-série 2 C Administration des domaines.

2 C 831-136   Contrôle des actes des notaires et sous-signée privée. Bureau de Larochemillay (1773-1791).

2 C 1222-1229   Contrôle des actes de notaires et sous-signée privée. Bureau de Moulins-Engilbert (1773-1789).

2 C 2040-2042   Tableaux alphabétiques des partages. Bureau de Château-Chinon (1738-1812).

2 C 2250   Tableau alphabétiques des partages. Bureau de Luzy (1707-1822).

2 C 2301   Tableau alphabétiques des partages. Bureau de Moulins-Engilbert (1730-1812).

Sous-série 3 E Registres des minutes notariales.

3 E 13-2   Étude de M. Perrot. Bureau de Moulins-Engilbert.

Sous-série 4 E État civil.

4 E 253   Larochemillay.

4 E 275   Saint-Jean-Goux.

4 E 255   Limanton.

Sous-série 1 F, Fonds Bruneau de Vitry.

Sous-série 2 F, Fonds Du Bourg du Bozas.

Série L Cahiers de doleances.

Tribunal de Moulins-Engilbert.

Série M Administration général.

Listes nominatives (1820, 1831).

4 M 1141   Rapports et correspondances des préfets et sous-préfets, état d'ésprit de la population.

6 M 1152   Reseignements géographiques et économiques.

6 M 1153   Recensements de la population.

6 M 1156   Statistiques agricoles (1815-1900).

6 M 1160   Mercuriales. Nevers (1813-1861), Département (1813-1900).

6 M 1162   Réponses aux questions proposées aux sous-préfets.

7 M 1161   Élévage et enquêtes sur les prairies.

7 M 1162   Rapports des sous-préfets sur la statistique bovine.

10 M 1164   Enquête sur le travail industrielle et agricole (1848).

Statistiques divers. Tableau de nombre et de la division des côtes comprisés aux rôles de la contribution foncier de l'année 1835.

Série Q   Registres des actes des notaires et sous-signée privée.

3 Q 5   Bureau de Château-Chinon (1791-1864).

3 Q 6   Bureau de Châtillon-en-Bazois (1792-1864).

3 Q 16   Bureau de Luzy (1792-1860).

3 Q 18   Bureau de Moulins-Engilbert (1790-1864).

Cadastre   140 Larochemillay.

142 Limanton.

III. Manuscripts deposited in the Bibliothèque municipale de Nevers.

1 N 1   Lièvre au terrier de Decize, Champvert, Gannay et dépendances (1775).

2 N 304   Sentence rendue au bailliage de Nevers au sujet des bordelages (1753).

2 N 326   Observations presentées pour Louis Ballerat, fermier, demeurant en la commune de Saint-Caise; contre le sieur François Paignon, proprietaire demeurant à Nevers (1809).

2 N 508   Rapport statistiques sur les routes départementales de la Nièvre (1834).

3 N 2284   Avis aux proprietaires et aux fermiers d'exploitations rurales pour multiplier le gros bétail et améliorer la race (1819).

Ms. 33   Liève déclaration des cens, rentes et bordelages dus au terrier de Saint-Baidière (1780).

IV. Manuscripts deposited in communal archives.

Archives municipales de Larochemillay. Listes nominatives (1841-1876).
Archives municipales de Limanton. Listes nominatives (1836-1876).

V. Published government documents.

Institute nationale de la statistique et des études économiques. *Nomenclature des hameaux, écarts ou lieux-dits: Nièvre.* Dijon, 1974.

Ministère de l'agriculture. *Enquête sur la situation et les besoins de l'agriculture.* Paris, 1866-1872. 38 vols.

——. *Album statistique agricole. Résultats généraux de l'enquête décennale de 1882.* Nancy, 1887.

Ministère de finances. *Nouvelle évaluations de revenue fonçier des propriétés non-baties.* Paris, 1884.

Ministère de l'instruction public et des beaux-arts. Comité des travaux historiques et scientifiques. *Notices, inventaires et documents. La Statistique agricole de 1814.* Paris, 1914.

Statistique générale. *Tableau des communes ayant une totale de 3,000 âmes et au-dessus, ou une population agglomerée de 1,500 âmes et au-dessus.* Paris, 1842.

——. *Résultats du dénombrement de la population en 1856.* Strasbourg, 1859.

——. *Résultats statistiques du dénombrement de 1866.* Paris, 1868.

——. *Résultats statistiques du dénombrement de 1872.* Paris, 1874.

——. *Résultats statistiques du dénombrement de 1876.* Paris, 1878.

——. *Résultats statistiques du dénombrement de 1881.* Paris, 1883.

——. *Résultats statistiques du dénombrement de 1886.* Paris, 1888.

——. *Archives statistiques du ministère des travaux publics, de l'agriculture et du commerce, publiée par le ministère secretaire d'état de ce départment.* Paris, 1837.

——. *Statistique de la France. Territoire et population.* Paris, 1853.

———. *Statistique de la France. Agriculture.* Paris, 1840-1841.

———. *Statistique de la France. Statistique agricole décennale de 1852.* Paris, 1860.

———. *Statistique de la France. Agriculture. Résultats généraux de l'enquête décennale de 1862.* Paris, 1868.

Tribunat. *Rapport fait par Bouteville, au nom de la Section de législature, sur le projet de loi concernant le contrat de société. Séance de 14 ventose, An 12.* Paris, 1804.

———. *Rapport fait au nom de la Section de législation par Chabot sur le première titre du IIIe livre du projet de Code Civil, relatif au succession.* Paris, 1803.

VI. Other published documents.

"Traité du révenue et dépenses de France de la'année 1607." In *Révue rétrospective au bibliothèque historique,* ser. 1, no. 4 (1834), pp. 84-103.

"Extrait du mémoire de la Généralité du Moulins en 1698." In Le Comte de Boulainvilliers, *État de la France. Extraits des mémoires dressés par les intendants du royaume par ordre du Roi Louis XIV.* London, 1750.

Biver, André and Destray, Paul. *Inventaire sommaire de la série 2 F, Fonds Du Bourg, du Bozas.* Nevers, 1932.

Boislisle, Antoine de. *Correspondances des contrôleurs des finances avec les intendants des provinces.* Paris, 1874.

Boucomont, Antoine. "L'Ancienne coutume du Nivernais," *Nouvelle révue historique de droit français et étranger,* 21 (1897), pp. 764-820.

Bourdot de Richebourg, Charles. *Nouveau coutumier général ou corps coutumes de la France et des provinces.* Paris, 1724.

Destray, Paul. *Inventaire sommaire de la série 1 F, Fonds Bruneau de Vitry.* Nevers, 1927.

Dupin, André Marie Jean-Jacques. *La Coutume du Nivernais accompagnée d'extraits du commentaire par Guy Coquille.* Paris, 1864.

Duvergier, J-B. *Collection complete des lois, décrets, ordannances, reglements et avis du conseil d'état.* Paris, 1825.

Fièvè, Joseph. "Note confidentielle sur le département de la Nièvre." In Guy Thuillier, *Aspects de l'économie nivernais au XIXe siécle,* pp. 495-498. Paris, 1966.

Flament, P. *Mémoire de la géneralité de Moulins par Jean LeVayer.* Moulins, 1912.

Gueneau, Victor. "Éxtraits des mémoires d'Isaïe Bonfils, proprietaire-agriculteur à Flez-Tazilly," *Mémoires de la société académique du Nivernais 7,* (1898), 60-104.

Lespinasse, Réné de. *Registre-terrier de l'évêche de Nevers, redigé en 1287, contenant les révenues des quatre châteaux de l'évêche, la liste des paroisses, les rôles des tailles, cens, coutumes et autre redevances.* Nevers, 1869.

Mavidal, Jerome, and Laurent, E. *Archives parlementaires de 1787 à 1860.* Paris, 1862-19--.

Marlière. A. *Statistique de l'arrondisement de Clamecy.* Clamecy, 1859.

DuMoulin, Charles. *Les Coutumes générales et particulieres de France et les Gaules, corrigées et annotées de plusieurs decisions, arrêts et autres choses.* Paris, 1615.

Nomazy, Réné de. *Le Chartrier de Rivière, fief de la baronnie de la Rochemillay en Morvan.* Nice, 1955.

Sagnac, Philippe, and Caron, P. *Les comités des droits féodales et de législation et l'abolition du régime seigneurial (1789-1793).* Paris, 1907.

Vassavière, A. *Procès-verbal de la généralité de Moulins dressés en 1686 par l'intendant Florent d'Argouges.* Moulins, 1892.

VII. Secondary Sources

Achalme, Lucie. "Les communautés de famille en Auvergne." *La Réforme sociale,* 53 (1907), pp. 603-628.

Anderson, Michael. *Family Structure in Nineteenth Century Lancashire.* Cambridge, 1971.

Andorka, R. "Peasant Family Structure in the 18th and 19th Centuries," *Enthnographie* 86 (1975), pp. 341-365.

André, L. *Les Sources de l'histoire de la France au XVIIe siècle.* Paris, 1938.

Anglade, Jean. *La Vie quotidienne dans le Massif Central au XIXe siècle.* Paris, 1971.

Appleby, Joyce. "Modernization Theory and the Modernization of England and America." *Comparative Studies in Society and History* 20 (1978), pp. 259-285.

Arensberg, Conrad. *The Irish Countryman.* New York, 1937.

Ariès, Philippe. *Centuries of Childhood: A Social History of the Family.* Trans. by Robert Baldrick. New York, 1962.

Aubenas, Roger. "Réflexions sur les 'fraternités artificielles' au Moyen Age." In *Etudes historiques à la mèmoire de Noël Didier,* pp. 2-11. Paris, 1960.

Bachelin, Henri. *Le Serviteur.* Paris, 1918.

——. *Le Village.* Paris, 1919.

Baron, L. *Terres cultivables, amendments d'engrais.* Paris, n.d.

Baron, Roman. "Le Bourgeoisie de Varzy au XVIIe siècle." *Annales de Bourgogne* 36, no. 143 (1964), pp. 161-208.

——. "La Garde du bétail par pâtre commune dans le nord du Nivernais aux XVIIe et XVIIIe siècles." In *Actes du 92e congrés nationale des sociétés savantes. Strasbourg et Colmar* pp. 9-26. Paris, 1970.

——. "Près, prairies et pâturages divers en Nivernais." *Révue internationale d'onomastique* 14, no. 4 (1962), pp. 261-274.

——. "Les Défrichements dans la toponymie nivernaise." *Extrait du bulletin philogique et historique du comité des travaux historiques et scientifiques* pp. 424-438. Paris, 1967.

——. "L'Histoire de Marcy avant la Révolution." *Bulletin de la société scientifique et artistique de Clamecy,* ser. 3, nos. 27-29 (1952-1953).

Bastid, Paul. *De la fonction sociale des communautés taisibles dans l'ancienne droit.* Tours, 1916.

Barral, J. A. *L'Agriculture de la Haute-Vienne.* Paris, 1884.

——. *Enquête sur la situation de l'agriculture en France en 1879.* Paris, 1880.

Baudiau, J-F. *Le Morvan, ou éssai géographique, topographique et historique sur cette contrée.* Nevers, 1854.

Baudiot, German. *Annuaire statistique administratif et commercial du département de la Nièvre.* Nevers, 1829.

Baudot, M. "Les Archives notariales en France: histoire et état actuel." *Gazette des archives* 40 (1963), pp. 5-50.

Berkner, Lutz K. "Inheritance, Land Tenure and Family Structure in Lower Saxony." In *Family and Inheritance. Rural Society in Western Europe, 1200-1800,* edited by Jack Goody. London, 1976.

——. "Rural Family Organization in Europe: A Problem in Comparative History." *Peasant Studies Newsletter* 1, no. 4 (1972), pp. 145-150.

——. "The Stem Family and the Developmental Cycle of the Peasant Household: An Eighteenth Century Austrian Example." *American Historical Review* 57, no. 2 (1972), pp. 398-418.

Berkner, Lutz K., and Shaffer, John W. "The Joint Family in the Nivernais." *Journal of Family History* 3 (Summer, 1978), 150-162.

Bigay, Alexandre. "Les Communautés paysannes de la région de Thiers." *Actes du 88e congrés nationale des sociétés savantes. Clermont-Ferrand,* pp. 843-851. Paris, 1964.

Biver, André. "La Vain pâture dans la Nièvre." *Bulletin de la Fédération des sociétés savantes du centre de la France* (1934-1937), pp. 191-198.

Blin, Leon. "De Paris à Lyon par la vallée de la Loire: Velleites routieres aux XVIIIe et XIXe siècles." *Actes du 84e congrés nationale des sociétés savantes. Dijon* pp. 148-167. Paris, 1960.

Blin, Emile. *Le Morvan, moeurs, coutumes, language, historiettes, légendes, croyances populaires, topographie, histoire.* Château-Chinon, 1902.

Bloch, Marc. *French Rural History: An Essay on Its Basic Characteristics.* Berkeley, 1970.

Bogros, Dr. *Histoire de Château-Chinon* (Château-Chinon, 1864).

Boichard, Jean. "Quelques éléments de la vie rurale entre Loire et Allier Propriété et exploitation du sol." *Révue de géographie de Lyon* 37 (1962), pp. 251-271.

——. *La Vie rurale entre Loire et Allier.* Paris, 1971.

Bois, Paul. *Paysans de l'Ouest.* Paris, 1960.

Boisseau, P. *Traité d'agriculture.* Cosne, 1887.

Bomber, B. "Paysages ruraux des bassin parisien meridional." *Information géographique* 22, no. 2 (1958).

Bonnamour, J. *Le Morvan, la terre et les hommes, éssai de géographie agricole.* Paris, 1965.

Bossuat, André. "Le Servage en Nivernais au XVe siècle d'après les registres du Parlement." *Bibliothèque de l'école des Chartes* 117 (1959), pp. 89-134.

Bouchard, G. *Le Village immobile, Sennely-en-Sologne au XVIIIe siècle.* Paris, 1972.

Boucomont, Antoine. *Des Mainmortes personnelles et réelle en Nivernais.* Paris, 1897.

Bourde, André. *The Influence of England on the French Agronomes, 1750-1789.* Cambridge, 1953.

Bourgoing, Adolfe de. *Mémoire en faveur des travailleurs et des indigents de la classe agricole.* Nevers, 1844.

Boutrouche, R. *Crise d'une société: Seigneurs et paysans du Bordelaise pendant la Guerre des Cents Ans.* Paris, 1947.

Braun, Rudolf. *Industrialisierung und Volksleben.* Zurich, 1960.

Brenner, Robert. "Agrarian Class Structure and Economic Development in Pre-Industrial Europe." *Past and Present* 70 (1976), pp. 30-75.

Brooke, Michael Z. *LePlay: Engineer and Social Scientist.* London, 1970.

Byrnes, Robert, ed. *Communal Families in the Balkans: The Zadruga.* Notre Dame, Ind., 1976.

Cabourdin, Guy. "Gabelles et démographie en France au XVIIe siècle." *Annales de démographie historiques* (1969), pp. 293-314.

Cahen, Léon, and Guyot, R. *L'Oeuvre législative de la Révolution.* Paris, 1913.

Caillot, Joseph. *La Coutume du Nivernais étudiée dans ses differences avec le droit commun coutumier.* Paris, 1857.

Campbell, J. *Honor, Family and Patronage: A Study of Institutions and Moral Values in a Greek Mountain Community.* Oxford, 1964.

Carimantrand, H. *Richesses agricoles de la France. Un domaine d'élévage et d'engraissement (Louance, commune d'Azy-le-Vif).* Dijon, 1907.

Chambers, J. P., and Mingay, G. E. *The Agricultural Revolution.* New York, 1966.

Chambray, Georges, le marquis de. *De l'industrie et de l'agriculture en Nivernais.* Paris, 1834.

——. *De l'entretien, l'amélioration et du faire-valoir des herbages.* Paris, n.d.

Chambure, E. de. *Un domaine du Morvand.* Nevers, 1854.

Chayanov, A. V. *The Theory of Peasant Economy,* trans. and ed. D. Thorner, R. E. F. Smith and B. Kerblay (Homewood, Ill., 1966).

Cheung, Steven. *The Theory of Share Tenancy.* Chicago, 1969.

Cheverry, Victor de. "Fermiers à communauté taisible du Nivernais." *Les Ouvriers des deux mondes* 5 (1885), pp. 3-50.

——. "Fin des communautés taisibles du Nivernais." *Unions du Nivernais et du Bourbonnais. Réunion régionale du 11 avril 1886* (1886), pp. 43-53.

Chevrier, V. G. "Quelques traits caracteristiques de la coutume du Nivernais dans ses rapports avec les coutumes voisines." *Mémoires de la société de l'histoire du droit bourguignon,* fasc. 23 (1962).

Chu, Solomon Shu-Ping. *Family Structure and Extended Kinship in a Chinese Community.* Ann Arbor, 1969.

Clampham, J. H. *Economic Development in France and Germany, 1815-1914.* Cambridge, 1921.

Coale, Ansley, ed. *Aspects of the Analysis of Family Structure.* Princeton, 1965.

Cognard, R. "Bazois et Morvan," *Révue d'Auvergne,* no. 411 (1963), pp. 36-48.

Cole, John W. "Social Process in the Italian Alps." *American Anthropologist,* 75, no. 3 (1973), pp. 765-786.

Collomp, Alain. "Famille nucleaire et famille élargie en Provence au XVIIIe siècle." *Annales. Économies, Sociétés, Civilisations* 27 (1972), pp. 969-976.

Coquille, Guy. *Histoire du pays et duché du Nivernais.* Paris, 1612.

——. *Questions et réponses sur les coutumes de France.* Paris, 1616.

Corbin, Alain. *Archaisme et modernité en Limousin au XIXe siècle, 1845-1880.* Paris, 1975.

Cornu, Paul. "Grèves des flotteurs sur l'Yonne aux XVIIIe et XIXe siècles." *Cahiers du centre* (1911).

——. "Introduction bibliographique à l'histoire nivernaise: Généralites, agriculture, flottage, forges, faïenceries, commerce." *Mémoires de la societé académique du nivernais* 17 (1912), pp. 305-317.

Cronzet, M. *Géographie de la Nièvre physique agricole, industrielle, commerciale et administrative.* Nevers, 1859.

Damas d'Anlezy, M. *En Nivernais: Étude de la production animale dans la canton de Saint-Benin-d'Azy.* Nevers, 1907.

Delafond, O. *Progres agricole et amélioration du gros bétail de la Nièvre.* Paris, 1849.

Delamare, M. *Statistique de l'arrondissement de Clamecy.* Clamecy, 1832.

Delord, Jeanne-Marie. *La Famille rural dans l'économie du Limousin.* Limoges, 1940.

Desai, I. P. "The Joint Family in India: An Analysis." *Sociological Bulletin* 5 (1956), 97-117.

Desert, G. "Viande et poisson dans l'alimentation des français au milieu de XIXe siècle." *Annales. Économies, Sociétés, Civilization* 30 (1975). 519-533.

Desforges, Antoine. "Curieuses déliberations des paroisses des environs de Châtillon-en-Bazois en 1790." *Mémoires de la société académique de Nivernais,* 33 (1941), 39-42.

——. "Notes et documents sur Saint-Parize-Le-Châtel." *Mémoires de la société académique du Nivernais* 30 (1931-1938), 98-115.

——. "Le Prix des denrées au début du XIXe siècle." *Bulletin de la société nivernais des lettres, sciences et arts* 24 (1935), 257-258.

——. *La Vie dans un coin du Morvan.* Paris, 1911.

——. "Coutumes relatives au mariage." *Révue de folklore français* 6 (1935), pp. 235-237.

Desmaisons, François. *Nouvelle traité des aides, tailles et gabelles.* Paris, 1666.

Despois, L. *Histoire de l'autorité royale dans le comte de Nivernais.* Paris, 1912.

Destray, Paul. "Contributions à l'histoire de l'association en Nivernais: La région de Clamecy." *Mémoires de la société académique du Nivernais* 24

(1922), pp. 1-32.

———. "Étude sur les vieilles associations nivernais." *Bulletin philologique et historique* (1920), pp. 370-389.

———. "Contribution à l'histoire de l'association en Nivernais: Qui peut vivre en communauté?" *Bulletin de la société nivernais des lettres, sciences et arts* 27 (1926), pp. 110-188.

Dion, Roger. *Éssai sur la formation du paysage rural français*. Tours, 1934.

———. *La Val de Loire: Étude de géographie régionale*. Tours, 1934.

Divale, William, and Harris, Marvin. "Population, Warfare and Male Supremacy." *Transactions of the New York Academy of Sciences*. (New York, 1975).

Dobb, Maurice. *Studies in the Development of Capitalism*. New York, 1947.

Douglas, William. "Rural Exodus in Two Spanish Basque Villages: A Cultural Explanation." *American Anthropologist* 72 (1977), pp. 1101-1114.

Drouillet, Jean. "Notes d'un folkloriste: Les coutumes de moisson en Nivernais." *Annales des pay Nivernais* 2 (1972), pp. 23-28.

———. *Folklore du Nivernais et du Morvan*. La-Charité-sur-Loire, 1959.

———. *Histoire de Saint-Benin-d'Azy*. Paris, 1936.

Dube, S. C. *Indian Village*. New York, 1967.

Dubroc de Segange, Comte. *Les anciennes communautés de cultivateurs dans le centre de la France*. Moulins, 1898.

Duclos, N. *Annuaire du département de la Nièvre*. Nevers, 1838-1843.

Ducrot, Lazare. *Le Nouveau traité des aides, tailles et gabelles*. Paris, 1643.

Dupin, André Marie Jean-Jacques. *Le Morvan: Topographie, agriculture, moeurs des habitants; état ancien, état actuel*. Paris, 1853.

Dussourd, Henriette. *Au même pot et au même feu. Étude sur les communautés familiales agricoles du centre de la France*. Moulins, 1962.

———. "Les Dissolutions des communautés familiales agricoles dans le centre de la France depuis le XVIIIe siècle jusqu'au Code Civil." *Actes du 89e congrés nationale des sociétés savantes. Lyon*, pp. 309-319. Paris, 1964.

Engels, Friedrich. *The Origin of the Family, Private Property and the State*. Translated by Eleanor B. Leacock. London, 1940.

Fanchy, M. "Visite au dernier survivant de la grosse communauté des Jault." *Bulletin de la société nivernais des lettres, sciences et arts* 28 (1930), pp. 78-82.

Fitch, Nancy. "The Demographic and Economic Effects of Seventeenth Century Wars: The Case of the Bourbonnais, France." Paper presented to the Social Science Historical Association Annual Meeting, Oct. 1977, Ann Arbor, Michigan.

Flamare, Henri de. *Le Nivernais pendant la Guerre des Cents Ans*. Paris, 1925.

Flandrin, Jean-Louis. "Repression and Change in the Sexual Life of Young People in Medieval and Early Modern Times." *Journal of Family History* 2, no. 3 (1977), pp. 196-210.

———. *Familles: Parenté, maison, sexualité dans l'ancienne société*. Paris, 1976.

Forster, Robert, and Ranum, Orest. *Family and Society*. London, 1976.

Fortes, Mever. Introduction to *The Developmental Cycle in Domestic Groups,* edited by Jack Goody. Cambridge, 1958.

Foster, George M. "What Is Folk Culture?" *American Anthropologist* 55 (1953), pp. 159-173.

Fraix de Figon, M. de. *Le Métayage en Bourbonnais au point de vue économique et sociale.* Dijon, 1911.

Garidel, J. de. *Notes sur le métayage complimentaire du travail intitulé le metayage au point de vue sociale.* Montlucon, 1885.

Garrier, G. "Les Enquètes agricole du XIXe siècle, une source contestée." *Cahiers d'histoire* 12 (1967), pp. 105-113.

Gaudemet, Jean. *Les communautés familiales.* Paris, 1963.

Gauthier, G. "Anciennes mesures du Nivernais comparées à celles du system metrique." *Bulletin historique et philogique du comité des travaux historique* (1904), 360-370.

Gauthier, Marthe. *La Nocle et ses seigneurs.* Bourbon-Lancy, 1968.

——. *Au Carrefour des trois provinces: Nivernais, Bourgogne et Bourbonnais; passé méconnu de la baronnie de Vitry-sur-Loire.* Bourbon-Lancy, 1966.

Gay, Francois. *La Champagne du Berry: Éssai sur la formation d'un paysage agraire et l'évolution d'une société rurale.* Bourges, 1967.

Gay, Jean-Lucien. *Les éffets pécuniaires du mariage en Nivernais du XVIe au XVIIIe siecles.* Paris, 1963.

——. "L'Application du droit des gens mariés dans la région de Clamecy pendant les trois siècles de l'Ancien Régime." *Société pour l'histoire du droit et les institutions des anciennes pays bourguignons, comtois et romands* 21 (1966), pp. 146-156.

Gille, Bertrand. *Les Sources statistique de l'histoire de la France.* Paris, 1964.

Gillet, P. *Annuaire du département de la Nièvre.* Nevers, 1809.

Glasson, M. "Communautés taisibles et communautés coutumieres depuis la rédaction des coutumes." *Révue d'histoire du droit français et étranger* (1899), pp. 527-538.

Goldschmidt, Walter, and Kunkel, Evalyn. "The Structure of the Peasant Family." *American Anthropologist* 73 (1971), pp. 1058-76.

Goode, William. *World Revolution and Family Patterns.* London, 1963.

——. *The Family.* Englewood Cliffs, N.J. 1964.

Goody, Jack, ed. *Family and Inheritance: Rural Society in Western Europe, 1200-1800.* Cambridge, 1976.

——. "Class and Marriage in Africa and Eurasia." *American Journal of Sociology* 76 (1971), pp. 585-603.

——. "Strategies of Heirship," *Comparative Studies in Society and History* 15 (1973), pp. 3-20.

——. "Domestic Groups." In *Anthropology,* Addison-Wesley Module, no. 28, pp. 1-32. Reading, Mass., 1972.

——. "Inheritance, Property and Marriage in Africa and Eurasia." *Sociology* 3 (1969), pp. 55-76.

——. "Marriage Prestations, Inheritance and Descent in Pre-Industrial Societies," *Journal of Comparative Family Studies* 1 (1970), pp. 37-54.

Gore, M. S. "The Traditional Indian Family." In *Comparative Family Systems,* edited by M. F. Nimkoff, pp. 226-235. Boston, 1965.

Gotteri-Grambert, Nicole. "Chassy-en-Morvan." *Mémoires de la société académique du Nivernais* 55 (1969), 29-54; 56 (1970), 29-38; 57 (1971), 43-66.

Goubert, Pierre. *Beauvais et le Beauvasis de 1600 a 1730.* Paris, 1960.

——. "Family and Province: A Contribution to the Knowledge of Family Structure in Early Modern France." *Journal of Family History* 2, no. 3 (1977), pp. 179-195.

Grantham, George. "The Diffusion of the New Husbandry in Northern France, 1815-1840." *Journal of Economic History* 38, no. 2 (1970), pp. 311-337.

——. "Scale and Organization in French Farming, 1840-1880." In *European Peasants and Their Markets,* edited by William N. Parker and Eric L. Jones, pp. 293-326. Princeton, 1975.

Greenfield, S. M. "Industrialization and the Family in Sociological Theory." *American Journal of Sociology* 67 (1961), pp. 312-322.

Gueneau, Victor. *Notes pour servir à l'histoire de la commune de Vandenesse.* Nevers, 1874.

Gueneau, Lucien. *L'Organisation du travail à Nevers aux XVIIe et XVIIIe siècles (1660-1790).* Paris, 1919.

——. *Les Conditions de la vie à Nevers (denrées, logements, salaries) à la fin de l'Ancien Régime.* Paris, 1919.

——. "Us et Coutumes du Morvan: Luzy." *Bulletin de la société académique du Nivernais* 1 (1881), 18-26.

Guillaumin, Emile. *Panorama de l'évolution paysanne, 1870-1935.* Moulins, 1936.

——. *En Bourbonnais: La propriété et l'agriculture, les moeurs, les diverses categories de travailleurs.* Paris, n.d.

——. *The Life of a Simple Man,* translated by Margaret Holden. London, 1919.

Hajnal, John. "European Marriage Patterns in Perspective." In *Population in History,* edited by D. V. Glass and D. E. C. Eversley, pp. 101-143. London, 1961.

Halpern, Joel, and Kerewsky, Barbara. *A Serbian Village in Historical Perspective.* New York, 1972.

Halpern, Joel. *A Serbian Village.* New York, 1967.

——. *Social and Cultural Change in a Serbian Village.* (New Haven, 1956).

——, and Anderson, David. "The Zadruga, A Century of Change." *Anthropologica* 12, no. 1 (1970), pp. 83-97.

Hammel, E. A. "The Zadruga as Process." In *Household and Family in Past Time,* edited by Peter Laslett and Richard Wall, pp. 335-373. Cambridge, 1972.

——. "Lineage Cycle in Southern and Eastern Yugoslavia." *American Anthropologist* 75 (1973), pp. 802-814.

——. "Household Structure in Fourteenth Century Macedonia." In *Mediterranean Family Structure*, edited by Jack Campbell. Forthcoming.

——, and Laslett, Peter. "Comparing Household Structure Over Time and Between Cultures." *Comparative Studies in Society and History* 16 (1974), pp. 75-79.

Hervé, G., and Hovelacque, H. *Recherches éthnologiques sur le Morvan*. Paris, 1894.

Homans, George C. *English Villagers of the Thirteenth Century*. Cambridge, Mass., 1941.

Hilaire, Jean. "Vie en commun, familie et ésprit communautaire." *Révue d'histoire de droit français et étranger* (1973), pp. 8-53.

——. *Le Régime des biens entre epoux dans la région de Montpellier du début du XIIIe siècle à la fin du XVIe siècle*. Montpellier, 1957.

Hohenberg, Paul. "Change in Rural France in the Period of Industrialization." *Journal of Economic History* 32 (1972), pp. 219-240.

Hsu, F. L. K. *Under the Ancestor's Shadow*. Stanford, 1971.

Hunt, David. *Parents and Children in History*. New York, 1970.

Imbart de la Tour, Joseph. *La Nièvre au point de vue agricole*. Nevers, 1892.

——. *La Crise agricole en France et à l'étranger*. Never, 1901.

——. *Réponse au questionnaire de la grand enquête agricole de 1888, notamment en ce qui concerne le Nivernais*. Never, 1888.

——. *Les Causes morales et économiques de la désertion des campagnes*. Paris, 1909.

——. *La Production de l'élévage et le commerce du bétail en France et à l'étranger*. Paris, 1905.

——. *Le Role sociale du proprietaire fonçier*. Paris, 1900.

——. *Étude économiue sur le département de la Nièvre*. Nevers, 1890.

Jacquart, Jean. *La Crise rural en Ile-de-France, 1550-1670*. Paris, 1974.

Joly, P. "Charrin." *Les Cahiers du centre* (1910).

Jones, Eric L. *Agriculture and Economic Growth in England, 1760-1815*. London, 1967.

——, and Wolf, S. J., eds. *Agrarian Change and Economic Development*. Cambridge, 1970.

Jouzier, E. *Économie rurale*. Paris, 1903.

Juillard, Etienne. *Histoire de la France rurale. Apogée et crise de la civilisation paysanne (1789 à 1914)*. Paris, 1976.

Kapadia, K. M. "Changing Patterns of Hindu Marriage and Family." *Sociological Bulletin* 3 (1954), 161-192.

——. *Marriage and Family in India*. Bombay, 1959.

Kaplan, Temma. *Anarchists of Andalusia, 1868-1903*. (Princeton, 1977).

Keesing, Roger M. *Kin Groups and Social Structure*. New York, 1975.

Kerr, Clark, et al. *Industrialization and Industrial Man: The Problems of Labor and Management in Economic Growth*. Cambridge, Mass., 1960.

Kerridge, Eric. *The Agricultural Revolution*. London, 1967.

Khera, Sigrid. "Kin Ties and Social Interaction in an Austrian Peasant Village with Divided Land Inheritance." *Behavior Science Notes* 7 (1972), pp. 349-365.

——. "Social Stratification and Land Inheritance Among Austrian Peasants." *American Anthropologist* 75 (1973), pp. 814-822.

Klapisch, Christinne. "Fiscalité et démographie en Toscane (1427-1430)." *Annales. Économies, Sociétés, Civilisations* 24 (1969), pp. 1313-37.

——, and Demonet, Michel. "A 'uno pane e uno vino': La famille rurale toscane au début de XVe siècle." *Annales. Économies, Sociétés, Civilisations* 27 (1972), pp. 873-901.

Klein, G. "L'Embouche en Bazois." *Année propédeutique* (1956), pp. 273-282.

Kroeber, Alfred. *Anthropology.* New York, 1948.

Kulkarni, M. G. "Family Patterns in Gokak Taluka." *Sociological Bulletin* 9 (1960), 60-81.

Labit, H. *Topographie médicale du département de la Nièvre.* Paris, 1892.

Labrousse, C. E., ed. *Aspects de la crise et de la dépression de l'économie français au milieu du XIXe siècle, 1846-1852.* Paris, 1956.

Landes, David S. *The Unbound Prometheus.* Cambridge, 1972.

Lang, Olga. *Chinese Family and Society.* New Haven, 1946.

Laslett, Peter, and Wall, Richard. *Household and Family in Past Time.* Cambridge, 1972.

Laslett, Peter. *The World We Have Lost.* London, 1971.

——. "Characteristics of the Western Family Considered Over Time." *Journal of Family History* 2, no. 2 (1977), pp. 89-116.

Lebrun, F. *Histoire de la pays de la Loire.* Toulouse, 1972.

Leguai, A. "Les Émotions et séditions populaire dans la généralité de Moulins aux XVIIe et XVIIIe siècles." *Révue d'histoire économique et sociale* 43 (1965), 45-65.

LePlay, Frederic. *Le Réforme Sociale.* Paris, 1864.

——. *Les Ouvriers Europeans.* Paris, 1877-1879.

LeRoy Ladurie, Emmanuel. *The Peasants of Lanquedoc,* translated by John Day. Chicago, 1974.

——, and Recurat, Jeanne. "L'État des vents des sel vers 1625." *Annales. Économies, Sociétés, Civilisations* 24 (1969), pp. 999-1010.

Lespinasse, C. de. "Dots de mariage de laboureurs en Nivernais." *Révue du Nivernais* 1 (1896-1897), 6-15.

Lespinasse, M. de. "Les Maisons-types dans la régions de Nevers." In *Enquête sur les conditions de l'habitation en France: Les Maisons-types,* edited by Alfred Foville. Paris, 1894.

Lespinasse, Réné de. *Le Nivernais et les comtés de Nevers.* Paris, 1909-1914.

——. "Notice sur les redevances routurieres du Nivernais appelées bordelages." *Bibliothèque de l'école de Chartes* (1868), pp. 140-55.

Levainville, J. *Le Morvan, étude de géographie humaine.* Paris, 1908.

Levy, Marion. "Aspects of the Analysis of Family Structure." In *Aspects of the Analysis of Family Structure,* edited by Ansley Coale. (Princeton, 1965).

Levy-Leboyer, Maurice. "La Croissance économique en France au XIXe siècle." *Annales. Économies, Sociétés, Civilisations* (1968).

Locke, Robert R. *French Legitimists and the Politics of Moral Order in the Early Third Republic* Princeton, 1974.

McArdle, Frank. "Another Look at Peasant Families East and West." *Peasant Studies Newsletter* 3, no. 3 (1974), pp. 11-14.

Madan, T. N. "The Joint Family: A Terminological Clarification." In *Family and Marriage,* edited by John Mogey, pp. 7-16. Leiden, 1963.

Mandelbaum, David G. *Society in India,* Berkeley, 1970.

Nicolle, Marcel. *Les Communautés de laboureurs dans l'ancien droit* Dijon, 1901.

Marion, Marcel. *Les Impôts directs sous l'Ancien Régime, principalement au XVIIIe siècle.* Paris, 1910.

Maron, Albert. "Une association agricole de l'ancienne France." *Réforme sociale* ser. 2, 10 (1890), 259-276.

Massé, Alfred. *Herbages et embouches.* Paris, n.d.

——. "La Vie rurale d'une paroisse rurale: Pougues de 1674 à 1795, d'après les registres de l'état civil." *Mémoires de la sociéte académique du Nivernais* 44 (1940-1941), pp. 16-47.

——. *Histoire du Nivernais.* Paris, 1938.

——. "Les anciennes communautés de vignerons et laboureurs en Nivernais d'après les archives notariales de Pougues (1775-1830)." *Mémoires de la société académique du Nivernais* 49 (1949), pp. 3-15.

Maumigny, J. de. *Étude sur Guy Coquille, publiciste et jurisconsulte.* Paris, 1910.

deMausse, Lloyd. *The History of Childhood.* New York, 1974.

Meplain, A. *Les anciennes coutumes successorales du Bourbonnais et du Nivernais.* Montlucon, 1885.

Merle, Louis. *La Métairie et l'évolution de la Gatine poitevine.* Paris, 1958.

Meunier, Paul. *La Nièvre pendant la Convention.* Nevers, 1895.

——. "Bailliage provincial-duché prairie de Nivernais." *Bulletin de la société nivernais des lettres, science et arts* ser. 3, no. 5 (1937), 72-125.

Meuvret, J. *Études d'histoire économique.* Paris, 1971.

——. "Les Amognes." *Annales de géographie* 35 (1926), 236-244.

Michaud, Réné. *Un ferme en Bazois.* Beauvais, 1910.

Millien, Achille. *Litterature orale et traditions du Nivernais.* Paris, 1906-1910.

Mingay, G. E. "The Size of Farms in the Eighteenth Century." *Economic History Review* 14, no. 3 (1962), 469-488.

——. *English Landed Society in the Eighteenth Century,* London, 1963.

Mirot, L. "Notes nour servir à l'histoire du Nivernais et du Donziais de 1360 à 1409 d'après les comptes de la Recette général et des châtellenies." *Bulletin de la société académique du Nivernais* ser. 3, no. 5 (1937), 132-160.

——. and Bossuat, André, "Les Limites et la réunion du Nivernais et du Donziais." *Bulletin de la société nivernais des lettres, sciences et arts* 29 (1937), pp. 689-704.

Mohler, Paul. *Le Servage et les communautés serviles en Nivernais.* Paris, 1900.

Monod, N. "Les Maisons-types dans la région de Montsauche (Morvan)." In *Enquête sur la conditions de l'habitation en France: Les Maisons-types,* edited by Alfred Foville. Paris, 1894.

Moore, Barrington. *Social Origins of Dictatorship and Democracy: Lord and Peasant in the Making of the Modern World.* Boston, 1966.

Moore, Wilbert E. *Industrialization and Labor: Social Aspects of Economic Development.* Ithaca, N.Y., 1951.

Monnot, Armand. "La Situation agricole du Nivernais avant 1789." *Révue du Centre,* mo. 61 (1934).

Morineau, Michel. "Y a-t-is eu une révolution agricole en France au XVIIIe siécle?" *Révue historique* 239 (1968), pp. 299-326.

——. "Note sur le peuplement de la généralité de Moulins." In *Hommages à Marcel Reinhard* pp. 475-503. Paris, 1973.

Morellet, J-N. *Du Servage dans le Nivernaïs du XVe siècle.* Nevers, 1840.

Morrison, William A. "Family Types in Badlapur: An Analysis of a Changing Institution in a Maharushtrian Village." *Sociological Bulletin* 8 (1959), pp. 45-67.

Mosely, P. E. "The Peasant Family: The Zadruga or Communal Joint Family in the Balkans and Its Recent Revolution." *The Cultural Approach to History,* edited by Caroline F. Ware, pp. 95-108. Nw York, 1940.

Mousnier, Roland. *Lettres et mémoires adressés au chancelier Sequier (1633-1649).* Paris, 1964.

——. *Peasant Uprisings in Seventeeth Century France, Russia and China.* New York, 1967.

Mukherje, B. N. "Family Structure and Laws of Residence, Succession and Inheritance Among the Vrali of Travencore." *Vanyajati,* 3 (1955), 99-104.

Murdock, G. P. *Social Structure.* New York, 1949.

Musset, Réné. "Les Statistiques agricoles français: Étude critique." *Annales d'histoire économique et socialé* 5 (1933), 284-291.

Myers, Charles A. *Labor Problems in the Industrailization of India.* Cambridge, Mass., 1958.

Naudin, A. *L'Industrie de l'élévage dans la Nièvre.* Paris, 1916.

Nee de la Rocelle, M. *Mémoire pour servir à l'histoire du département de la Nièvre.* Paris, 1827.

——. *Commentaires sur la coutume du bailliage et comte d'Auxerre.* Paris, 1829.

Newell, William. "Agricultural Revolution in Nineteenth Century France." *Journal of Economic History* 33 (1973), pp. 697-710.

Nimkoff, M. F. "Is the Joint Family an Obstacle to Industrialization?" *International Journal of Comparative Sociology* 1, no. 1 (1960), pp. 109-118.

——, and Middleton, Russell. "Types of Family and Types of Economy," *American Journal of Sociology* 66 (1960), pp. 215-225.

Quesnay, François. "Fermiers." In *Oeuvres économiques et philosophiques de F. Quesnay,* edited by Auguste Oncken (New York, 1888), 159-192.

Parish, William L., and Schwartz, Moshe. "Household Complexity in Nineteenth Century France." *American Sociological Review* 37 (1972), pp. 154-173.

Pasquet, Joseph. *En Morvan: Souvenirs du bon vieux temps.* Château-Chinon, 1967.

Pazzis, Comte de. *Enquête sur la situation du bétail dans le département de la Nièvre.* Paris, 1875.

Pellault, H. *L'Art de s'enrichir par l'agriculture en créant des prairies.* Paris, 1844.

Peyronnet, Jean-Claude. "Famille élargie ou famille nucleaire? L'Éxample du Limousin au debut du XIXe siècle." *Révue d'histoire moderne et contemporaire* 22 (1975), pp. 568-582.

Plakans, Andrejs. "Familial Structure in the Russian Baltic Provinces." In *Sozialgeschichte der Familie in der Neuzeit Europas,* edited by Werner Conze, pp. 000-000. Stuttgart, 1976. 346-362.

———. "Peasant Farmsteads and Households in the Baltic." *Comparative Studies in Society and History* 17 (1975), pp. 2-35.

———. "Identifying Kinfolk Beyond the Household." *Journal of Family History* 2, no. 1 (1977), pp. 3-27.

———. "Seigneurial Authority and Peasant Family Life: The Baltic Area in the Eighteenth Century." *Journal of Interdisciplinary History* 5 (1975), pp. 629-654.

Poitrineau, A. *La Vie rurale en Basse-Auvergne au XVIIIe siècle, 1726-1789.* Paris, 1966.

Porshnev, Boris. *Les Soulevements populaires en France au XVIIe siècle.* Paris, 1963.

Prieur, M. *Histoire du district de la-Charité-sur-Loire.* Nevers, 1937.

Prieuret, C. "Une association agricole en Nivernais: Histoire de la grosse communauté des Jault, 1580-1847." *Bulletin de la société nivernais des lettres, sciences et arts* 27 (1927), pp. 333-383.

Rabb, Theodore K., and Rotberg, Robert I., eds. *The Family in History, Interdisciplinary Essays.* New York, 1971.

Rameau, H. "La Censive nivernais d'après la coutume de 1534." *Mémoires de la société pour l'histoire des droit de pays bourguignons, comtois et romands,* fasc. 30 (1970-1971), pp. 205-219.

Raveau, Paul. *L'Agriculture et les classes paysannes: Les transformations de la propriété en Haut-Poitou au XVIIe siècle.* Paris, 1926.

Remond, Nicolas. *Sommaire traité du revenue et dépense des finances de France, ensemble les pensions de nos seigneurs et dames de la cour.* 1622.

Redfield, Robert. *Peasant Society and Culture.* Chicago, 1965.

———. *The Little Community.* Chicago, 1965.

Renault, Ernest. *Contribution à l'histoire de Moulins-Engilbert.* Nevers, 1909.

Robin, Theodore Taurin. *Guide théoretque et pratique des cultivateurs.* Nevers, 1861.

Rouppel, Gaston. *La Ville et la campagne au XVIIe siècle. Étude sur la population du pays dijonnais.* Paris, 1955.

Roy, G. *Observations sur le commerce du département de la Nièvre à l'époque du 1er mai 1811.* Nevers, 1811.

Sabean, David. "Aspects of Kinship Behavior in Rural Western Europe Before 1800." In *Family and Inheritance. Rural Society in Western Europe, 1200-1800,* edited by Jack Goody and Joan Thirsk, pp. 96-111. London, 1976.

Sagnac, Philippe. *La Législation civile de la Révolution Français (1789-1804): Éssai d'histoire sociale.* Paris, 1898.

Saint-Jacob, Pierre de. *Les Paysans de la Bourgogne du nord au dernier siècle de l'Ancien Regime.* Paris, 1960.

Saint-Phalle, M. le marquis de, and Pinet de Maupas, M. *Enquête sur les besoins et la situation du l'agriculture. Réponses fait au questionnaire général.* Nevers, 1867.

Sarriau, H. "Notes sur deux éditions des coutumes du Nivernais." *Bulletin de la société nivernais des lettres, sciences et arts* 17 (1900), pp. 000-000. ser 3, 18 (1900), 472-475.

Sauzet, L. *Du Métayage en Limousin.* Paris, 1897.

Shah, A. M. "Changes in the Indian Family: An Examination of Some Assumptions." *Economic and Political Quarterly* 3 (1969), pp. 8-21.

Shanin, Teodor, ed. *Peasants and Peasant Societies.* London, 1971.

Shorter, Edward. *The Making of the Modern Family.* New York, 1975.

Simon, J. *Statistique de la commune de Fretoy.* Château-Chinon, 1883.

Slicher van Bath, B. H. *The Agrarian History of Western Europe.* London, 1963.

Smelser, Neil. *Social Change in the Industrial Revolution.* Chicago, 1969.

Stirling, Paul. *The Turkish Village.* New York, 1965.

Taverna, M. "Une Ville affamée: Nevers pendant la Révolution." *Mémoires de la société académique du Nivernais.* 21 (1921), 80-110.

Tawney, R. H. *The Agrarian Problem in the Sixteenth Century.* London, 1912.

Terline, Baron J. de. *L'Agriculture dans l'Amognes à la fin du XVIIIe siècle d'après la relation contemporaire inedité de J-C. Flamen d'Assigny.* Nevers, 1927.

Thaubault, Roger. *Education and Social Change in a Village Community.* New York, 1972.

Thienneaut, Philippe. *La Crise actuelle de l'agriculture.* Clamecy, 1886.

Thomas, William L. *Man's Role in Changing the Face of the Earth.* Chicago, 1956.

Thuillier, Andre. "L'Évolution de l'élévage en Nivernais de 1820 à 1852." *Actes du 93e congrés national des sociétés savantes. Tours,* pp. 95-143. Paris, 1971.

——. "Un Village du Morvan sous la Convention: Semelay de 1793 à 1795." *Actes du 87e congrés nationale des societés savantes. Poitiers,* pp. 233-268. Paris, 1963.

——. *Économie et société nivernaises au début du XIXe siècle.* Paris, 1974.

Thuillier, Guy. *Aspects de l'économie nivernais au XIXe siècle.* Paris, 1966.

——. "Pour une histoire des travaux ménages en Nivernais au XIXe siècle." *Révue d'histoire économique et sociale* 50 (1972), pp. 238-264.

Toutain, Jean-Claude. *Les transports en France de 1830 à 1965.* Paris, 1967.

——. "La Consommation alimentaire en France de 1789 à 1964." *Économies et sociétés. Cahiers de l'I.S.E.A.* 5, no. 11 (1971).

——. "Le Produit de l'agriculture français de 1700 à 1958." *Cahiers de l'institut de science économique. Histoire quantitative de l'économie français,* 1961.

Tricot, Albert. *Étude sur l'allodialité en Nivernais.* Paris, 1904.

Tudesq, André-Jean. *Les Grandes Notables en France.* Paris, 1964.

Tupin, L. "Les Anciennes communautés de laboureurs et la coutume du bordelage dans les paroisses de Magny-Cours du XVe au XVIII siècles." *Bulletin de la société nivernais des lettres, sciences et arts,* ser. 3, no. 5 (1909), pp. 195-237.

Wallerstein, Immanuel. *The Modern World-System: Capitalist Agriculture and the Origins of the European World Economy in the Sixteenth Century.* New York, 1974.

Weber, Eugen. *Peasant into Frenchmen. The Modernization of Rural France, 1870-1914.* Stanford, 1976.

Weinberger, Stephen. "Peasant Households in Provence: ca. 800-1100." *Speculum* 48 (1973), pp. 247-257.

Wharton, Clifton R., ed. *Subsistence Agriculture and Economic Development.* Chicago, 1969.

Wheaton, Robert. "Family and Kinship in Western Europe: The Problem of the Joint Family Household." *Journal of Interdisciplinary History* 4 (1975), pp. 601-628.

Wolf, Eric. *Peasants.* Englewood Cliffs, N.J., 1966.

Wolf, Margery. *The House of Lim.* New York, 1968.

Wolkowisch, M. "L'Élévage dans le Bazois." *Annales de géographie* 55 (1946), pp. 206-210.

——. *L'Économie régionale des transports dans le centre et le centreouest de la France.* Paris, 1960.

Wrigley, E. A. "The Process of Modernization and the Industrial Revolution in England." *Journal of Interdisciplinary History* 3 (1972), pp. 225-260.

Wylie, Laurence. *Village in the Vaucluse.* New York, 1957.

Van Gennep, Arnold. *Manuel de folklore français contemporaine.* Paris, 1943.

Vannereau, abbe G. *Le District de Moulins-Engilbert pendant la Révolution.* Cosne, 1962.

Varagnac, Andre. *Civilisation traditionnelle et genres de vie.* Paris, 1948.

Vilar-Berrogain, Gabrielle, ed. *Guide des recherches dans ldes fonds d'enregistrement sous l'Ancien Régime.* Paris, 1958.

Villenaut, Ad. de. "Registres-terriers des seizième et dix septième siècles." *Bulletin de la société nivernais des lettres, sciences et arts,* ser. 3, no. 5 (1892), 77-84.

Villeroy, Felix. *Manuel de l'éléveur de bêtes à cornes*. Paris, 1861.

Young, Arthur. *Travels in France During the Years 1787, 1788 and 1789*. New York, 1969.

Yver, Jean. *Egalité entre héritiers et exclusion des enfants dôtés*. Paris, 1966.

Zeldin, Theodore. *Conflicts in French Society*. London, 1970.

——. *France, 1848-1945*. London, 1973-1978.

Index